SO YOU WANT TO
SING FOLK MUSIC

So You Want to Sing

Guides for Performers and Professionals

A Project of the National Association of Teachers of Singing

So You Want to Sing: Guides for Performers and Professionals is a series of works devoted to providing a complete survey of what it means to sing within a particular genre. Each contribution functions as a touchstone work for not only professional singers, but students and teachers of singing. Titles in the series offer a common set of topics so readers can navigate easily the various genres addressed in each volume. This series is produced under the direction of the National Association of Teachers of Singing, the leading professional organization devoted to the science and art of singing.

So You Want to Sing Music Theater: A Guide for Professionals, by Karen S. Hall, 2013

So You Want to Sing Rock 'n' Roll: A Guide for Professionals, by Matthew Edwards, 2014

So You Want to Sing Jazz: A Guide for Professionals, by Jan Shapiro, 2015

So You Want to Sing Country: A Guide for Performers, by Kelly K. Garner, 2016

So You Want to Sing Gospel: A Guide for Performers, by Trineice Robinson-Martin, 2016

So You Want to Sing Sacred Music: A Guide for Performers, edited by Matthew Hoch, 2017

So You Want to Sing Folk Music: A Guide for Performers, by Valerie Mindel, 2017

SO YOU WANT TO SING FOLK MUSIC

A Guide for Performers

Valerie Mindel

Allen Henderson
Executive Editor, NATS

Matthew Hoch
Series Editor

A Project of the National Association of
Teachers of Singing

ROWMAN & LITTLEFIELD
Lanham • Boulder • New York • London

Published by Rowman & Littlefield
A wholly owned subsidary of The Rowman & Littlefield Publishing Group, Inc.
4501 Forbes Boulevard, Suite 200, Lanham, Maryland 20706
www.rowman.com

Unit A, Whitacre Mews, 26-34 Stannary Street, London SE11 4AB

British Library Cataloguing in Publication Information Available

Library of Congress Cataloging-in-Publication Data

Names: Mindel, Valerie, 1946- author.
Title: So you want to sing folk music: a guide for performers / by Valerie
    Mindel.
Description: Lanham, MD : Rowman & Littlefield, 2017. | Series: So you
want to sing | "A Project of the National Association of Teachers of Singing."
    | Includes bibliographical references and index.
Identifiers: LCCN 2016045303 (print) | LCCN 2016048239 (ebook) | ISBN
    9781442265615 (pbk. : alk. paper) | ISBN 9781442265622 (electronic)
Subjects: LCSH: Singing—Instruction and study. | Folk music—Instruction
and study.
Classification: LCC MT820 .M657 2017 (print) | LCC MT820 (ebook) | DDC
    782.42162/043—dc23
LC record available at https://lccn.loc.gov/2016045303

∞™ The paper used in this publication meets the minimum requirements
of American National Standard for Information Sciences—Permanence of
Paper for Printed Library Materials, ANSI/NISO Z39.48-1992.

Printed in the United States of America

CONTENTS

LIST OF FIGURES

FOREWORD

So You Want to Sing Folk Music: A Guide for Performers is the seventh book in the NATS/Rowman & Littlefield So You Want to Sing series and the fourth book to fall under my editorship. For this title, we have engaged folk singer and pedagogue Val Mindel, who travels internationally presenting her workshops to both experienced folk musicians as well as newcomers to the style. She brings a lifetime of experience singing and teaching folk music to these chapters, and her wisdom is evident throughout this volume.

While some topics in the So You Want to Sing series present us with dozens of prospective authors from which we must pick, folk music is a genre that seems to exist somewhat separately from the traditional voice-teaching community. In conversation with NATS colleagues, I initially had difficulty identifying who would be the "right" author for this book. Then one day during a phone conversation with Jeannette LoVetri, I heard the answer to my months-long, open-ended question: "If you are thinking about a book on folk music, you really have to get Val to write it." Jeanie could not have been more correct, and these pages you are about to read resoundingly affirm that Val Mindel is the perfect author for this topic.

Like other books in the series, there are several "common chapters" that are included across multiple titles. These chapters include a chapter on voice science by Scott McCoy, one on vocal health by Wendy LeBorgne, and "Using Audio Enhancement Technology" by Matthew Edwards (author of *So You Want to Sing Rock 'n' Roll*). These chapters help to bind the series together, ensuring consistency of fact when it comes to the most essential matters of voice production.

The collected volumes of the So You Want to Sing series offer a valuable opportunity for performers and teachers of singing to explore new styles and important pedagogies. I am confident that voice specialists, both amateur and professional, will benefit from Val Mindel's important resource on singing folk music. It has been a privilege to work with her on this project. This book is an invaluable resource for any performer who has ever been interested in adding folk to their stylistic vocabulary.

Matthew Hoch

ACKNOWLEDGMENTS

Thanks to the following people—musicians, writers, and more—who gave me their thoughts and their time in interviews during 2015 and 2016, the period when this book came together. I could not have done this without them. Special thanks to my editor husband, Michael Miller, who lent his expertise and good humor to the project repeatedly during that time and never once said anything but "Great!"

Scott Ainslie
Sam Amidon
Roy Andrade
Tony Barrand
Kate Brislin
Debra Clifford
Laura Cortese
Patty Cuyler
Jeff Davis
Julie Dean
Emily Eagen
Tim Eriksen
Sara Grey
Sabra Guzman

Jefferson Hamer
Ginny Hawker
Kate Howard
Elizabeth LaPrelle
Kip Lornell
Jeannette LoVetri
Brian MacNeill
Ruth Ungar Merenda
Emily Miller
Gerry Milnes
Jesse Milnes
Keith Murphy
Joe Newberry
Brian Peters

John Roberts
Anna Roberts-Gevalt
Lissa Schneckenburger
Mark Simos
Mark Slobin
Moira Smiley
Mollie Stone
Nora Jane Struthers
Suzy Thompson
Jeff Warner
Charles Williams
Flawn Williams

INTRODUCTION

For someone who has rarely thought of the term "folk music" since the heady days of the 1960s folk revival, it was a bit daunting to think of writing a book on how to sing it. It's true that I do sing (a lot), and the material I sing can often be described as folk, although usually another descriptor, such as "early country," comes into play, and the places I work often have the word "folk" in their names somewhere. But in much of what I do and teach, the folk music part of it blurs into country music or blues or gospel, and I suspect this is the case for any five American "folk" singers you might find on YouTube. Still, over the months I've worked on this book, I've come to have a new respect for the term. It really encompasses the idea that there is a music that we all can sing and maybe on some level own a little. Everyone gets to do it. There's a sea of people who sang it before us, and a still-to-emerge sea of people who will want to keep singing it after we're gone, and it's always the music itself that is front and center. We can sing it for a while, and for that while we want to sing it the best that we can. A book like this can help.

There's also the performance aspect of the So You Want to Sing series from the National Association of Teachers of Singing (NATS), which focuses on contemporary commercial music in its many guises. Although performing was rarely the impetus for many folk musicians of my generation, who fell into performing as a natural extension of what they were already doing for fun, these days more and more musicians starting out have their sights on the lights. It's a tricky, daunting, competitive, and sometimes rewarding business. But the thoughts and advice of young folk musicians today who are deep into the business can make it more manageable. That too can help.

And then there are the many students I teach in my workshops and classes and music camps. They always have questions about singing the kind of music I do. They want to learn new songs, of course, and they want to learn all the good harmonies, but they also want the "how to" part of it: how to sound like the singers they admire, how to find their own harmonies, how to do the rolls and wiggles and slips and slides and setups and voice flips and all the other ornaments that are woven into the singing of the oldsters, and how to not lose their voice in the process. And while it's difficult to address these "how tos" in a book—folk music is typically learned and passed down by ear—this book can help shine a light on a possible way forward.

I've been obsessed with music that can be termed "folk" since I was in grade school and fell in love with the cowboy ballad "Streets of Laredo." And when guitar seemed a critical part of it all I was an early adopter, driving my family crazy while I figured out the rudiments. I've been in many bands, including the Any Old Time String Band, which was one of the first all-women string bands that bubbled up in the surge of players re-creating the old music in the 1970s. I've played in many places, to both small and large audiences, I've been through the trials of recording on both vinyl and CD, and I've been teaching this music in some way or another for more than thirty years. So while I haven't necessarily thought about folk music as folk music, I've been in its thrall for a long time.

But more important is that I've walked the talk. In the early years of my performing life I sang without much guidance, and although I consulted voice coaches at various times, I more or less let nature take its course. Then I started having real vocal problems—understandable if you teach five music camps in a row without a break. I felt that I was missing notes. I consulted an otolaryngologist who sent a camera down my throat to look around and told me, "If you want to keep doing the amount of singing you're doing, you need help." This is where Jeannette LoVetri came in. Jeanie has been a voice teacher for more than forty-five years, and she's the director of the Voice Workshop in New York City and the creator of Somatic Voicework™. Jeanie teaches a functional approach to the voice, concentrating on what's going on physically. Under her guidance I learned how to work with my voice to make it a stronger, more dependable, and tuneful instrument. So I believe you too can enhance not only what you sing but also how you sing—and not lose that natural way of singing that is so much a part of folk music. You'll still sound like yourself, only in sharper focus.

Learning any aspect of folk music is largely a self-directed task, and one that involves a lot that's not going to be found on any page. But a book like this, which offers sound vocal advice as well as a clear-headed look at the business side of things and a bit of history to keep you grounded, can be a valuable companion on your journey.

Before reading the book from cover to cover, however, I suggest reading around in it, stopping at parts that seem interesting to you and absorbing what you can. You might want to tackle the chapters on vocal and harmony techniques, for example, at a slower pace than the chapter on various aspects of folk music history. Or you might want to go to a specific problem you're facing at the moment—intonation issues, for example. You'll find a section that addresses that, and that might be your first spot to linger. At some point it will seem like a good idea to read this book from cover to cover, but that's not necessary in order to learn from it. The main thing is to keep singing!

For additional information, go to the NATS website at www.nats.org.

ONLINE SUPPLEMENT NOTE

So You Want to Sing Folk Music features an online supplement courtesy of the National Association of Teachers of Singing. Visit the link below and click on the button for the So You Want to Sing series to discover additional exercises and examples, as well as links to recordings of the songs referenced in this book.

http://www.nats.org

A musical note symbol ♪ in this book will mark every instance of corresponding online supplement material.

1

YOU KNOW IT
WHEN YOU HEAR IT

Drop the word "folk" and just call it real old honest-to-god American singing.

—Woody Guthrie, from the official
Woody Guthrie website

What is this thing called "folk music" that has beguiled people through the centuries? If you ask twenty people you'll get twenty different answers. Yet people involved in the genre usually have some idea that a certain sound can be called folk. They may not agree on what that sound is, but they're clear on what it's not: it's not classical music, it's not jazz, it's not rock, it's not pop, it's not some other clearly defined category. It's, well, folk.

And this is where things start to blur. If you're a fiddler, folk music means one thing; if you're a folklorist it means another; if you're a songwriter it means something else entirely. Today many folk musicians have opted for other labels—"traditional" or "roots" or "vernacular" or "Americana" or even "folk-based"—because the term "folk" doesn't really describe them or communicate what they do.

The important thing is not to get bogged down in the terminology. If you identify with folk music in some form, or develop a passion for it, or feel compelled to sing it, then what it's called is beside the point. You know it when you hear it.

A WAY TO LOOK AT IT

But despite the mushiness of the term, if you're going to sing folk music in any of its guises, you'll need to come to some understanding for yourself of what that means. In general, definitions fall into one of two camps.

The anonymous, worn-by-years-and-use camp: Many folk scholars over the years have limited the term "folk song" to songs that are anonymous in origin or have origins that are obscured by time and passage through generations of singers. Even when an author is known, as in the songs of nineteenth-century songwriter Stephen Foster, the feeling is that if it comes out of the past, has stood the test of time, has been accepted into a community, and been shaped by those who have given voice to it over the years, then it reaches the standard of folk music.

Along with this focus on the past is the idea that it's important to retain the marks of that earlier time, to preserve the folk song as a bit of history. The "re-creationists" set up in this camp, those enthusiastic (or possibly obsessive) fans of early recorded folk music who work to learn everything they can from the original recording—each word, each note, each inflection, each breath.

The you-know-it-when-you-hear-it camp: This takes a more "functional" view of folk music. A song can be old or newly minted or commercially recorded as long as it carries with it a folk aura—a sense of timelessness, a sense of some sort of community (geographical, chronological, or of shared interests or experiences), a feeling of being vital today. Oscar Brand, a folk singer and writer on all things folk, called it a "well-handled feeling" in his 1962 book *The Ballad Mongers*. "As far as I'm concerned a folk song is distinguishable by a special sound, a kind of 'simple noise,'" he wrote.

In Brand's view, "Big Rock Candy Mountain" is a folk song, even though Harry "Haywire Mac" McClintock, who recorded it in 1928, claimed authorship. Today, almost ninety years after McClintock's recording, most of us would agree, especially after it was featured in the Coen Brothers' film *O Brother, Where Art Thou?*

It's in this more inclusive definition of folk song that singer-songwriters find a place to stand, alongside musicians who sing songs they've borrowed from a variety of musical streams, from 1900s Tin Pan Alley to 1920s commercial hillbilly to 1930s gospel to 1950s country and beyond.

Today, with the wide array of music surrounding us, if you identify as a folk musician it's probably as much your approach to what you sing (your process) and your performance (your singing style) as the actual songs you sing that define who you are.

FOLKS ON FOLK MUSIC

"American folk songs . . . are the oral history of our country. They reveal traditions and beliefs that we cannot discover in any other way. They are the honest voice of people saying, 'This is what I think is important, this is my place in the world, this is how I feel about being here.' There's value in this far beyond the music."

Alan Lomax in his article "Getting to Know Folk Music."

"One of the best things about folk music is that you can . . . talk about everything that's happening—groundhogs to lords and ladies—from 300 years ago to what happened yesterday on the picket line."

Mike Seeger on being honored by the Society for American Music in 2003.

"American folk musics clearly speak to our soul and provide us with inspiration and comfort. . . . What's old becomes new again, if you live long enough."

Kip Lornell, *The NPR Curious Listener's Guide to American Folk Music.*

"Every folk song starts out being made up by someone, but going through lots of people, it changes. It's the cumulative effect of all of those changes, large and small, that makes it a folk song. . . . Sure, you can know who wrote the original version, years ago and miles away, but not who wrote the version you're singing, or hearing now, because . . . lots of people helped to write it."

Michael Cooney, a "singer of old songs," in his article "What Is Folk Music."

DOING YOUR HOMEWORK

In any definition, folk music reflects the people and places and cultures and times it has passed through, and—in my view, of course—the best folk musicians pay homage to that. This means understanding something about that journey and the history that helped create the music you're trying to absorb, whatever folk form that takes.

The history of folk music, however you want to parse it, is a huge topic and the subject of many fine books and recordings, and people who love both history and folk music will never lack for something to fill their days. But you don't have to become a folk music scholar, unless that sort of research appeals to you. For most folk musicians, it's usually a piece of music, rather than a history book, that lights the fire. You stumble upon something you feel passionate about—a song or a tune—and it compels you to follow its tracks back from musician to musician, source to source, listening to the people who have also been passionate about it, who perform it, who have perhaps learned it from someone who learned it from a family or community member, and then tracking the music further to archives and texts from ever distant periods and places. Do this enough times and a historical picture starts to emerge. What's important is to understand enough about the music you're singing to give it context.

Here we're focusing on American folk music, primarily in the English language. And because my interests rest more in the rural South, that region gets additional weight. But it doesn't really matter what catches your ear. The process is the same, and in these days of digital media you can start digging by just rattling your fingers on a computer keyboard. Soon you'll be drawn beyond the Web to the people who sing the songs, the tradition bearers or those who learned from them; you'll hunt through field collections, find recordings to listen to, and then dig some more. It's not hugely different from what you might do as a musical scholar, but here the emphasis is on absorbing the music and finding the information that gives it that context. It's the rare folk musician who doesn't tip his or her hat to those who have gone before.

A FEW THINGS TO THINK ABOUT

If you look at where American folk music comes from, you inevitably get to the music of the people who came willingly from Europe (specifically the British Isles) and the music of those who came unwillingly from Africa (largely West Africa). There were of course many other influences at play—the Hispanic cultures in the American Southwest, the Germanic cultures in the Midwest, and traditions of the various Native American populations across the country add richness and variety to the mix—but these two peoples and their music give you a place to start.

Of the waves of immigrants to arrive on the east coast in the early years of America, the immigrants who came from Scotland via northern Ireland—the Scots-Irish—to settle in Pennsylvania, Virginia, and points south and west arguably had the most to do with what we think of today as "traditional" American folk music. These settlers brought with them ballads that were generations in the making as well as hymns and popular songs of the day—whatever appealed to them or was meaningful in their lives. In the isolation of their new homes this music continued—augmented by inspired songsters but retaining much of the character that came with it over the ocean.

THE SCOTS-IRISH AND APPALACHIA

If you claim a Scots-Irish heritage, as do many people in Appalachia, your ancestors likely left the lowlands of Scotland to settle in Ulster, in northern Ireland, and then, when that proved less than ideal, emigrated to America. They were in good company: Between 1718 and 1800 an estimated two hundred fifty thousand people emigrated from Ulster to the New World.

These intrepid settlers brought their music with them, particularly songs whose origins even then sometimes traced back centuries and across borders. Many of the songs were the old ballads of the sort that Cecil Sharp and other collectors of the early 1900s were so avidly collecting. But they also brought scores of songs that wouldn't fit into this category—hymns, topical songs, children's songs, political songs, love songs, and "broadside" songs that they or family members had purchased on the streets of the cities and towns they came from or through.

For a fascinating and detailed look at this migration, check out Fiona Ritchie and Doug Orr's book *Wayfaring Strangers: The Musical Voyage from Scotland and Ulster to Appalachia*.

At the same time, the music of the people transported from Africa as slaves made its mark. Analyses of the Trans-Atlantic Slave Trade Database estimate that by the mid-1800s some half a million Africans had been brought to America, and with them came the polyrhythms, the "call and response" songs, the ring shouts, and other musical forms of their native lands. Here, enslaved, they listened and adapted and created, evolving new musical forms, including, with the increasing influence of Christianity, spirituals, which some scholars view as the first true American folk song form.

Eventually and inevitably, despite segregation and racial divides, these musical forces wound into one another, giving generations of scholars something to argue about and providing us musicians with a rich heritage to explore. It's inspiring to know that every time we flat a third or slide between two notes or blur a downbeat or feather the end of a phrase, we're standing on the shoulders of singers who came before.

SONG COLLECTORS

> I got into folk music because when I was in seventh grade, Frank Warner came to my school and did a program the year or so after "Tom Dooley" was a big hit. I was sitting two-thirds of the way back in the auditorium expecting to be bored to tears, but there was a man and he had a banjo and pictures about all the travel he had done. One of the songs he sang was "Tom Dula" and I was absolutely astounded to realize that here was the man who had gone into the mountains and found this old song and brought it out to the rest of the world.
>
> —singer Jeff Davis

Folk song collectors have had an immeasurable influence on our ideas about folk music. Their preferences have become our reality and, in many cases, our inspiration. A short list of collectors, at least in America, will include the names of Francis James Child, Cecil Sharp, and Alan Lomax, even though Child and Sharp had their sights and efforts firmly fixed on British music. In recent years these collectors and their collections have been the focus of folk projects, recordings, and tours by dedicated young musicians—closing yet again the circle that links the past to the present.

Francis James Child, born in 1825, was a Harvard University professor of English who had a decades-long obsession with British ballads, which he defined as narrative songs in lyric verse. In his search for ballads Child set the bar extremely high, since he believed true ballads were all but dead, thanks to the influx of printed commercial music and other influences. Although an American, Child had little use for anything made in America. But he was a meticulous researcher, and his years of research resulted in *The English and Scottish Popular Ballads*, a masterwork published in ten parts between 1882 and 1898. The completed work included 305 titles and some thirteen hundred variants, along with copious annotations, but it was strictly words only—no music. It is common now to see references to "Child No. *X*" on a song that may have an entirely different title, different verses, and a different setting than what Child documented. But the connection is there. For example, "The Two Sisters That Loved One Man," sung by North Carolina singer Lee Monroe Presnell for song collectors Frank and Anne Warner in 1951, can be linked to Child's ballad No. 10, "The Twa Sisters," even though the details of the crime in question have changed. Scholars trace the song's origins back to Scandinavia sometime before the 1600s. Today you can go to YouTube and hear such folk musicians as Tim Eriksen and Molly Andrews sing their own versions of the ballad to their twenty-first-century audiences.

Cecil Sharp was another of the seminal collectors with a deep interest in British ballads, but in keeping with the newer trends in collecting (it was the early twentieth century) he collected tunes as well as songs. Traveling from England with his assistant Maud Karpeles, Sharp made three forays into Appalachia in the summers of 1916, 1917, and 1918. His inspiration was Olive Dame Campbell (the subject of the 2000 movie *Songcatcher*), a pioneer of folk song research in the region. "My sole purpose in visiting [the United States] was to collect the traditional songs and ballads which I had heard from Mrs. Campbell, and knew from other sources, were still being sung there," he wrote in the introduction to his two-volume *English Folk Songs from the Southern Appalachians*. This impressive work eventually comprised 274 songs and 968 tunes collected from traditional singers in the mountains of Virginia, North Carolina, Kentucky, and Tennessee.

One of the differences between Sharp and Child was Sharp's method of collecting. Sharp, unlike Child, was not averse to going into the community to find songs, especially if he thought the singers were isolated enough to have versions of songs unsullied by modern influences. Appalachia proved a fertile ground. "I discovered that I could get what I wanted from pretty nearly everyone I met, young and old," he wrote. "In fact, I found myself for the first time in my life in a community in which singing was as common and almost as universal a practice as speaking." To capture that singing, Karpeles would take down the words in shorthand while Sharp notated the tunes.

But Sharp, like Child (and many collectors of the time), was also blinkered by his prejudices. He collected the songs that fit his expectations—specifically songs with English or Scottish roots—and ignored those that didn't fit. Thus he ignored material from African Americans, who made up a significant portion of the population of Appalachia at the time, and songs from white community members that were of more recent vintage or seemed in some way insignificant to him. He also ignored the large body of religious songs that were such an integral part of the communities he visited. But for any fledgling folk singer with an interest in Appalachian ballads, Sharp's collection is an important resource.

Alan Lomax and his father John are probably the collectors who have done the most to further the cause of folk music in the United States.

John Lomax first gained recognition in the field in 1910 with the publication of *Cowboy Songs and Other Frontier Ballads*, the result of extensive fieldwork he did as a Harvard graduate student under mentor George Lyman Kittredge, who had himself been mentored by Child. "Home on the Range" came from this collection as well as countless other songs that we can't imagine not knowing.

Alan Lomax began working with his father in their song-collecting travels in 1933, at age eighteen, and from their thousands of miles on the road and thousands of hours of recordings, they produced two books that are still must-haves in the library of any serious American folk singer: *American Ballads and Folk Songs*, published in 1934, and *Our Singing Country*, published in 1941. John Lomax died in 1948, but Alan's career continued over six decades, during which he made an incalculable contribution to American and world folk music.

Unlike earlier collectors, the Lomaxes had a particular interest in the songs of African Americans, but like earlier collectors they also wanted songs that were unadulterated and that had the least contact with "jazz, the radio and with white men." It was in the segregated prison farm camps, the Lomaxes wrote in the introduction to *American Ballads and Folk Songs*, that conditions were ideal. "A life of isolation, without books or newspapers or telephone or radio, breeds songs and ballads," they wrote. The Lomaxes actively sought "made-up" songs, and at the same time they omitted "the beautiful English ballads that it has been America's good fortune to inherit," reasoning that the people in these ballads had "lived and died and had most of their folk stature before they came to this country." Thus, they explained, these old ballads wouldn't reflect much of the social history of America.

A notable exception was the inclusion of a version of "Barbara Allen" by a convict they recorded. He had transformed the old English ballad into a tale of the American West, changing "Barbara" to "Bobby," giving her a buckskin pony and burying her, after much "squallin' and holl'in'" in the sands of the Arizona desert. It was the folk process at work.

The books that resulted from the Lomaxes' extensive research were meant for singers rather than scholars. So instead of presenting and annotating the many variants, they created song composites, bringing together the best stanzas and even the best lines from a number of singers and sources for their book. "No one person probably has ever sung entirely a number of the songs as herein printed," they explain in *American Ballads and Folk Songs*, "but all the words given have been sung by some people."

The melodies, they are careful to explain, were transcribed exactly as a particular version was presented, an homage to the power they found in the presentations of the singers they encountered. "No lover of folk songs who hears the untutored ballad singer render them fails to realize that the music is more vital for the total effect than the words," they write. But understanding that no two musicians would hear or notate a melody in exactly the same way, they invite anyone who shares their interest to listen to the original recordings archived at the Library of Congress. Over the course of the Lomaxes' careers, they donated more than ten thousand recordings. You can find at least some of those recordings online today at the American Folklife Center at the Library of Congress.

TRADITIONAL VERSUS APPALACHIAN

The notion of "traditional" American folk music seems to conjure up the term "Appalachian," even if the song in question is from Arkansas singer Almeda Riddle or Eleazar Tillett of the Outer Banks of North Carolina or New York's "Yankee John" Galusha, or if it merely sounds old.

Appalachian music in fact comes from Appalachia (pronounced "apple-at-cha" by most residents), a geographical region that covers some two hundred five thousand square miles, following the spine of the Appalachian Mountains, which extend from northern Mississippi to southern New York. It includes all of West Virginia and parts of twelve other states: Alabama, Georgia, Kentucky, Maryland, Mississippi, New York, North Carolina, Ohio, Pennsylvania, South Carolina, Tennessee, and Virginia. Some 42 percent of the people of the region live in a rural setting, according to the Appalachian Regional Commission, compared with 20 percent of the national population.

Appalachian music has had, and continues to have, a huge influence on our musical identity, but it doesn't have to be traditional to be Appalachian. Meanwhile, traditional music can come from anywhere—and any time period. "It doesn't just mean it's come from the past," says folklorist Gerry Milnes. "To exist it has to happen in the present," he says. "Once-popular songs can become folk music too, if the values expressed are accepted and the songs repeated through generations."

BALLADS AND BROADSIDES

What's a Ballad?

Folklorists, historians, and song collectors tend to have strong (and sometimes opposing) ideas of what a ballad is. But most agree that the old ballads have certain characteristics in common: their authorship is unknown, they have weathered time and the passage through many hands and mouths and regional idiosyncrasies, and they have remained recognizable and generally consistent through that passage. They tell their tales in an objective, journalistic, almost unsentimental fashion using an economy of language (unimportant text is easily lost over time), and like all good stories, they dwell on the dramatic, dispensing with extraneous background details.

American ballads are latecomers to the ballad world. "The Ballad of Jesse James," for example, is about events that took place after the Civil War. The ballad tells the story of outlaw Jesse and his brother Frank, who murdered, robbed, and generally marauded throughout Kansas and Missouri in the postwar years, stealing from the rich and, if the song is to be believed, giving to the poor, until in April 1882 gang member Robert Ford shot Jesse for the reward money. Soon after he was killed, Jesse became the subject of at least one many-verse ("ten-foot") poem, and the ballad followed. His life and deeds have sparked interest in a string of singers since, from Bascom Lamar Lunsford, who recorded it in 1924, to Woody Guthrie, Eddy Arnold, the Pogues, and Bruce Springsteen. Indeed, it turns up in John Lomax's *Cowboy Songs and Other Frontier Ballads*, published in 1910.

As an aside, Jesse was a considerable singer, and also a relative of Ozark ballad singer Almeda Riddle (her father's grandfather was a brother of Jesse's father). "I didn't know him," she says in her book, *A Singer and Her Songs*, "but my Grandfather Wilkerson fought with him through the [Civil] War, and he said that he was one of the finest ballad singers he'd ever heard.

"Jess was an outlaw and that wasn't good," Almeda continues, "but these things happen." For Almeda and many of us, if you're a good singer you're forgiven many things.

There are scores of American songs that can be pointed to as authentic ballads, if your definition is at all flexible. "Frankie and Johnny," based possibly on a murder that took place in St. Louis, Missouri, in 1899, fits, although Bill Dooley, a St. Louis songwriter of the day, is thought to have planted the song's seed. We also have ballads of very clear authorship. I'm particularly fond of Jean Ritchie's "West Virginia Mine Disaster," about the Hominy Falls mine disaster of 1968. As a singer, you can make up your mind what to sing and what to call it, as long as you're communicating.

What about Broadsides?

If you get into ballads at all, you'll run across the term "broadside ballad." The term refers to the ballads printed on broadsheets (paper printed only on one side) that were sold on the streets in England in the seventeenth and eighteenth centuries. Aimed to appeal to the "lower classes," they were cheaply printed, cheaply purchased, and hugely popular. Along with old ballads and newer ballads detailing tabloid-style news of the day (the birth of deformed babies, for example), broadsides also featured songs popularized by professional entertainers, stories, poems, political treatises, and so on. "You would not just *see* broadside ballads on walls or in hands," writes Eric Nebeker in his essay, "Heyday of the Broadside Ballad." "You would also hear them. They were sung in groups in the alehouse, sung individually by a ballad monger, sung at work by apprentice and master, sung in the fields by milkmaids and farmers. Printed with the names of familiar tunes to which they could be sung, broadside ballads were more than art, more than text, and more than song . . . [and] they were available to all."

Our forebears could tuck a favorite broadside into their belongings on their journey to America. Songs that migrated in this written form tended to experience less of the folk process than songs that made the journey in people's memories.

For a colorful picture of what broadside ballads were and something of their history, read the full text of Eric Nebeker's essay at the University of California, Santa Barbara, online archive.

GIMME THAT OLD-TIME RELIGION

If you're involved in American folk music, it's impossible to ignore the wide stream of religious song that courses through the genre, from psalmody, shape-note compositions, and lined-out hymns to spirituals, ring shouts, and elaborately composed gospel pieces. Religion was a driving force in the lives of many of our American ancestors, and songs that echoed that religion were often all they sang, since many believed that secular songs were an invitation to the devil.

Today, those considerations aren't in play for most of us, but if you're setting out to sing American folk-based music, you'll eventually have to figure out your comfort level with "God" songs. There have been folk and traditional singers throughout the past century whose focus has been entirely on gospel songs—from the gospel blues singer Washington Phillips, who recorded in the 1920s, to the evangelical Cooke

Family, who are still recording today (worth a listen if only to admire Jeanette's cut-through-anything, no-holds-barred delivery). Meanwhile, folk music camps and festivals often feature a gospel singing session on Sunday mornings, attended by enthusiastic participants of all religions and creeds, and many folk musicians typically add some sort of "gospel" material to their concert sets, enjoying the rhythms and the opportunities for harmonies and spontaneous participation.

So how to keep the various forms and factions straight? Kip Lornell, in *Exploring American Folk Music*, covers sacred and religious folk music succinctly yet comprehensively from both the African American and Anglo-American perspective. For our purposes and the space we have, I'm offering a quick look at a few important forms you'll run across.

SHAPE-NOTE

Fans of the 2003 film *Cold Mountain* may remember Nicole Kidman and the congregation in the little church singing "I'm Going Home" (it's on YouTube if you need a refresher). At the start the congregation sings a seeming jumble of syllables, which soon organize themselves into powerful harmonies. They are "singing the shapes"—going over the harmony parts by singing the syllables associated with the shaped note heads they see in front of them. Because the parts—soprano, alto, tenor, bass—sing different notes, the syllables are different, hence the jumble. The name for what they're doing is "shape-note," and it's usually defined as a cappella community singing of hymns in three- and four-part harmony.

Shape-note uses four distinct shaped note heads—*fa* (a triangle), *sol* (a circle), *la* (a square), and *mi* (a diamond)—to indicate intervals. The system is meant to be an aid to sight singing, easily intuited by people who can't read music. Because the note heads are on the appropriate lines and spaces of a musical staff and indicate rhythm, it's also comprehensible to people who can.

This type of singing started in New England in the early 1800s and quickly spread throughout the South and beyond. Back in the day, armed with *The Sacred Harp* (which came out originally in 1844 and boasts the subtitle "The Best Collection of Sacred Songs, Hymns, Odes, and Anthems Ever Offered the Singing Public for General Use"), itinerant singing teachers could come into a community and quickly get everyone singing in glorious harmony. As a pastime it was accessible, fun, and, given the subject matter, usually on the right side of whatever restrictions the religious community placed on musical pursuits. Today, thanks in part to *Cold Mountain*, this highly social form of singing is once again enormously popular, with shape-note conventions and singing groups, both casual and performance-based, springing up across the country and abroad. Indeed, whenever I teach in England and Scotland I find eager singers clutching their copies of *The Sacred Harp* and looking to gather a group to sing this full-throated music.

According to the Sacred Harp Musical Heritage Association's website, the term "sacred harp" refers to the human voice, the voice we're born with. *The Sacred Harp* itself was only one of more than one hundred oblong hymnbooks published in the United States in the mid-1800s. It has been continually updated, and copies of the 1991 "Denson" edition are readily available. You can find other, lesser-known collections in secondhand shops and, of course, on eBay.

Meanwhile, there are scores of composers who are writing songs in the shape-note tradition and format. A stellar collection of such works is *Northern Harmony,* edited by Larry Gordon and Anthony Barrand, which includes songs written by teenage composers, veterans of the teen singing camp Village Harmony.

Other shape-note books still in use today include *Christian Harmony*, which uses a seven-shape notation that is more prevalent in the South. On a song-collecting trip through West Virginia in 2000 with my daughter, Emily Miller (pictured on the cover of this book), we had the opportunity to visit ballad singer Rita Emerson, then eighty-eight, at a senior center and join her and a group of her contemporaries in singing from *Christian Harmony*. The singing was true and thrilling, despite the ages of the voices joining in, but what was remarkable was the singers' complete independence from their books, which everyone carried and opened dutifully to the appropriate page as the hymn number was called. It was clear the singers needed neither the words nor the notes, as they knew the songs by heart, but having their books spread before them was part of this regular and welcome social singing.

CAMP MEETING SONGS

In the early decades of the nineteenth century, about the same time that shape-note singing was, as we say now, "trending" in America, camp meetings were getting their start, propelled by the fervor of the evangelical Second Great Awakening. The first big one took place in Cane Ridge, Kentucky, in August 1801 and reportedly attracted ten thousand to twenty thousand people—many of whom traveled for days to get there. The draw was the prospect of experiencing real preaching (ordained ministers were hard to come by on the American frontier), visiting with other people, catching up on news, and generally enjoying the various aspects of life in a large unruly gathering. It wasn't quite Woodstock, but some of that fervor was clearly evident. The preachers—often several of various Protestant denominations were on the roster—exhorted the crowd to embrace the Christian life and cast away sin, often winding themselves and gathered penitents into bouts of ecstasy. (If the preacher didn't finish up by rolling on the ground, one report said, he was "just lazy.") Singing was a huge part of this hubbub, and while printed collections of camp meeting songs and hymns abounded as the popularity of these events swelled, typically few hymnals or printed word sheets were in evidence at the meetings themselves. Many people couldn't read, and reading by torchlight or bonfire was iffy at best. And although some singers knew scores of hymns by heart, spontaneity and improvisation were the order of the day. It wasn't unusual for a song to rise on the spot out of a phrase in the sermon. In this uprising of song African Americans excelled. Although seating was segregated, whites and blacks could hear and sing with each other, providing an opportunity for cross-cultural musical exchange. When the white farmer went back to his field, the song that lingered could be a spiritual. A good portion of the songs we think of as camp meeting songs in fact have their origins in slave songs and spirituals. You'll hear them at folk festivals, sing-alongs, and other social singing gatherings. The songs tend to have simple, easy-to-pick-up words, often featuring mother-father-sister-brother verses, and easy-to-intuit tunes. An example of the sort of song that could well have been sung at a camp meeting is "Down in the Valley to Pray" (sung by Alison Krauss in the soundtrack to the movie *O Brother, Where Art Thou?* as "Down to the River to Pray"). While longtime fans of Doc Watson's singing of this song might feel petulant about the word changes, that sort of lyric fluidity was—and continues to be—indicative of the style.

HILLBILLY HARMONY AND COUNTRY GOSPEL

In the rural South, where religion was often at the center of daily life, there wasn't a lot of distinction between what you sang in church and what you sang around the house. The big difference was that in church there were many voices, while at home there were only a few, so that when you sang "in parts" at home you were more likely to be holding a part on your own. This is a likely factor in the development of the close harmony that became a hallmark of old-time, early country, country gospel, bluegrass, and all the styles that fit under the "country" umbrella. If you pull on cowboy boots when you perform and include "country" and "harmony" in your folk identity, you're undoubtedly mining the material of those early old-time players and singers—and in the process the hymns and songs that they brought home with them from church.

To give you an idea of what a big part country gospel played in old-time music, look at the list of songs from the Bristol Sessions in summer 1927. Of the seventy-six recorded performances Ralph Peer gleaned from two weeks of recording, thirty-one were gospel, including "Are You Washed in the Blood" (the Dixie Mountaineers), "Old Ship of Zion" (Ernest Phipps and his Holiness Quartet), and "Where We'll Never Grow Old" (Alfred Karnes), a song that still crops up in folk gospel singing sessions today.

A number of groups who became popular on records, radio, and the performing circuit in the rural South based much—and sometimes all—of their repertory on gospel music, often taking their songs and harmonies straight from the hymnals they sang from in church—or what they remembered of them. Others forged new ground, reworking old songs and writing new ones.

A prolific author of country gospel was Albert E. Brumley, who wrote the ubiquitous "I'll Fly Away." He was helping his family pick cotton back on the family farm in Oklahoma and someone was singing "If I had the wings of an angel." Brumley said it was a desire to fly away from that cotton field that inspired the song, which he started in 1929 and finished in 1931 (lest you think songwriting is an immediate process). The song became immensely popular and was a million-seller for the gospel group the Chuck Wagon Gang, which recorded it in 1949. Among Brumley's other hits are "Turn Your Radio On," recorded by the Blue Sky Boys, and the bluegrass standard "Rank Strangers to Me," recorded by the Stanley Brothers.

SPIRITUALS, GOSPEL SONGS, AND AFRICAN AMERICAN RELIGIOUS MUSIC

In the same way that "Appalachian" has come to mean almost anything that sounds old, ballad-like, and hard-edged, regardless of its age or origins, "gospel" has come to mean anything that mentions "God" or "Je- sus" or "heaven." But in African American song, there are distinctions between spirituals and composed hymns, jubilee quartet material, and elaborate modern gospel pieces. If you're interested in singing these songs, it helps to know the difference, if for no other reason than be- cause spirituals don't have an identified author, while hymns and more modern songs typically do.

Spirituals grew up on the plantations among the enslaved populations. And although their typically simple texts seem to refer to God and heaven, they also often carried other, more secret meanings. "Wade in the Water," for example, has a coded message that urged people trying to escape to the North to "wade in the water" so the dogs used by the slave hunters couldn't track their scent.

Spirituals aren't all alike. John Wesley Work, an important early col- lector of African American folk songs and spirituals, saw three distinct types: call-and-response songs such as "Shout for Joy" in which the leader might sing, "Early in the morning" or "Oh, Lord" or, at Christ- mastime, "Mary had a baby," and the congregation would answer "shout for joy"; songs featuring long phrases and slow tempos, such as "Nobody Knows the Trouble I've Seen," sung solo or in groups; and fast-paced, highly rhythmic good-feeling songs such as "The Old Ark's a Moving (or "Movering") and "Old-Time Religion."

There wasn't much in the way of formal harmonies—"no singing in parts" is the way the authors of the 1867 compilation *Slave Songs of the United States*, William Francis Allen, Charles Pickard Ware, and Lucy McKim Garrison, put it. "Yet," they say, "no two appear to be singing the same thing."

This harmonization became more formalized in the decades after the Civil War with, among others, the Fisk Jubilee Singers, out of Fisk University in Nashville. They brought worldwide attention to such songs as "Wade in the Water," an arrangement of which the group published in 1901.

Composed gospel hymns began to take their place in African American religious repertory around that time. Among the composers of the day, the Methodist minister Charles Albert Tindley was a standout. A prolific writer and composer, he was the author of such iconic hymns as "Leave It There," "We'll Understand It Better By and By," "Stand By Me," and "I'll Overcome Someday." This last song, which he wrote in 1901, was transformed at mid-century into "We Shall Overcome," an anthem of the civil rights movement.

There are innumerable stellar recordings of Tindley's songs in the world of gospel music, and folk music continues to borrow from his work. "What Are They Doing in Heaven," recorded in 1927 by the gospel blues singer Washington Phillips, accompanying himself exquisitely on a sort of zither-like instrument called a "manzarene," has recently enjoyed considerable popularity, performed by musicians as various as Abigail Washburn, Mavis Staples, Vince Gill, and the Be Good Tanyas. In fact, the comfortable gentleness of Tindley's songs has made them a favorite among secular folk, world music, and hospice choirs as well as such groups as the African American performance ensemble Sweet Honey in the Rock. *Beams of Heaven: Hymns of Charles Albert Tindley (1851–1933)*, published in 2006, includes all forty-six of his songs.

From Tindley it's a pretty direct step to Thomas Dorsey, who is considered by many to be the father of modern African American gospel music, but this is where gospel music really takes a giant step away from its folk origins and is a subject unto itself.

African American gospel quartets, meanwhile, experienced a boom in popularity in the 1930s. The Golden Gate Quartet was considered a pioneer of this new type of jubilee singing, which historian Kip Lornell describes as "up-tempo," featuring "vocal effects, high rhythmic interest, strong lead vocal, and a 'pump' bass."

Today you can hear the influence of jubilee quartets in groups such as the Nashville Bluegrass Band, which has recorded with the African American group the Fairfield Four, and Doyle Lawson (in particular, check out Doyle Lawson and Quicksilver's 1981 recording *Rock My Soul*).

For a deep look into African American harmony and history, you can't go wrong with Ysaye Barnwell's *Singing in the African American Tradition*, a four-CD collection of choral and congregational music taught in detail by Barnwell, a phenomenal singer, teacher, and scholar, and a member of Sweet Honey in the Rock for more than thirty years.

THE BIG BANG

As historian Bill Malone points out, there's a direct line between the southern rural folk music that caught the ear of collectors such as Cecil Sharp and John and Alan Lomax and the music that record companies categorized as "hillbilly" and began recording in the early 1920s. The commercial success of these early efforts proved that there was a market for folk/country music. Fiddlin' John Carson's "You'll Never Miss Your Mother Till She's Gone," recorded in New York City in 1923, sold a million copies, for example, and there were others. So it wasn't a huge step for the Victor Talking Machine Company (later RCA Victor Records) in 1927 to send talent scout and producer Ralph Peer south to set up a temporary recording studio to record hillbilly musicians. The place Peer chose was Bristol, a town that straddles the Tennessee-Virginia state line. For two weeks Peer recorded artists, both acts he had arranged in advance and some surprises culled from responses to newspaper notices inviting musicians to audition. Much great material was recorded in the course of the jam-packed schedule, but the two acts that went on to rock the American music world were singer/yodeler Jimmie Rodgers from Mississippi and the Carter Family—Sara, Maybelle, and A. P. Carter—from Virginia. In hindsight, music historians began to understand the importance of this particular recording event and started referring to it as "the Bristol Sessions" or "the Big Bang of commercial country music." For an in-depth look at all this, check out *The Bristol Sessions*, a collection of writings about the sessions edited by Charles K. Wolfe and Ted Olson.

A few facts:

The Bristol Sessions took place over two weeks between July 25 and August 5, 1927.

Producer Ralph Peer, under the auspices of the Victor Talking Machine Company, recorded nineteen acts, resulting in seventy-six recordings of acceptable "takes."

Of the seventy-six takes, thirty-five could be considered traditional, including the first-ever recordings of "Skip to My Lou, My Darling," which became a popular children's song, the murder ballad "Pretty Polly," and "The Longest Train I Ever Saw," performed and recorded by subsequent artists as "In the Pines."

Gospel songs such as "Old Ship of Zion" accounted for thirty-one of the takes; instrumentals accounted for only seven (Peer vastly preferred vocals). The Bristol Sessions were in fact the first recording sessions to emphasize songs and vocal music.

The sessions had little in common with the collecting efforts of people like the Lomaxes, who started their work a few years later. Wolfe points out that they were "a calculated exercise in recording and marketing an emerging commercial art form within a bustling Southern city" rather than a means to preserve some sort of pure Appalachian folk music. Nevertheless the sessions stand as an important start to country music as we've grown to understand it, and country music has always had folk at its heart.

CLOSE HARMONY AND THE BROTHER DUETS

In the years that followed the 1927 Bristol Sessions, old-time music surged in popularity, and along with it an interest in close-harmony singing of the sort that rural people were hearing on their records and their radios. The Carter Family became hugely popular as well as the "brother duets"—"DNA harmony" duos such as the Blue Sky Boys, the Monroe Brothers, the Delmore Brothers, the Dixon Brothers, and the Louvin Brothers who recorded in the 1930s or 1940s up into the 1950s. Instrumentation typically featured guitar, mandolin, and perhaps fiddle, and repertoires ranged from gospel to ballads, sentimental songs, and material the musicians wrote themselves. Alton Delmore and Ira Louvin were particularly gifted songwriters, and it's the rare old-time vocal jam today that doesn't include a song or two they wrote. In particular, Alton Delmore's "Blues Stay Away from Me" is a must-know if you sing old-time early-country songs.

There were sister groups as well, such as the Bowman Sisters, daughters of fiddler Charlie Bowman, in the 1920s, the Girls of the Golden West (Millie and Dolly Good) in the 1930s and 1940s, and the Davis Sisters, who weren't really sisters but sounded like it, in the 1950s. These groups didn't think of themselves as folk, but their material rose from the sources or at least the life circumstances that Alan Lomax and others were collecting in their field recordings. The difference was that these acts were scrabbling to make a living at it. Today most folk-based, country-flavored harmony groups listen avidly to these early country harmony singers, and their vocal chops remain an inspiration.

THE FOLK REVIVAL

Some people who read this will think I still haven't gotten to what they consider the "real" American folk music—the music of Woody Guthrie, Pete Seeger, and the Weavers and on to Bob Dylan, Joan Baez, and the folk stars of the 1960s. To these people, most likely baby boomers, "folk" is that musical supernova that took place in the late 1950s and early 1960s when folk music burst into the consciousness of the public at large and then fizzled and fragmented into all the factions that make it so difficult to figure out today.

But as brightly popular as the folk performers who made up that popular folk flash were, they don't seem to have captured the ear and re-creationist obsessions of twenty-first century folk musicians in the way that the tradition bearers of the time—Jean Ritchie, Bill Monroe, Doc Watson, Maybelle Carter, and others—have done, even though many were listening to and learning from these tradition bearers and bringing considerable musical acuity to the task. Today's folk musicians just don't seem to be reviving the revivalists. This doesn't mean that Joan Baez, with her still-amazing voice, doesn't fill auditoriums or that in gatherings of people of a certain age, background, and purpose "If I Had a Hammer" isn't pulled out, but young aspiring folk musicians aren't studying the stalwarts of the urban folk revival with the intensity and exacting detail that they are applying to the singing of, say, the Louvin Brothers or Texas Gladden. And the "dangerous" songs of social protest that so inspired young musicians and so horrified "the establishment" back in the day just don't make it onto many set lists. We sing the songs of 1960s folk in homage as these old musicians slip away, but that's about it.

Tastes change. Our current understanding of the American folk sound is a sound that is more hard-edged and more ornamented, with more vocal twists and turns, than what many folk singers were doing at the height of the revival. Generally speaking, we want a straight tone; we don't want vibrato. We want "speakerly" singing—singing that's an extension of how we talk. We don't want long-held "singerly" notes that carry on at the end of phrases—they put too much attention on the singer, while the song itself takes a backseat. And while we all would love to capture Joni Mitchell's ease with shifting registers—her word yodels—we'd rather practice the technique using, say, a Hank Williams song. Women have found their chest voices in today's folk music, and men their falsettos. It's just a different time.

But folk musicians are inevitably a product of what has gone before, and the 1950s–60s folk revival inevitably colors what we as folk singers do and who we are. So it bears pausing for a moment on that heady time.

A NEW FOLK CONSCIOUSNESS

The seeds of the folk revival were planted in the 1930s, when people began conceiving of folk music differently. Instead of seeing it as history, people began looking at it as something happening right now. A "dynamic art" was how Charles Seeger, father of the Seeger clan and an important folk scholar of the day, saw it—a process of losing old songs and acquiring new ones and embracing hybrids and songs from such commercial sources as hillbilly music. You sang a folk song, this "functional" reasoning went, not because it was a piece of history but because it was somehow relevant to your life and the lives of your listeners. Even if you weren't *of* the folk in question, you could absorb the music and make it yours. This is still what drives many of us to sing folk songs, even if we spend hours delving into their past, and this is what allowed the singers over the next thirty years to embrace songs and tunes and reshape and repurpose them for their own times and issues. Also, given the hard times of the Depression, folk music was something to rally around, and the government took note. In *Romancing the Folk: Public Memory & American Roots Music*, folk historian Benjamin Filene points out that it was during this period that folk music received government funding for the first time, in various projects designed both to make work and to capture our rich and diverse folk heritage. An important piece of this was the 1937 funding of the Archive of American Folk-Song, under the auspices of the Library of Congress, with young Alan Lomax as a full-time employee.

LEAD BELLY

In the 1930s and 1940s audiences in New York City were awed by an African American singer and ex-convict who went by the name of Lead Belly. Born around 1889 in Louisiana as Huddie Ledbetter, Lead Belly earned his nickname from fellow laborers on Southern work gangs because, Alan Lomax wrote, "he could set the pace for the cotton-picking gangs all day and make music for the barrel-house dances all night."

John and Alan Lomax "discovered" Lead Belly at the Louisiana State Penitentiary in 1933 during a song-collecting foray into the South. "We were hunting ballads and we found a folk artist," Alan wrote later in an essay, "Lead Belly's Songs." "We became possessed." John Lomax brought Lead Belly up to New York on his release from prison the following year and introduced him and his music to the city's folk scene.

Lead Belly proved to be a passionate performer, combining a clear "far-carrying" voice with powerful guitar playing. The particular guitar he played was a battered green twelve-string Stella that came to him from Mexican street singers in Dallas, but, as Lomax wrote, "the music Lead Belly created for it was the folk history of East Texas and back-woods-Louisiana slave dance tunes, children's games, songs, cotton-picking chants, field hollers, early ragtime, the western Negro ballads, early blues."

A lot has been written about Lead Belly's life in New York City and the far-from-smooth relationship he had with John Lomax in particular. Although he was able to eke out a living with his music and was a central figure in the left-leaning folk scene, he didn't become widely known until after his death in 1949, when the Weavers topped the charts with his "Goodnight Irene." But he's a key figure in the American music of the mid-twentieth century, and many of his songs—"The Midnight Special" and "The Rock Island Line," for example—still define what many people think of as folk music.

WOODY GUTHRIE

With the 1940s, folk singers with a clear "voice of the people" agenda took center stage. First among these was Oklahoma songster Woody Guthrie, a charismatic singer/guitar player with a huge, restless talent and a penchant for making up songs anytime, anywhere. In the mid-1930s, drought and massive dust storms had combined with the general poverty of the Depression to make life impossible for farmers and many others across the Great Plains. Thus Woody and thousands of his neighbors hit the road looking for ways to support their families. In February 1940 Woody's hard traveling landed him in New York City. It was a time when the young city-bred folk singers were ardent cheerleaders for the "common man," and, as his son Arlo Guthrie said later, "here was Woody, the commonest man." They were in awe. Woody was dripping with songs—about his travels and the people he came across, mostly working people and those simply trying to get by. During the months that followed he recorded *Dust Bowl Ballads*, a semi-autobiographical set of songs describing what happened during the Dust Bowl crisis that included "Dusty Old Dust" (later known as "So Long, It's Been Good to Know You") and "I Ain't Got No Home in This World Anymore," which was based on an old gospel song but in Woody's hands was more about how the working class got the short end of the stick.

Woody was many things, and he said, sang, and wrote many things, and to many he was the singing voice of folk protest. "If the fight gets hot, the songs get hotter. If the going gets tough, the songs get tougher," he said, and still people who are moved to protest in song, no matter the genre, find inspiration in Woody and his music. For more flavorful Woody quotes, along with a succinct biography and many Woody facts, check out the official Woody Guthrie website; for a more detailed look at this great man, read Joe Klein's *Woody Guthrie: A Life*.

PETE SEEGER, THE ALMANAC SINGERS, AND THE WEAVERS

Another folk singer of the period who reached iconic status was Pete Seeger, son of Charles and half-brother to Mike and Peggy (each of whom made their own marks in the folk world). Over his sixty-plus-year career, Pete became a beloved household name across the country, and his importance to what we loosely think of as American folk music can't really be overstated. He was something of an instrumental virtuoso, developing a vibrant style on banjo and both six- and twelve-string guitar, and his complex instrumental arrangements encouraged scores of young would-be folk players to take their instruments seriously. At the same time he was a lifelong activist, embracing causes from the labor movement to civil rights, Vietnam War protests, and environmentalism. A member of the Communist Party for a time in the 1940s, he was hauled before the House Un-American Activities Committee in 1955 but refused to discuss his personal and political associations. As a result he was charged with contempt of Congress and sentenced to jail (the verdict was eventually overturned on appeal). He went on to stand on the stage of countless liberal events and causes, always urging the audience, whether two dozen, two hundred, or twenty thousand, to sing along.

Pete set out on the folk path soon after dropping out of Harvard in 1938. In 1940 he helped create the Almanac Singers, an energetic young folk group with strong leftist, pro-union leanings. The group, which included at various times Woody Guthrie, Lee Hays, Millard Lampell, Alan Lomax's sister Bess Lomax Hawes, Cisco Houston, and Josh White, mined folk material from all over, enthusiastically bringing the music of the people to the people, if primarily the people of New York City. The Almanacs believed fervently in the power of folk songs to change the world and in writing songs to inspire that change, getting everyone both onstage and off to sing along.

Pete also helped create probably *the* stand-out folk group of the late 1940s and early 1950s, the Weavers, who enjoyed a crazy meteoric nation-wide success and then, after being blacklisted during the anticommunist hysteria of the early 1950s, a crazy dizzying fall from grace. The Weavers—Pete Seeger, Lee Hays, Ronnie Gilbert, and Fred Hellerman—had a more upscale (i.e., well-dressed and well-rehearsed) approach than the Almanac Singers, and some said they were more pop than folk, but like the Almanacs, they sang folk songs from all over with great energy and high spirits, and they clearly had what the public wanted. Their 1950 top-of-the-charts hit "Goodnight Irene" sold two million copies in four months. "Some people in the trade believe that no other song ever sold so fast in so short a time," *Time* magazine reported. The song was one that Lead Belly sang, but the Weavers sanitized it for general audiences, removing a reference to morphine and changing "I'll get you in my dreams" to "I'll see you in my dreams." Still today, it's a common closing choice for that everyone-on-stage final number at a festival.

With the song came fame, accompanied by rave reviews, television appearances, and nightclub offers. But although the Weavers soft-pedaled their politics in favor of what Pete called "a good song," they were black-

DRESSING FOR PERFORMANCE THEN AND NOW

The Almanac Singers of the early 1940s took an "of the people" approach to their music and also to their performances. They tended to wear whatever clothes they happened to have on.

"It wasn't that we were trying to look poor—we were!—but we hadn't thought of ourselves as dressing up or dressing down, dressing any way in particular," Bess Lomax Hawes recalls in David King Dunaway and Molly Beer's book of interviews on the folk revival, *Singing Out*. "We had the same kind of naïveté when we started to make it. . . . We didn't have any presentation; we just straggled up to the microphone and started to sing."

Today you can see the same youthful dishevelment, change-the-world-through-music drive, and good-time energy in the string bands that swarm summer gatherings such as the Mount Airy Fiddlers Convention in North Carolina or the Appalachian String Band Festival in Clifftop, West Virginia. What goes around comes around.

listed and bookings dried up. The group finally disbanded in 1952. Their Christmas Eve 1955 Carnegie Hall reunion concert would be the next thing in their future.

FOLK MUSIC GOES MAINSTREAM

That 1955 Weavers concert, immortalized in a live recording, marked what some see as the beginning of the *real* folk revival, but the 1958 release of the Kingston Trio's "Tom Dooley" really lit the folk fire. The song was a murder ballad, "Tom Dula," collected by Frank and Anne Warner from Frank Proffitt of North Carolina; the Kingston Trio added a dramatic recitation—"when the sun rises tomorrow, Tom Dooley must hang"—three-part harmonies, and Caribbean rhythms. (Harry Belafonte had recently had a runaway hit with his 1956 *Calypso* album.) Listening from the vantage of the twenty-first century, it's hard to imagine ever being swept away by the song or for that matter by the Kingston Trio, especially after hearing Frank Proffitt's low, sweet voice, and incomparable banjo or the gritty string band rendition that G. B. Grayson and Henry Whitter recorded way back in 1929. (Take a break from reading this and check out all three; they're on YouTube.)

In the early 1960s, the world of folk music, specifically urban folk-based music, started growing with a sort of supercharged musical energy. Boston, Washington, Chicago, and Los Angeles all sprouted folk scenes. But, for many, New York City's Greenwich Village was the scene of scenes. The Village was chockablock with cheap rents, cheap eats, and places to play at every level, from Washington Square on Sundays to pass-the-hat houses to top-of-the-folk-heap clubs, and scores of young musicians slung their guitars (uncased, of course) on their backs and went. A fair amount of documentary footage from the time exists (check out the 2012 film *Greenwich Village: Music That Defined a Generation*) as well as many books and articles, not to mention Internet forums and the like, so I'll leave the sleuthing to those with a particular interest. The Village produced dozens of singer-songwriters, and indeed anyone wanting to write songs would do well to listen to some of the greats who came out of that time: Phil Ochs, Tom Paxton, Eric Andersen, Buffy Sainte-Marie, and of course Bob Dylan.

Dylan arrived in New York in 1961, a nineteen-year-old singer/guitarist with a voracious musical appetite and eclectic musical tastes but an ear for folk music. He played folk music, he said later, "because I had to make it somehow. . . . I played guitar, that was all I did." According to reports, those beginning months were hardly stellar, with missed opportunities and a lukewarm reception (performers just getting started should take heart), but when Dylan began focusing more on his own songs his career took a sharp turn toward runaway success.

Bob Dylan had a rare talent, but by all reports he listened to all sorts of music with an obsession and focus that seem a vital part of musical genius in any generation. His attention to and admiration of the music that went before him is a lesson for any aspiring songwriter.

"These songs didn't come out of thin air," he told the audience in his speech accepting the MusiCares Person of the Year 2015 award. "I didn't just make them up out of whole cloth. [They] all came out of traditional music: traditional folk music, traditional rock & roll, and traditional big-band swing orchestra music."

He went on to say: "I learned lyrics and how to write them from listening to folk songs. And I played them, and I met other people that played them, back when nobody was doing it. Sang nothing but these folk songs, and they gave me the code for everything that's fair game, that everything belongs to everyone. For three or four years, all I listened to were folk standards. I went to sleep singing folk songs. I sang them everywhere, clubs, parties, bars, coffeehouses, fields, festivals. And I met other singers along the way who did the same thing, and we just learned songs from each other. I could learn one song and sing it next in an hour if I'd heard it just once.

"If you sang 'John Henry' . . . as many times as I did, you'd have written 'How many roads must a man walk down?' too." (For the complete text of this speech, which *Rolling Stone* rightly calls "riveting," go to the *Rolling Stone* website.)

Bob Dylan was probably *the* voice of 1960s folk music, but he was in good company. Many in the urban folk revival were using their music artfully and boldly to spotlight social injustice and get people thinking about things differently. Joan Baez sang and worked to foster civil rights, Buffy Sainte-Marie championed the cause of Native Americans, while Phil Ochs and Tom Paxton spotlighted the plight of American youth who stood to be conscripted to fight in Vietnam. But by this point things were fragmenting. In 1965 Bob Dylan famously went electric onstage at the Newport Folk Festival, polarizing the folk community and further blurring the definition of what could be called "folk." The times they were a-changin'.

There is a lot more to know about this vibrant and odd time, but it's enough to understand that if you write songs and identify with the "folk" genre, you're standing on ground cleared by those earlier singer-songwriters of Greenwich Village and elsewhere.

WHICH SIDE ARE YOU ON?

Protest songs and the people who sing them are as American as, say, "Yankee Doodle," which our rebellious forefathers in the Revolutionary War era sang in defiance of the British who would mock them. Skip to the mid-1800s and you have the Hutchinson Family Singers of New Hampshire, who used four-part harmony arrangements to deliver to audiences their views on hot-button topics of the day—abolition, workers' rights, women's rights, and temperance. Fifty years down the line, labor activists such as Joe Hill, who was famously tried and executed for murder in 1915, wrote and repurposed hymns and songs as part of their unionizing activities. Coal mine unionizing efforts in Kentucky and West Virginia into the 1930s also found melodic support with singer/activists such as Aunt Molly Jackson, who wrote "I Am a Union Woman" and the moving "Poor Miner's Farewell."

From the 1940s and on into the 1960s, everyone with the slightest interest in "folk" seemed to be writing or adapting protest songs, but those of the Civil Rights Movement were especially prominent. These "freedom" songs drew from many sources, including spirituals, gospel songs, and chants, and they included the iconic "We Shall Overcome" (from Charles Tindley's "I'll Overcome Someday"). Joan Baez was front and center among Northern singers who went south to lend their voices to the struggle. But African Americans in the South were also using songs to create community and resolve. A particularly moving collection of these songs, many recorded live in mass meetings in churches, came out in 1997 on a Smithsonian Folkways collection: *Voices of the Civil Rights Movement: Black American Freedom Songs 1960–1966.*

"THE QUEEN OF FOLK MUSIC"

In his MusiCares speech in 2015, Bob Dylan calls Joan Baez "the queen of folk music then and now," and to many she was and is. In the 1960s urban folk revival she was a star among stars. She had a voice that soared and shimmered and a presence that brought a hush to crowds numbering in the thousands. And she rose quickly through the folk firmament. In 1959 singer Bob Gibson had her join him onstage at the Newport Folk Festival, and by November 1962 she was on the cover of *Time* magazine. She became legendary both for her work onstage and at the forefront of such causes as civil rights, free speech, and nonviolent protest. In her music she paid homage to traditional singers and their songs and at the same time embraced the new songs and emerging songwriters (she famously championed Bob Dylan in his early career). "Joan Baez is often touted by classical singers as the folk singer they love because of her high resonance," says New York singer Emily Eagen, who straddles both worlds.

THE FOLK OF FOLK MUSIC

Running through the exuberant energy of the urban folk music revival was a continual stream of people who could be thought of as "tradition bearers"—the people some viewed as the *real* folk of folk music. These were musicians, mostly from the rural South, who sang and played music from where they grew up. Singers as various as Jean Ritchie and Doc Watson, Roscoe Holcomb and Dock Boggs, Almeda "Granny" Riddle and Hedy West traveled to folk clubs and universities and festivals large and small, sharing this other side of folk music with enthusiastic listeners.

At the same time, thanks in part to the release in 1952 of Harry Smith's three-volume (six records in all) set *The Anthology of American Folk Music*, young musicians began studying the music of the old-time musicians who came before them. Not all of these young obsessed musicians were in New York, although many folk revival histories center on that city. One player out of Washington, D.C., was Mike Seeger, who in 1958 joined with Tom Paley and John Cohen to form the New Lost City Ramblers, a band predicated on the desire to play the music of the rural Southeast that they had all been listening to and learning for years.

"The Ramblers were profoundly respectful of the music that they heard on old records, and they strived mightily to present 'authentic' faithful recreations of the material they had chosen," Bill Malone writes in his biography of Mike Seeger, *Music from the True Vine*. But he goes on to point out that the band faced some of the same issues that young people doing old music face today. "If they strayed too far from the music of their old-time heroes, they would lose the support of the traditionalists," he writes. "But if they labored too hard to sound exactly like them, they ran the risk of being accused of 'slavish imitation' or of 'slumming' in poor white culture."

But the New Lost City Ramblers showed it could be done, leading the way for a blossoming of old-time string bands such as the Highwoods String Band, and on the West Coast a band I helped found, the Any Old Time String Band. We were all women and all accomplished instrumentalists, and we had an exceptional lineup of singers, giving the band a particular place in the old-time music of the day.

Another stream flowing concurrently through the revival years was bluegrass. Although it's doubtful that any of the early bluegrass artists— Bill Monroe, Earl Scruggs, Carter and Ralph Stanley, Jimmy Martin— ever thought of themselves as folk musicians, their music became the focal point for numerous "citybillies" at the time.

Bluegrass was at "the very core of the folk music heyday," Eric Weissberg said in Robbie Woliver's *Hoot: A 25-Year History of the Greenwich Village Music Scene*. "It got a lot of people out to concerts who wouldn't have gone to other types of music concerts. If you liked it at all, you liked it a lot."

Bluegrass was something new, and Bill Monroe is generally credited as being its founder. In the mid 1940s he formed the "Blue Grass Boys" (named for Kentucky, his home state), which featured banjo hot-shot Earl Scruggs, guitarist Lester Flatt, and Monroe's high-tenor lead singing, as well as tight harmonies, virtuosic mandolin and guitar, and a pushing, front-of-the-beat rhythm anchored by a standup bass. Alan Lomax gave the music his seal of folk approval in a 1959 article in *Esquire* magazine, "Bluegrass Background: Folk Music with Overdrive." "Out of the torrent of folk music that is the backbone of the record business today, the freshest sound comes from the so-called bluegrass band," he wrote. Among the bluegrass musicians in addition to Monroe who caught the ears of the new aficionados were the Stanley Brothers (Carter and Ralph), Mac Wiseman, the Stoney Mountain Boys, and the Osborne Brothers, who in 1960 began performing bluegrass on college campuses, giving the new genre a new audience.

FAMILY MUSIC: JEAN RITCHIE, DOC WATSON, ALMEDA RIDDLE

Many traditional singers come from families of musicians to whom they acknowledge a debt. Among these, Jean Ritchie and Doc Watson are particularly well known and are featured on numerous recordings that are readily available, including one of a 1963 concert they did together at Folk City in New York. *The Watson Family*, which also came out in 1963, is a particularly moving collection of old songs, tunes, and ballads, featuring Doc and his wife, Rosa (their duet "Your Long Journey" remains one of the saddest parting songs ever), and her father, fiddler Gaither Carlton. The Ritchie family is acknowledged both in a 2003 recording, *Jean Ritchie: Ballads from Her Appalachian Family Tradition*, and in a small book that Jean wrote, *Singing Family of the Cumberlands*, which includes not only stories of her childhood but words and music for forty-two songs. Meanwhile, many of Jean's own songs are included on a tribute album, *Dear Jean: Artists Celebrate Jean Ritchie*, issued in 2015.

Almeda Riddle is less of a household name among the nonfolk public, but any singer who aspires to sing American ballads should listen to her (much is available online) and, in addition, read *A Singer and Her Songs: Almeda Riddle's Book of Ballads*. The book is a compilation of transcribed interviews with "Granny" Riddle covering all manner of singerly topics, from where she got various songs to her opinions on how to sing them.

AM I A FOLK SINGER?

Fast forward to today and you'll find that the image of "folk singer" has some baggage. Many musicians who could gather under the folk umbrella prefer other descriptors. Even Pete Seeger, the quintessential American folk singer in many people's eyes, grew to dislike the term. "According to the pop definition, to be a folk singer you have to be a (white) person on stage with an acoustic guitar singing a song in English—a song you just made up," he wrote in his autobiography *Where Have All the Flowers Gone.* "I use the phrase as little as possible now."

Others take the view that you can't really be a folk singer unless you're a tradition bearer. For these folks, real folk music made an end run around all the urban revivalists—the singers and songwriters of the folk craze of the 1950s and 1960s—to deliver the torch to such bred-in-the-bone musicians as West Virginia's Hazel Dickens and North Carolina's Ola Belle Reed (both exemplary singers and songwriters of recent years, and very much "of the people"). "One cannot join the 'folk'; one must be born into the culture," writes historian Bill C. Malone in his seminal book *Country Music, U.S.A.*

Fortunately, today we don't have to get into the argument of who is and who isn't a folk singer. It's enough to know that these factions exist. Most singers use the term "folk" only as a way to communicate with people who don't work in the genre, to conjure an image like the one Pete Seeger disliked, but without the negativity—simple music, straightforward singing, and acoustic instruments. Then, if there's an opportunity, they qualify with terms such as "roots," "vernacular," "Appalachian," "old-time," or the currently popular "Americana."

SO WHAT DOES ALL THIS MEAN?

Folk music has in its very concept the notion of history—of times and events and heartaches past and the people who have come through them, who have used their music to bring some understanding or joy or community feeling or even simply entertainment to their lives. Even in this quick look at a small portion of one country's music you can feel the richness of the folk form. Whether you're aspiring to become a folk singer or you're already deeply involved in some aspect of the music, knowing that there's a history behind you can give you a place to stand and a point from which to take new paths.

Alan Lomax once wrote: "Under the smooth, bland surface of popularized folk songs lies a bubbling stew of work songs, country blues, field hollers, hobo songs, prairie songs, spirituals, hoedowns, prison songs and a few unknown ingredients. This is the varied voice of our people crying out because they have something important to say."

So when you pluck that old folk song out of the crowd, and you go through all that's involved in working it up to sing, and you do your due diligence, tracing it back and listening to others who have handled it, you're helping those people speak out, and maybe yourself as well.

COLLECTIONS TO EXPLORE

Folk song collections abound. Here are a few I've used from time to time. This list is in no way exhaustive—it's merely a prod to get you out there hunting and listening to songs.

From the Ballad Hunters

The English and Scottish Popular Ballads. This is the culminating work of Francis James Child's ballad-collecting efforts in the nineteenth-century collection—305 ballads with variants that passed Child's criteria of being suitably old and unsullied. The collection or portions of it are available through booksellers, and various websites address the ballads in different ways. One of these lists some ten thousand recordings, dividing them by title—useful if you're intent on hearing various approaches to a particular ballad. There are countless recorded renditions of Child ballads on both sides of the Atlantic, depending on your vocal tastes. A relatively new recording is *Child Ballads*, by Anaïs Mitchell and Jefferson Hamer, which earned a spot on NPR's list of "Top 10 Folk and Americana Albums of 2013." In addition to being a good listen, the album shows you how two young singers chose to approach this very old body of work.

English Folk Songs from the Southern Appalachians. This two-volume collection was the result of the song-gathering journeys of English collectors Cecil Sharp and Maud Karpeles into southern Appalachia in 1916–1918. The two volumes together comprise 274 songs and 968 tunes culled from that material. Again there are various online sources, but this is an instance where it just feels right to hold the printed book in your hands.

For an intriguing exploration into Sharp and Karpeles's travels in the United States, try to catch a multimedia presentation of *Sharp's Appalachian Harvest*, researched and presented by well-known (to the folk world) singers Jeff Davis and Brian Peters. They use songs, photos, and more to evoke these seminal song-collecting journeys, and they have issued a CD as well.

African American Songs

Slave Songs of the United States. This anthology from 1867 was edited by William Francis Allen, Charles Pickard Ware, and Lucy McKim Garrison and reprinted by Dover. It includes a number of songs we've come to regard as standards, such as "Michael, Row the Boat Ashore" and "Jacob's Ladder" as well as extensive descriptions of how the songs are sung. For example:

"The leading singer starts the words of each verse, often improvising, and the others, who 'base' him, as it is called, strike in with the refrain, or even join in the solo when the words are familiar.

"When the base begins, the leader often stops, leaving the rest of his words to be guessed at, or it may be they are taken up by the other singers. And the basers themselves seem to follow their own whims, beginning when they please and leaving off when they please, striking an octave above or below . . . or hitting some other note that chords so as to produce the effect of a marvelous complication and variety and yet with the most perfect time and rarely with any discord."

American Negro Songs and Spirituals. This collection, by African American collector John W. Work of Fisk University, came out in 1940 and has also been reissued. In this collection of 230 songs, Work includes spirituals, blues, work songs, hollers, jubilees, and social songs. He also includes extensive notes and comments. Where applicable, the songs include harmonization—choral parts that give you some idea of how the songs might have been sung.

Singing in the African American Tradition. Taught by Ysaye Barnwell, a fabulous singer, educator, and longtime member of the vocal group Sweet Honey in the Rock, this four-CD instructional set has her explaining a series of African American songs, settling them into their historical niches and then singing them in all their parts so that singers and their singing friends can recreate them. It originally came out in 1989 (Home-spun Tapes) and remains a must-have for community choir leaders. Ysaye also gives excellent (and quick to fill up) workshops around the country and abroad. Keep an eye out.

From the Lomaxes

Cowboy Songs and Other Frontier Ballads. This, John Lomax's first work, is the result of his work as a Harvard graduate student, but it was born out his childhood in Texas and his longtime love of the songs he heard as a child. This collection of songs, with a handwritten (complete with ink blotches) foreword by Theodore Roosevelt, includes many songs we know without knowing how we know them—"Home on the Range" and "Whoopee-Ti-Yi-Yo, Git Along Little Dogies" are but two of them. Some have the tunes written out as well.

American Ballads and Folk Songs and *Our Singing Country.* These two collections from John Lomax and his son and collecting partner Alan Lomax are pretty much indispensable for anyone interested in traditional American music.

Lomax Archives Online

The Association for Cultural Equity now has more than seventeen thousand recordings from the Lomax collection available. The American Folklife Center at the Library of Congress is also a source for record-ings. It takes some stick-to-it-iveness to get to the right place; the magic words are "audio" and "online."

Children's Folk Songs

American Folk Songs for Children, American Folk Songs for Christ-mas. Ruth Crawford Seeger, wife of Charles Seeger (patriarch of the Seeger clan) and mother to Mike, Peggy, Barbara, and Penny, was a renowned modern composer who joined her husband in his keen inter-est in American folk music. These two books of songs, arranged and compiled by Ruth Crawford Seeger, are useful for their songs and also for Ruth Seeger's approach to singing them, which she details at length.

Mike and Peggy recorded ninety-four of their mother's songs in 1977, a collection that is now available on CD.

Frank and Anne Warner

Traditional American Folk Songs. Anne Warner culled the songs included in this hefty book, which came out in 1984, from the collecting trips she and her husband Frank made starting in the late 1930s. Their trips were relegated to vacation time, since they had jobs, but they managed in that time to travel down the Atlantic seaboard, from New Hampshire to North Carolina and westward into southern Appalachia. They recorded some one thousand songs in all, bringing to light such iconic ballads as Frank Proffitt's "Tom Dula." The Warners spent considerable time with the singers who sang the songs they collected, learning about their lives and how and where they had come to know what they sang. This book allows us to tag along on these trips.

Two CD compilations of the original recordings have come out of the Warners' work: *Her Bright Smile Haunts Me Still: The Warner Collection, Volume I* and *Nothing Seems Better to Me: The Music of Frank Proffitt and North Carolina: The Warner Collection, Volume II.*

Smithsonian Folkways

Smithsonian Folkways Recordings is the nonprofit record label of the Smithsonian Institution, which took over the Folkways Records catalog in 1987 after the death of founder Moses Asch. Asch, a larger-than-life character in the New York folk scene in the mid-twentieth century, launched Folkways in 1948 and issued more than two thousand albums over the years. From the start the Folkways sound was a far cry from the slickly commercial albums of the day, reflecting Asch's eclectic tastes. He recorded variously such well-known musicians as Woody Guthrie and Pete Seeger and less well-known artists such as the Six and Seven-Eighths String Band from New Orleans and the Poplin Family of Sumter, South Carolina. The now-vast catalog is a seminal resource for all things folk. What's more, Smithsonian Folkways keeps in place Asch's policy that all the Folkways titles ever issued are always available. If it's not in stock they'll print you your very own copy on request (and a modest payment).

An added note: Smithsonian Folkways has just acquired the Arhoolie Records catalog, with a similar promise to keep them all in print, so now that immense body of recordings is accessible through the label.

Harry Smith

The Anthology of American Folk Music. This is the famous compilation edited by Harry Smith and often referred to simply as "the Harry Smith anthology." It's a three-volume, six-record, eighty-four-track set that came out on Folkways in 1952, when Smith was only twenty-nine, culled from his vast collection of 78 rpm recordings from the 1920s and 1930s. Track No. 1 was "Henry Lee," by Dick Justice, and track No. 84 was "Fishing Blues," by Henry Thomas. In between came old-time, early country, blues, Cajun, fiddle tunes, shape-note, and more. Folkies of the 1950s and 1960s inhaled it all. Bob Dylan and Joan Baez both recorded songs they found there. "The anthology was our bible," folk musician Dave Van Ronk wrote, looking back on those years. "We all knew every word of every song on it, including the ones we hated." Today the anthology is beguiling a new generation of listeners. Lance Ledbetter, founder of Dust-to-Digital, a relatively new label that releases excellent compilations of old records (check out "Goodbye, Babylon"), recalls staying up all night when he first got hold of the anthology. "I felt like I was going into this big, beautiful house for the first time," he says. "I got to look out all the windows and hear all the sounds, and it was just a life-altering event." Harry Smith has himself become something of a folk hero, and various festivals honor the man and his anthology. The Harry Smith Frolic, for example, takes place every July in Massachusetts and features, among other things, a midnight reenactment around a campfire of an album in the anthology. Smithsonian Folkways has reissued the entire collection in a six-CD set with the original notes as well as "essays, appreciations, and annotations" relating to the anthology.

The Digital Search

You can, in your hunt for songs, choose to let your fingers do the walking—something I do regularly. Although some of the online collections are not particularly user-friendly, there are sometimes real people at the collections who can help if you have something specific in mind. It's good to keep notes on where you've been and what you've found. By not doing that I've sometimes lost gems that I had uncovered on some midnight foray.

In terms of collections, the Library of Congress (American Folklife Center at the Library of Congress) has a huge amount of material. In addition, universities and other scholarly organizations are continually digitizing their archives and making new collections available online. Berea College in Kentucky houses a collection of Alan Lomax's Kentucky recordings, and Missouri State University has the Max Hunter collection of Ozark material. Another source for Ozark songs is the John Quincy Wolf Collection of Ozark Folk Songs. With any dedicated sleuthing you're bound to uncover enough to keep you sitting in front of your computer for hours and days.

Many other collectors have contributed mightily to the body of American folk song in the past century. One of the giants of today is folklorist and record producer Chris Strachwitz, who has just turned over his Arhoolie Records catalog—some three hundred fifty albums of Tex-Mex, blues, bluegrass, Cajun, and much, much more, the result of decades of recording—to Smithsonian Folkways. And the Smithsonian Folkways site itself is always worth a scroll around.

For a list of websites referred to in this chapter, visit the companion page to this book on the National Association of Teachers of Singing website, www.nats.org/. ♪

Collecting Today

You too can be part of the song collecting process that has contributed so much to our musical heritage. For excellent pointers on how to do this, check out Kip Lornell's *Exploring American Folk Music: Ethnic, Grassroots, and Regional Traditions in the United States*. He provides an excellent how-to guide in the third chapter, "Fieldwork in Twenty-First Century America."

2

VOCAL NITTY-GRITTY

Remember that the point of singing is to enjoy making music in front
of (and sometimes with) others. You might need to work very hard
in order to learn how to make this happen every time. That is the
purpose of studying—to improve not only your skills, but your ability
to enjoy being a singer.

—Jeannette LoVetri, longtime voice teacher and
creator of Somatic Voicework™

At some point, most of us who sing want our voices to behave in
some way that's different from how they are behaving. We want to
sing higher, lower, louder, freer—with more ring, more brightness,
more power, more stamina. We may have a sound quality in mind or a
particular singer we hope to emulate, but the bottom line is we want to
sing better.

Just identifying that as a goal is an important first step. The next step,
of course, is doing something about it. Right away, for many "folkies"
there's the fear that vocal training will somehow destroy our authentic
folk sound, change our voice, make us sound "like an opera singer"—the
most oft-voiced fear among folk musicians seeking vocal help. But of
course singing is like any instrument (folk or otherwise)—it responds to
information and lots of intelligent practice.

A CASE IN POINT

Folk musician Lissa Schneckenburger started fiddle when she was six years old and went on to the New England Conservatory for violin. "I also sang," she says, "just for my own enjoyment, but I was dissatisfied with my performances whenever I sang solo. My voice just wasn't there." She figured she just didn't have the "right kind of voice," but then in conservatory she had an epiphany. "I actually witnessed friends of mine actively working on their voices," she recalls. "I could literally hear the development from month to month to month. I thought, maybe there's no such thing as having a good voice or a bad voice, maybe it's just like the violin; you have to work at it."

Lissa buckled down to the task of becoming a better singer. She worked on her own and tried various teachers, but things began to shift when she moved to New York and started working with Jeannette LoVetri, a voice teacher for more than forty-five years, director of the Voice Workshop in New York City, creator of Somatic Voicework™, and coincidentally the teacher who has had the most to do with my own personal journey of vocal self-discovery. "She was very direct and practical with all my technical questions," Lissa says. "I would sing a particular song and say, 'I keep going out of tune on this word every single time' or 'This particular ornament I want isn't clear,' and she would say, 'Oh, this is the reason, and this is how you work on it, and this is a strengthening exercise, and this is another strengthening exercise to get at it from a different angle,' and I would go home, work on it for a couple of weeks and go back to her with more questions."

Gradually things changed. Lissa recalls noticing that she could sing louder ("I've always had a small voice," she says, "and I still do, but it used to be prohibitive"). Then she noticed that her range got broader ("That was a nice benefit!"), and stylistic details that she was having trouble with became more accessible ("I really love very ornamented English, Scottish, and Irish ballads, and those ornaments improved"). It was a gradual process, but in the end Lissa found out that in fact she *did* have the right kind of voice. Check her out on YouTube.

A JOURNEY OF SELF-DISCOVERY

However, if you're like many folk musicians, and you're timid about presenting yourself to a teacher, you're in luck. Folk music is for self-starters. You'll find (or write) songs you want to sing; you'll listen to sounds and singers you admire and hear ornaments and styles you want to incorporate into your own singing. This process of listening, absorbing, imitating, and experimenting is what folk music is all about. But it's not just songs that you can work on as you develop your craft; you can also start to absorb good vocal technique.

"Technique is being able to do whatever you want," says New York singing teacher Emily Eagen. Your way to good technique might in fact be a teacher, or a book like this one, or simply exploring singing through recordings and trying things out. The main thing is that you can figure out what you need.

How do you learn good vocal technique? While there are websites that can teach you lick for lick the guitar backing for Gillian Welch's "Orphan Girl" or a mandolin solo for "I'll Fly Away," there's really nothing (that I've found) that's aimed at singing techniques for folk musicians. And to further complicate things, it's really difficult to cull the general singing advice you need from the many, many sites and blogs that want to tell you what's what. It's not that these websites are wrong. While misinformation *is* everywhere, solid vocal advice is as well, but for the independent student the sheer wealth of it is confusing—and sometimes contradictory. What we can do here is give you enough information that you can get started, and your ongoing path will be clearer.

A word of caution, though: In this process of self-discovery, you need to pay scrupulous attention to how what you're doing feels. "If your voice feels good and sounds good, it probably is good," says vocal coach Jeannette LoVetri, "If it feels bad and sounds good, something is wrong," she says. "If you can't make yourself sound good or feel good, go get help from a skilled singer or teacher. If that doesn't help, seek out an otolaryngologist or throat specialist and get examined right away. Vocal problems that are ignored can lead to serious issues down the road, both vocal and in general health." In other words, don't do something that hurts, and if it does hurt, get help. In singing there's no gain in pain.

DO I NEED A TEACHER?

If you're in a quandary about how you're singing—if you have a particular problem or your voice gets tired mid-concert or you simply, as one of my students said, want to "not suck so bad," a vocal teacher can help. And of course, those of us who teach singing see the merits of working with a teacher—from simply benefiting from an objective set of ears and eyes to learning an organized, stepwise approach to singing better. There are plenty of teachers who want to take you down the classical road to an art song or an aria, but there are more and more teachers who, like Julie Dean in Charlotte, North Carolina, take a more functional approach, teaching technique and helping singers to realize the music they themselves choose. In much the same way you might choose a doctor, you can choose a teacher who feels right for you. Try a lesson or two, explain what you hope to gain, and see if the fit is right.

And you don't need to be a beginner to get something from vocal coaching. "I've worked with a lot of singer-songwriters in recent years, people who've been singing for a long time," Julie says. "When they get some instruction or they get some guidance or they just get some knowledge about what they are doing, it's really helpful."

EVERYONE NEEDS A HELPING HAND

Mention Joan Baez and what comes to mind is her extraordinary, clear soprano. Her voice in the 1960s had an easy, natural quality, and it continued to serve her well over some five decades of performing. But when she reached her early seventies, she says, her voice got "unmanageable." "I didn't hate it, but I hated being preoccupied with trying to get a high note right, not getting to what I wanted to hear," she told the *Guardian* in a 2014 interview. Finally she consulted an ear, nose, and throat specialist, and "we concluded that I was so busy trying not to hear the current voice (especially the high notes) that I just locked everything up. He then sent me to his vocal therapist, a lovely young woman who opened up a whole new toolbox. After two lessons I went on tour and the entire group noticed the change. The voice returned and the notes started to come back."

It's a lesson to take to heart for any aspiring folk singer. If something's wrong with your voice—even if, like most of us, you don't have a voice like Joan Baez's—you can work to fix it.

STANDING STRAIGHT AND TALL

The first factor in good singing technique is a good singing posture. It sounds so simple, but like most folk singers I brushed aside this part of singing for a long time, even as really excellent teachers tried to point out the error of my ways. Deep down I didn't want to look like some caricature of a "classical" singer. So even as I diligently worked on other aspects of good vocal technique, I continued to collapse my chest (doing the guitar player's hunch) and jut my chin out. It wasn't until I really began trying to figure out why some days I could sing effortlessly with a free, ringing tone, and other days I couldn't, that I began shifting around how I was standing (and sitting), and my singing became much more consistently what I wanted.

What is good singing posture? It is pretty much common sense, echoed by every vocal teacher I've talked to, as well as a couple of physical therapists: Stand straight and tall, with nothing locked or tense and your feet comfortably placed about shoulder-width apart. You can think specifically about relaxing other areas—your eyes, face, jaw and tongue, neck, shoulders. If "relaxing" seems impossible, think instead of "releasing"—different words trigger different things for different people. Check that you're not drooping, though. The idea is more of engaged relaxation. Emily Eagen describes it as "buoyancy," which works for me.

One problem with singing and playing an instrument is the tendency to wrap yourself over or around your instrument in some way. A microphone just exacerbates the situation. So check that your chin is back far enough that your head is over your shoulders, not over your guitar, and is level. I've found it useful to think about lengthening the back of my neck, which corrects my tendency to slouch and jut my chin. This one small adjustment can release whatever issues I might be having that day in shifting from low to high notes. If you sit to sing—and there are occasions when folk musicians do this—you can still adjust yourself to create that feeling of upright, aligned buoyancy. Note that these body alignments are all really subtle and should not look or feel at all forced or weird. Also—and this is the hard part—you need to practice them so that they're second nature. Just knowing about good posture isn't enough.

BREATHING, AIRFLOW, AND BREATH SUPPORT

For folk musicians, breathing for singing can be hard to pin down and still harder to do. Airflow is something we never think about, and breath support is just one of life's mysteries. While you're not likely to be called on to sing long passages over an orchestra without amplification, as opera singers are, some control of your breathing and an understanding of what you're going for can help make you a more flexible, resonant, and in-tune singer. Even without studying the physiology of singing, which we won't go into here, you can actually accomplish quite a lot if you incorporate breathing into your practice routine. Like good posture, good breathing really does help you sing better.

Jeannette LoVetri describes breathing for singers very succinctly: "Inhale with the idea that you are breathing down into the bottom of the lungs, which extend down into the lower part of your ribs. While you are singing, try to keep your rib cage expanded (it will want to collapse as your lungs deflate) and pull your abdominal muscles slowly in and up. Keep singing while you work on all of this." In short, your chest remains lifted and open while you're breathing and singing, and all the real action happens in your abdominal muscles.

If you're having trouble getting that "lifted" feeling, teacher Kate Howard suggests imagining a rubber ring around your chest. As you breathe in, the ring fills up, and when you sing or breathe out, it remains inflated. "This image helps you to keep the chest inflated as you sing and stops any droop," she says. "Another way is to imagine tennis balls under your armpits; with your arms relaxed and out, it gives more space in your chest." Meanwhile, if you're having trouble locating those abdominal muscles, try pressing your hands together in front of you, as if you're squeezing an egg. You'll feel the pull below your navel. Or do a couple of sit-ups.

And while we're thinking about muscles, take a moment to feel the horseshoe of intercostal muscles across your mid-back and sides under your ribs. These are what keep that lifted chest position, and you'll hear singing teachers talk about them, so it's useful to know where they are and what they do. See figure 6.2.

"Airflow" is a term to describe the air you exhale as it moves up through your larynx (the vocal apparatus in your neck) into your throat and up into your mouth, allowing you to create sound. As singers we want this airflow to be steady and consistent, which is where exercises such as the hiss breath come in. The real work of breathing and control-ling airflow is to keep things low in your body. From your rib cage north, everything is as relaxed and free of tension as possible. ♪

Breath management—the term I like to use instead of "breath support"—has to do with the balance between the air you take in and the air you expel. You take in a moderate amount of air on your inhale, and you expel a measured but smaller amount of air on your exhale. Another way of thinking of it is managed air pressure. By engaging your abdominal muscles you can manage your airflow in a steady stream while your throat remains open and your chest lifted. This air pressure works to "support" your singing, allowing your vocal apparatus to do its work freely without your throat, neck, shoulder, and jaw muscles getting into the act, choking your sound.

How much of this breathing work do we need as folk musicians? Really not a huge amount, but good breathing like good posture is wo-ven into our ability to make beautiful (and loud) sounds, so it's worth

RECEIVING SOUND

I don't use a lot of images in my teaching, but some can be useful. One that I first heard from Kate Howard when we were co-teaching Village Harmony teens was the idea of pulling the sound in to you instead of pushing the sound out away from you.

"Folk singers tend to push their voice out," she says. "What a lot of clas-sical singers are taught is to receive the sound, which counteracts pushing and also helps the brightness of the sound." Emily Eagen expresses it an-other way: "The best singers sing to, not away from, the body; it's always as if you're bringing it back in, you're never pushing out. Don't think of the voice as a bellows. You're not squeezing air out to make sound—it's the opposite." Bringing the sound toward you instead of sending it for-ward can help straighten your tone as well, says Charles Williams, so if you're struggling with too much vibrato, the image of "receiving sound" may be something to play around with.

incorporating breathing exercises into your practice so that you can breathe in a "singerly" fashion. You want it to all happen automatically, with nothing forced or tense. One beginner mistake I see is people taking huge breaths in, which sort of jams up the entire breathing mechanism. You don't need to fill your lungs or gulp air in any way. Less is more. The idea is to breathe efficiently and in a way that enhances your singing rather than hobbling it.

These descriptions I've given you here have to do with what it *feels like* when we breathe for singing—something to get you thinking about it. What really goes on anatomically is somewhat more complex and fascinating. For a more detailed exploration, see chapter 6.

RESONANCE, VOICE PLACEMENT, AND VOLUME

Resonance is one of those singer terms that you'll hear in folk circles and will have a basic understanding of, but would likely be hard-pressed to define. *Merriam-Webster's Dictionary* defines "resonance" as "a quality imparted to voiced sounds by the resonance-chamber action of mouth and pharynx [the space of your throat and mouth coupled together as a bent tube] configurations." It's created by sound pinging off hard surfaces and amplified by hollow spaces that create a resonating chamber. Where I live in the Vermont woods, there's a downy woodpecker that rat-a-tats on the corner of our metal roof every spring. He's staking his territory and using our house as a very effective resonating chamber to announce his claim.

We have various resonating chambers in our bodies, and singers over the centuries have learned to exploit them. These are principally located in our head—our sinus cavities (behind the nose) and our mouth, in particular the hard palate (the bony plate located in the front roof of the mouth). We articulate sound with our tongues, and if we have created the sound just right it pings off these cavities and projects effortlessly. This is the goal. There are numerous highly prized but non-singerly sounds made in the folk world that exploit these resonating spaces (check out the annual National Hollerin' Contest at Spivey's Corner, North Carolina, for some fine examples of projected vocal resonance), but resonance is particularly critical for singers.

So how do you find resonance? It's a question of "moving" your sound to where you can feel it vibrate. In the folk world we talk about voice "placement," but as with many things in singing, we're talking about a feeling, not the physical actuality. You can't actually move or place your voice anywhere. But if you make an exaggerated *mmmm* sound as much toward your nose as possible and then let it drop back a tick to where you can feel the vibrations around the bridge of your nose and under your eyes, you've found the resonance that's at the center of most American roots music. It's somewhat nasal—in fact nasal resonance is one of the biggest differences between a folk/country and classical singing—but the sound you produce feels "forward," like it's more in your sinuses, as if you could taste it and say "yummmm." You should be able to pinch your nose and still make the sound, an activity that singer Moira Smiley has her workshop students do to find this placement. In folk-speak we call this sound "forward," but, as Emily Eagen points out, "it's not due west, it's northwest"—above the mouth.

Much like with your voice, you can't physically "move" your resonance, but you can play around with it. If, for example, you "move" your resonance to your sinuses, really activating them, you'll eventually discover what Emily calls "a plumb line" down to your chest. "It's like an alignment," she says. "Suddenly your chest starts resonating too because your air column and your voice column are basically as stacked as they can be.

"Medieval architects would sometimes set a window so at the moment the sun is just right it makes a pattern on the floor," Emily continues. "That's what it's like. When I get my sinus resonance just right there is no up or down—it's all resonance."

This alignment, once you find it, is easy to relocate when you're singing in the shower, but during performances, when factors such as microphone placement weigh in, it can be elusive. This is why you practice it, so you can find the alignment easily and be aware and make adjustments when you find that you've contorted yourself for a performance situation.

Another way to think about resonance is to go for what singer and teacher Charles Williams calls "tone in the bone." "The basic thing is the placement of the voice—'tone in the bone,'" he says. "If you put your fingers on your cheekbones (by your nose) and your forehead and hum, you'll feel the vibration. That's nature's loudspeaker, and that's where your voice should be placed. If you think in terms of your eyes and your nose—not closed off so it's nasal, but, yes, in the nose—you're not pushing in your throat." He continues, "If you're in the resonance you'll project naturally—you won't need to push or press or dig in the chest or try to give a lot of volume. Less is more." If you're having trouble finding this particular resonance, Charles recommends that you bend, with legs well planted and apart, so that your face is parallel to the floor, and hum. "You can feel the sound falling into your face," he says. "That's where you want it." Once you've got it, he says, practice maintaining the placement as you gradually straighten up so you can remember and keep your humming in that resonant place. Making witchy sounds, as nasty and ugly as possible, also helps. You won't sing that way, but making those sounds reinforces where you want your sound to be. Moira Smiley points out that your body is like a stack of amplifiers, and you can learn to aim your sound to engage each one. Playing with non-singing sounds helps, such as "yoo-hooing" as if you're hailing a friend.

What to take away from all of this? First, resonance is a good thing, whatever style we're singing, and it is an absolute good in folk singing. You may be one of those lucky singers who have already discovered how to make your voice resonant without ever thinking about it in those terms. You just know how to do it. For example, Suzy Thompson, a bandmate of mine in the Any Old Time String Band, has always had a powerful ringing voice, and I noted recently that her daughter Allegra, a singer in her own right, has much the same resonance—and I doubt whether "resonance" crosses either singer's mind from year to year. But if you have on your singing wish list a desire to be louder, to project more, to have a clearer, more ringing tone, then playing around with these ideas is worthwhile. Remember, think forward—"so far forward it's a revelation to find it," is the way Emily Eagen puts it. As well as promoting good tone and volume, it releases the pressure on the back of the tongue and throat, always a desirable result.

NEGOTIATING YOUR REGISTERS

Vocal registers are different sound qualities associated in untrained singers with pitch range, and among my folk students they're cause for some confusion. The way we're going to approach it here is through the terms "chest," "head," and "mix." The low notes are your "chest" register

RESONANCE: MORE OF THE STORY

Recently I asked Jeannette LoVetri, New York vocal teacher extraordinaire, to explain this thing called "resonance" that looms so large in vocal technique. She was able to help me delve a little deeper into what's actually going on when we create resonance, and the important role vowels play.

"When we talk about resonance we need to think in terms of instrumental resonance: I can play a note, and it will vibrate a string and bounce off a sounding board—that's what we think of in terms of resonance in, say, a piano," she explains. "In order for me to get a different sound I can hit it harder or softer, because sound decays. That's true of the voice as well, because we run out of air. How we enhance resonance is a combination of things—making the most efficient shape we can for the vowel in our throats and our mouths, which includes the tongue and the jaw, on any given pitch at a specified volume.

"The pitches are given, so the variability is in how you do the vowel. Most people when they start to sing only do the kinds of vowels they do in normal conversational speech, which works at conversational volume and in conversational pitches, meaning right in the middle of their pitch range and not too loud. The louder you sing or the higher you sing or the lower you sing, the more you have to do something more with the vowel sound than you would when you talk. And the only directly available way to do that is to open your mouth.

"Over time if you've been taught to think about vowels as acoustic space, the back of the throat and back of the mouth start to respond and stay responsive as you sing, so if you're thinking of a smile and you're thinking of a yawn and someone is saying to you imagine that you can smile in the back of your mouth, that instruction is going to have some impact on the sound. What it does is boost the acoustic energy in the vowel sound so it seems like there's more resonance.

"Each vowel has its own little costume that it wears. The simplest version is that the *ee* is the smallest shape that we make, therefore it has the highest energy, the most 'tweeter,' and *oh* and *ah* are the lowest and have the most bass. We make the sounds flow together by equalizing the vowels, which we do by changing their shape. To bring in more treble on the low vowel, an *ah* or *oh*, we smile. When we smile the corners of the mouth retract and that shortens the length of tube between the mouth and the vocal cords. Shorter makes it smaller and smaller makes it brighter. To go the other way, to bring more bass into the *ee*, we make the tube longer by extending the lips, dropping the jaw or perhaps imitating a "Santa Claus" sound (or doing all of those in some combination), which brings out the bass.

"Volume is the final contributing factor to resonance. Volume is a breathing issue, and its enhancement comes from being able to take a deep breath with as little extra physical movement as possible, to keep the rib cage from collapsing, and to balance that against increased abdominal effort or pressure or contraction while you exhale the air. If a person is able to learn to do that, to counter the collapse and strengthen the exhale as the pressure in it decreases, we perceive that as loudness, and sometimes loudness enhances resonance. Not all loud sounds are maximally resonant, but if you're louder it is more likely that I'm going to hear you and get an idea of what pitches you're on."

(think strong speech), the high notes are your "head" register ("falsetto" in men), and the notes in the middle are your "mix," or varying mixtures between head and chest. These register shifts occur as we sing up and down the scale and the muscles in the larynx shift to accommodate the various pitches: they're powerful and full in our speaking chest voice and warm and pleasant in our "singerly" head voice, and doing a coordinated action between the two for the mix. For American folk musicians, who typically sing in the higher part of their chest range but may have to access their head register to accommodate an arrangement or a particular harmony, it's this vocal shifting of gears or "break" between the two registers that causes problems. In classical singing much emphasis is placed on a smooth transition between registers and strengthening the area around the transition notes between the registers. In folk singing we aren't necessarily looking for that smoothness (we like to exploit vocal cracks), but we do need strength in that area to negotiate those difficult "bridge" notes, because they tend to be weaker and often not as in-tune as we'd like. And that takes specific work. That means working on the register you don't use predominantly, which for women these days is often the head register.

"Most people are going to sing in some kind of a chest mix," says Jeannette LoVetri. When the chest range tops out—at a G or A♭ in women and at E or F in men—the voice will go flat or get tight or loud. "But if a singer is going to develop some capacity, even with a break, to at least keep going, they have to understand what the head register is and use it, even just to sing around the house." Working with both chest and head, or falsetto, will give singers an idea that there is someplace to go. If this seems entirely mysterious to you, try consulting a voice teacher who enjoys folk styles.

Adding low or high notes is a common item on a singer's wish list. Here again vocal coach Jeannette LoVetri offers advice. To raise your range, she says "sing lightly in an easy sound, allowing your throat to

VOCAL PILATES

If you're like most folk singers, one thing on your short list is to enhance the middle of your voice when you're moving from chest to head. As we've talked about, the point is to get the muscles to work together.

The first thing to find is that place where your voice wants to flip (around G or A♭ in women and at E or F in men). Sing a gentle five-note pattern (up the degrees of the scale from 1 to 5 or "do" to "sol") in this part of your range and you'll find where that flip naturally occurs.

Once you've got that information, practice short slides up and back through the area. Very forward nasal sounds such as *ng* and *nn* and *mm* work particularly well, as do hums. Go slowly and remember to be gentle. If you find yourself pushing or straining, stop, have a talk with your voice or throat, and start over again with renewed relaxation.

When you've become good at this, when your voice is really forward and you've got all your vocal ducks in a row (relaxed, forward tongue, and so on) you'll find that you can start to make that slide effortless and. without a break. Your muscles have figured out how to coordinate. And if you need the break, for example, for a word yodel, put a little speed on the slide and usually it will come back. Keep the breath pressure steady as you slide, and be sure the volume is even from low to high. Start with an *ee* first, then go to *ah* or *aw*. If the break doesn't come back, drop your voice back a notch, more to mid-mouth, and try again. That's where I can dependably get a vocal break. It takes playing around with, though, so figure out what works for you.

THE TERMINOLOGY TANGLE

In researching this chapter I found that while vocal teachers stand on a few basic, unified ideas, their ways of talking about them can vary wildly. Vocal teacher Julie Dean helped me untangle the terminology. "A lot of confusion comes about because there are a bunch of different terms for the same thing, depending on what technical school you belong to," she says.

"You can talk about singing in your chest register, singing with front muscle action, singing with your speaking voice muscles or even singing predominantly with the thyroarytenoid muscle. It's all the same.

"Most of the singer-songwriters I work with don't understand head and chest, so we work on it in terms of strengthening two different sets of muscles," she explains. "Basically we're strengthening the speaking voice muscles, to get the singer to be able to sing louder on higher pitches, and we're also strengthening the falsetto (false voice, like Julia Child or Marilyn Monroe) muscles in the throat, and then working for coordination with the two muscle groups.

"My analogy is a baton handoff in a relay race," she continues. "When it gets too hard for the speaking voice muscles to work on higher pitches, they just drop the baton, and then the falsetto muscles have to run to pick up the slack. That's when we hear what we think of as a break (or crack) in the voice. When the muscles get stronger, and coordinate better, we get a smoother handoff, or a clear strong sound as the pitch rises."

relax on the way up while gently putting more pressure on the muscles of the abdomen. If this is done carefully, it will help to raise vocal range."

To lower your range "relax your throat as much as possible, allow the jaw to fall down and sing sustained pitches such as *ohhh* and *ahhh* at the lowest pitches you can sustain. Gradually try to make them sound louder by pressing harder on the belly muscles.

"Long slides on lip trills and tongue trills can be helpful both going up and going down," she says. "Since it is possible to squeeze high notes, just singing them without some care and attention to comfort would be a bad idea. Low notes can be swallowed or pushed if done incorrectly and that can cause other problems. It's best to develop range slowly, a little at a time."

WHAT'S TRENDING

Trends come and go, even in folk music. For example, there are trends about which register you sing in, or what's considered a "good" folk voice. At the height of the 1950s and 1960s folk revival, Jean Ritchie, Joan Baez, and Joni Mitchell all sang in their head voices, while guys like Doc Watson, Tom Paxton, and Fred Neil stayed solidly in their middle chest range. Of course, on the country side of things we had such magnificent chesty women singers as Sara Carter, Kitty Wells, Wanda Jackson, and Patsy Cline, while across the gender divide Bill Monroe, the father of bluegrass, was building a career on his falsetto, but in general, men sang low and women sang high. That has done a flip, possibly because at the peak of the women's movement, women came to view low, chesty voices as empowering. Often the women who end up in my classes have come back to singing in their middle years after not singing much, so their voices have lost some of their high notes and the head voice is weak. It's harder to get to and harder to maintain. Meanwhile the guys, especially those who want to sing with their female friends, are finding that having a solid middle-lower range just doesn't work that well in close harmony. They need to be up in the higher parts of their range (that "high lonesome sound"), and even have some falsetto accessible, in order to accomplish what they're hearing.

AM I IN TUNE?

If you worry about whether or not you sing in tune, you're in good company. This is probably the biggest secret (or not so secret) worry of singers starting out, and it can really be distracting and confidence draining, so your best strategy is to tackle it straight on.

Tuning—intonation—problems are generally caused by lack of coordination in the vocal system, says Jeannette LoVetri. "Singers use the throat and mouth as a resonating tube, learning to tune to the pitch of various vowels and various volume levels," she says. "It's easy to have poor control over all these ingredients, particularly in specific pitch ranges, and that will affect intonation. Training and practice should take care of this unless the problem is severe." This sounds fairly technical, but the bottom line is that intonation is something you can improve.

Typically, if you want to become a professional singer, you already know that you can "match pitch"—sing the same note that someone else is singing. If in fact you can't, there are singing teachers who can work with you and help you train your voice to do that, but it takes time and a lot of consistent work. There are no quick fixes.

But if you've come far enough to be thinking about becoming a professional folk singer, you probably sing in tune most of the time—and you also probably sing out of tune some of the time. The trick is to figure out when, where, and why you're going out of tune so that you can fix the problem. Eventually the out-of-tune moments will be few and the in-tune moments many, and you can let the worry go.

Singing "out of tune" can mean different things. It can mean that you're singing some "cents" (a term you'll find in the audio world) below the pitch—singing "flat"—or above the pitch—singing "sharp"—or it can simply mean that your sense of the middle of a particular pitch doesn't jibe with your accompanying instruments or your fellow singers. It can also mean that you're making your vowels differently than your bandmates, or that you've got some vibrato going that doesn't match up with your singing partner's. Because there are so many ways to not match up pitch-wise, and because singers tend to take pitch problems so personally, I tend to avoid the terms "sharp" and "flat." Those particular terms often convey a lot more negativity than the situation requires. It's more constructive simply to determine where the trouble spots are and to try to fix them.

TYPICAL INTONATION TROUBLE SPOTS AND QUICK FIXES

Poor Posture: Posture, as we've said, has everything to do with good singing technique, and it plays a role in intonation as well. If you haven't incorporated posture into your practice routine, take a moment to check that everything feels loose, that you're standing tall and straight and nothing feels locked. You want your singing to be as free of tension as possible, and much of that comes from your posture and how you breathe—low, rhythmically, and easily into the bottom of your lungs.

Choir leaders work on intonation problems with their singers all the time, and much of their advice can be useful to the solo or band singer as well. Victoria Hopkins, a chamber choir leader in Britain, advises her singers to pay particular attention to lifting the sternum and elongating the back of the neck, taking care not to raise the chin above the point of level. "As the head comes into position, the pitch will improve," she says. "A raised chin leads to collapsed shoulders and chest, which leads to poor breathing and support, which leads to bad intonation."

She, like many choral leaders, also urges a relaxed, "smiley" face. "The quickest way to sing flat is to let the face sag," she says. For many folk singers, smiling while singing might feel artificial, but I've found that even if I don't smile, per se, if my face feels engaged, like I've just had a pleasant surprise, my singing is brighter and slight pitch problems go away.

Another British choir leader, Kate Howard, adds a useful tuning tip. "Some of it is the way your eyes are," she says. "If you look up you tend to sing sharp, and if you look down you tend to sing flat. If you look in the middle you'll generally start to sing more in tune." This, like raising your hand a bit on a note where you tend to go flat, doesn't have much to do with what's actually going on physically with your singing, but it does make you mindful of the trouble spot. In any case, you're not going to sing your most in tune if you're looking down at words or chords on paper, or checking to see where your fingers are on the guitar neck.

Lack of Pitch Awareness: This usually stems from lack of attention rather than faulty hearing. "If you don't quite know what notes you're going to sing, that's often at the root of intonation problems," says Emily Eagen. "When you clarify what the actual notes are, a lot of tuning issues get resolved." The fix can be as simple as figuring out where the 1 (the root, or the "do") is, getting that pitch firmly in mind, and making a mental check of where it occurs, so you've got a home-base note to come back to. And you can do that with any repeated note, so you have in mind what the pitch is meant to be each time it occurs. Other strategies involve noting the half steps—in a C major scale, the steps from E to F, and from B to C—and practicing them, or finding problematic jumps. A tendency to overshoot when you go down a fourth is particularly troublesome, as is not quite making it up to the third or seventh in a scale. This is particularly quirky in folk music, because we often flat the third or seventh of the scale to add a bluesy feel, and we often scoop up or slide to and from notes. It's worth checking when you're bending a note that you're getting where you mean to go (usually the true pitch of the note in question).

Another issue that comes up with traditional singing and traditional music in general is "the note between the notes," that is, the notes between the half steps, where no notes exist in the Western classical model—for example, a pitch between C and C♯. Some people call them "quarter tones" (a term that can mean different things to different musicians), and some call them "neutral" pitches. The more you work in the world of traditional music, the more sensitive you'll become to these pitch variances. It's enough to know at the outset that they're there.

Dropping Pitch at the Ends of Phrases: As you run out of breath, your pitch drops, so if you're finding this to be a problem, check how you're breathing going into the phrase or word in question. It helps to remember to breathe evenly, rhythmically, and frequently, and check that you're not doing some sort of odd breathing, such as a gasp breath, right before the problem phrase, as that can shake up your intonation. Another strategy is to think of singing past the end of a line, so the phrase ends purposely rather than dying for lack of air.

Intonation Problems on Specific Words: Specific words can be problematic, particularly with regard to the shape of the mouth. North Carolina singing teacher Julie Dean talks about this at length. "Sometimes it depends on the word," she says. "Maybe it's a particular vowel where someone is always going flat. For example, syllables that end with *r*, *l*, and *n* require the tongue to go up and back. If the tongue is changing in the middle of a word, that can affect the intonation of a pitch." Julie suggests singing the melody line on a single vowel, perhaps with a cork held in your teeth so the tongue is stabilized. Once you get the word in tune on the vowel you can reintroduce the consonants.

Intonation Problems on Specific Notes: Specific notes can also be problematic, especially if they're at a register shift or at the top or bottom of your range or the end point of a dramatic interval leap, such as a sixth or an octave. Planning how to negotiate those notes and then practicing what you want to do is helpful. If I'm having a particular problem with a note at the point I would shift from chest register, I will take the key of the song down to where the problem disappears and then gradually work back up, paying attention to how bright my vowels are, the register shift, and whether I want to exploit or erase the yodel-like voice crack.

A Few Useful Tips: Changing key can be helpful for general intonation problems as well. In the choir world, a tried-and-true cure for sinking in pitch is to raise the key a half step or whole step. This also works in folk singing. At the very least it will often put your vocal break in a different, more manageable place in the melody. Intonation fixes can be found in lowering the key as well. Sometimes, once you fix things in the new, lower key you'll find that you can go back to the old, higher key and the problem is gone.

Imagery can also be helpful in improving intonation, although what works for one person won't necessarily work for another. If you notice that you have a tendency to overshoot the mark on descending and ascending lines, try counteracting this by thinking "up" as you go down and "down" as you go up. Hand motions to put your body into this sort of opposite thinking can augment the effect—you raise your hand (gently) on downward passages and lower it on upward passages.

A more musically technical way to deal with difficult jumps is to practice nailing down all the scale pitches that you're leaping over, so that you really know the ground you're meant to cover. If you've got an octave jump in a song, practice singing the scale from the note you start on to the note you end on. Pay particular attention to the half steps. I find that singers will often let half steps slide to something more akin to three-quarter steps, which will pull an entire phrase out of tune.

THERE'S ALWAYS A FIX

The most important thing about singing "in tune" is to understand that it's simply one factor of musicianship, and that if you're singing "out of tune" it's something you can fix. First, though, you have to learn to hear it. If something sounds muddy or "not right" or if someone—a band-mate, family member, or singing coach—tells you you're singing "flat," pinpoint (or ask them to pinpoint) the spot, record yourself, and check it out. Test the pitch you're singing against a guitar (tuned to pitch) or piano. Is it the same? If it isn't, what's off about it? Is it just that one note or did you go off someplace before that? Work back, testing what you've sung against the guitar. Even if you spot your problem notes, you should also check your beginning and ending notes, and the notes you're sing-ing at each chord change, to determine if you're staying with your ac-companying instrument throughout the song. Keep playing the correct pitch or pitches and match them, singing them on a single vowel, such as [a]. This will help you develop your ear and also show you particular problem spots. At that point you can work with the various strategies we talk about here to get your singing pitch perfect or close to it. Along with this basic ear training comes the understanding that singing "out of tune" isn't a character flaw, but rather simply a part of your musician-ship that you can work on. It's like car trouble; find the problem and do whatever it takes to fix it.

FEELING THE UNISONS

If you're singing with someone else and intonation seems to be a prob-lem, practice unison exercises. I give several in the chapter on singing harmony because I find singing unisons such a valuable first step in that process, but you don't really need a specific exercise. Just make a habit, whenever you sing with someone or with the radio or a CD, to really focus on creating an exact unison. It's a process of opening your ears and singing in complete lockstep. If the person you're singing with is actu-ally in the room, it helps to make eye contact, getting your attention off yourself so that you're just a channel, and reflecting back what you hear. Let your mouth respond. "The idea," says Emily Eagen, who is also a big proponent of unisons, "is to get away from a preconceived idea of what you're *supposed* to do when you sing."

FOLK-SPECIFIC TECHNIQUE

> To sing this music effectively the singer . . . must not *try* to sing; that
> is, he must not try to impress people with his voice or voice culture.
>
> J. W. Work, in introduction to
> *Folk Songs of the American Negro*, 1907.

While good general vocal technique can improve your skills as a folk
singer, there are specific ways in which techniques in folk singing differ
from singing in other genres.

Not all folk voices are the same, of course, so not all singing techniques apply to every folk voice. For example, in the United States many
women who sing folk music today sing in their high chest voice, while
in Britain many women, particularly if they sing Celtic music, use their
head voice, often quite high. But of course there are women folk singers in Britain who sing in their chest voice (think of the fabulous Norma
Waterson) and in America who sing in their head voice (memorably Joan
Baez, but also legends who are no longer with us, such as Jean Ritchie
and Texas Gladden). Meanwhile, someone who thinks of herself as a
"traditional" singer might be going for a different sound than someone
who sings a lot of country harmony, and someone who's concentrating
on singing harmony might be looking for a different sound than someone who identifies as a singer-songwriter. And we haven't even stirred
into the pot the blues, or Cajun music, or any of the currently popular
world music styles such as Georgian or South African. There are no
absolutes, but there are certain mind-sets.

As singer Moira Smiley sees it, the central characteristics of the folkie
voice come out of such concepts as honesty, humility, introversion, and
not showing off, along with a little rebelliousness and a quiet fierceness.
"Those things are very central," she says. What vocal technique gives this
folk voice, she says, is "vocal control without a homogenized sense of what's
correct, musicality without buying into some sort of specific 'right' sound."

We'll deal with specific vocal styles and ornaments in a moment, but
there are a few things in folk music that are markedly different from
what you might be taught in a classical setting and that are worth noting.

OPEN WIDE? MAYBE NOT!

Most vocal teachers I've worked with emphasize opening your mouth in various ways, usually more than you're initially comfortable with, but many singers on the vernacular music circuit in America hardly open their mouths at all and sound great. Is there some sort of peculiar anatomy that they all share that allows them to do this? Not really. Rather they've learned to create a bright sound with minimal help from their lips. "There's no need to be flapping your lips in the breeze," says vocal coach Charles Williams, who has observed this phenomenon in a lot of accomplished folk singers he has worked with. "Most people open their mouths too much, and they lose that focus, that 'tone in the bone.'" He goes on to explain, "You don't have to be moving your mouth around to articulate." New York teacher Emily Eagen describes it as "throwing your voice to the front of your face." "You see so many people with the 'bluegrass deadpan,'" she says. "Their faces are really still, and that's actually how their resonance gets the most active. If you calm the lower half of your face, you realize how much you can do with the upper part. Your tongue is in the middle and upper part of your mouth, definitely not pulling back. . . . It connects you with your upper resonance. You have to experiment and find it." If that feeling of stillness seems elusive, think about ventriloquism, a notion that has come up in interviews a number of times in the course of doing this book. But heed Emily's caution: "The danger," she says, "is that if you're not opening your mouth, your jaw will be tight and that's not what you want either. You want a floating jaw."

And a "floating jaw," like an "open throat," is not something most folk singers typically think about. Vocal coach Jeannette LoVetri pinpoints the problem. "I can say 'open your throat,'" she says, "but what does that mean? How do I get more open? The first thing to open is what you can see and feel, and that is your mouth." Therein lies the dilemma. So in this journey of musical self-discovery you'll have to find out what works best for you.

SINGING OUT OF SPEECH

A truism in folk singing is that you "sing out of speech." What does that mean? At its simplest it means singing the way you talk, and folk singing today is definitely conversational rather than singerly. It's mostly in your chest register rather than your head register, although there are people who talk and sing predominantly in their head register. And although this speech-like singing is more elongated than regular speech, you rarely hear long-held notes at the ends of phrases or such embellishments as a swell in volume or a blossoming of vibrato. You're using the same cadence you

KEEPING IT STRAIGHT

In most styles of American vernacular music, you don't want vibrato. The ideal is a straight tone, and if you don't already do it, it can sometimes be difficult to accomplish. It takes a lot of vigilance and vocal control, and in fact spectrographic studies have suggested that vocal sounds, even ones that we perceive as "straight," rarely are. There's always some vibrato, but it's been minimized. In any case, it's difficult for most folk singers to control their vibrato—to either get it or get rid of it. A small amount of vibrato, a microscopic fluctuation, is not immediately noticeable and can sometimes make matching pitch a little easier. But in folk music, an obvious wide vibrato is not going to work.

Getting rid of a well-established vibrato takes dedication. "It has to do with paying attention to the very end of a phrase," says Emily Eagen, who admits she's worked hard to eliminate hers. "You may start off straight, but the end will quiver because you lost support. Really good straight tone takes a lot more muscle tone." Going soft and breathy will also reduce vibrato, but that's not a sound we go for much in American folk music.

A strategy for reducing vibrato that teacher Kate Howard uses with her students is to think of what you might yell as you fall off a cliff, a sort of descending cry. If you're doing it right, there won't be any vibrato. I like the *ee* vowel for this (like the last half of the Cajun yell, *ah-ee*), but other vowels work, too. Once you feel the place that the cry is happening, try it on a single, level tone. If you can keep the vibrato away, start adding a real musical pitch. Success? Then try a little scale passage, perhaps going up or down the scale degrees to a third or a fifth. The point is to find the "no vibrato zone" in the cry and then move that into your singing.

Another thing to think about is a perfectly flat tongue (of course, forward behind the front teeth and relaxed). One singing teacher described this tongue position to me as like a "piece of liver just lying there" but that perhaps is not an image you want to carry around with you.

would when you talk, and it is sometimes easier to activate if you think of speaking with a melody rather than singing out of speech. Classically trained singers have the biggest difficulty with this sort of singing. In my experience, they're drawn to singing the folk songs, but they have a hard time letting go of those aspects of their training that make them sound, well, classical. Coach Julie Dean, in working with such singers, has them speak phrases and then turn the phrases into song. "I try to get them to be as conversational as possible, close their mouths more," she says.

Emily Eagen finds that in making the speech-to-singing transition it helps to elevate your speaking pitch. "It doesn't have to be refined, it just has to be up there . . . full-bodied speech that you can turn into song," she explains. "That's what singers like Elizabeth LaPrelle [a young American traditional singer with startling vocal power] seem to be doing, going straight from speech to song, but there's an extra charge in the speech; the speech is activating the same things that you want in the singing. You're already talking in the notes you're going to use."

However, Emily points out, this sort of speech-like singing isn't exactly how you talk. "It's more resonant," she says, "and because there's a rhythm you have to somehow make your peace with vowels and use them to your advantage. That ties into pitch. The pitch is carried by vowels, so if you say 'sing like you speak' that can trigger a whole lot of things that you then have to adjust to."

STYLES IN FOLK MUSIC

Much of what characterizes folk music has to do with singing style. "If you take away song text and basic melody from a performance, what is left is singing style," explains music historian Charles Wolfe in the liner notes to the New World Records CD *I'm on My Journey Home*, which is a survey of folk vocal styles. "In some kinds of formal music, this is rather little; in most kinds of folk music, it is usually a great deal." But because folk music isn't formal, there isn't an agreed-upon, standard vocabulary, and terms borrowed from the classical genre often don't really work. "Many folk performers do things with their voices that have little or no relationship to formal music," Wolfe points out, "and it is difficult and misleading to describe those things with terms borrowed from formal music." What you can do is pay specific attention to certain style aspects of folk singing that help differentiate one piece of music or one folk sub-genre from another so that when you encounter these things in the context of a song, you'll know what you're hearing.

Rhythm is huge. Ask any five folk musicians what's the most important thing to get right in your music, and four will say rhythm. "Rhythm" covers many things, from the pulse or "groove" to the beat and what part of it is emphasized. Syncopation, speech cadences, anticipations and lags, and peculiarities resulting from breathing patterns and extra syllables are all part of the rhythm package. Phrasing enters into it, too. The pulse or groove is that repeated pattern of beats that gets your head bobbing and your toe tapping and in slower music helps you organize the music internally into something satisfying and expected. It also allows the savvy musician to play with those "ear" expectations, to anticipate a beat or lag behind it, to insert syncopated passages or vary phrasing or in other ways to surprise the listener (and fellow musicians). Meanwhile, where the beat is emphasized in this pulse varies from musician to musician, genre to genre. Bluegrass musicians play far (sometimes far, far, far) ahead of the beat. Blues musicians can amble lazily behind it. Country singers often sing against a particular off-beat shuffle (boomba CHUKa, boomba CHUKa) that promotes two-stepping around a dance floor, whereas the square-dance caller may keep the dance going with a more even auctioneer-like patter that toggles between speech and song. Pay attention to what's going on rhythmically in the music that sticks in your head. Try to set your metronome to it to see how it matches up. Of course, folk music these days is often recorded to a metronome track, which evens things out, but in older recordings you can see how some singers have a rhythm that seems to breathe (goes in and out of sync with the metronome), while others keep the steady rhythm going but play with the phrasing so that their singing overlays the basic rhythm rather than emphasizing it. Still others, particularly singers who are used to singing unaccompanied, throw all pretense of rhythm to the wind and just sing free-form. If you listen with rhythm foremost in your mind, you'll discover a lot.

Phrasing is part of overall rhythm, in that speech patterns have an inherent rhythm, but it deserves thinking about on its own merit. Folk singers have all sorts of variations in phrasing, ranging from the New England ballad singer who sings unaccompanied and keeps a very square meter within a phrase but then pauses, breaking the meter, in between phrases, to the ballad singers in southern Appalachia who use a more free-form style that British collector Cecil Sharp describes as "dwelling arbitrarily upon certain notes of the melody, generally the weaker accents. This practice, which is almost universal, by disguising the rhythm and breaking up the monotonous regularity of the phrases, produces an effect of improvisation and freedom from rule, which is very pleasing." Other phrasing oddities have to do with emphasizing odd words or syllables to drive the underlying pulse. In the Stanley Brothers' version of "Let Me Walk, Lord, by Your Side," for example, in the very first line "In *our* church on Sunday morning," the emphasis is on "our," which is also the highest pitch in the phrase. That's repeated in the chorus: "Steer *me* on the righteous pathway." This emphasis has everything to do with the character of bluegrass singing; to phrase the song another way would strip it of that flavor. ♪

Melodic variation is another major aspect of folk singing. Typically, folk singers don't look at written music. As they sing a song, they'll likely change the melody from verse to verse, phrase to phrase—either purposefully, for emphasis or to help the listener stay with the plot of the song, or merely as the result of the human (often unconscious) need to create. I'm reminded of those tribal rugs where the weaver has started with a pattern at one end and by the time she or he gets to the other end, the pattern has become something else. So when you're listening to music you're passionate about, pay attention to how and where things change and try to figure out what the variations do for the song. If you can, listen to different renditions of a song by a singer you're passionate about, listening for how he or she changes things up or evolves the song over time.

Musical taste plays a role. Too much melodic variation upsets the listener's sense of the underlying continuity in a song. This may be what you want, but it tends to be unsettling. There's a reason little children say "do it again." Repetition is satisfying.

The other thing to note is that in a lot of social singing situations, such as shape-note singing or community choirs, the idea is that you're one of a group of people on a part singing the same thing, whether or not it's written down. You won't be popular if you decide to change things willy-nilly.

Ornaments, at least in traditional music, are significant in differentiating one style of folk music from another, or even one singer from another within a style, and for many of these ornaments there is no name, per se, for what the singer is doing. You can only describe it—how a singer approaches a note, for example. In a lot of southern American music, a singer will slide up to or off of a note. He or she might also scoop up to the note, which involves a dip in pitch between two notes. This is used a lot if two notes in a phrase are the same, to give definition to the second note—in American roots music it's rare to find a singer singing a string of notes of the same pitch without inserting some sort of ornament to break up the string. Other word ornaments are more subtle, such as a note that bounces off the pitch of the previous word to the higher pitch of the new word. Emily Miller, an American traditional and country singer (shown on the cover of this book), advises working on ornaments in the context of a song where they're stylistically appropriate. "In old-time music the most important ornaments are things you wouldn't really even think of as ornaments, like doing a quick little step up to a note at the beginning of the word," she says. "So instead of starting at your goal note, the melody note at the start of a song, for example, you start on the step below and do a little step up into it. It's not a slide; it's a step up, or that's what I call it. It's usually on the first note of a phrase, and acts to present the phrase." Emily also points to what she calls "a three-note cascade" on a word where the top note is the most important and the other two are the ornament following it. The point, she says, is to work on it until it sounds believable, so that the ornament actually *is* an ornament and not part of the melody.

The ornament my students are always keen to learn is the little flip or release at the end of a word that you hear in many southern mountain (Appalachian, Ozark) singing styles. Emily describes it as "singing in chest voice in a powerful way and letting your voice flip into head at the end of the word, but not actually to a different pitch. It's just letting your voice go from chest into head voice." It's also been described as "feathering": using a glottal stop to add a little "hook" to the end of the note, but for most folk singers a "glottal stop" is more difficult to comprehend than simply shifting registers. Note that when you start to practice this, your pitch will inevitably rise with the shift from chest to head, which makes the flip more prominent than you actually want. The more relaxed you become, the less this will happen. Note also that this flip is a "sometimes" thing. Listen specifically for how often (or more specifically how infrequently) traditional singers employ this ornament. It's easy for students, once they get it, to overdo it.

While we're on the subject of shifting registers, it's useful to look at word yodels, which involve a rapid shift between head and chest, invoking the crack that happens with the register shift. "Often you can add a little voice break at the beginning of a word to add emotion," says Emily. Try it on words starting with a vowel or an *h*. Hank Williams was a master of the "word yodel," and you can hear examples in almost any of his recordings. Check out "Lovesick Blues" or "Weary Blues from Waiting."

There are also a host of ornaments that you'll find in Celtic singing, multiple notes on a syllable that mimic the turns and rolls and cuts you might hear from fiddles or pipes. Gaining control of these so that they are clear and in tune is a project for a considerable hunk of your practice time. The idea is to execute them lightly and gracefully. In fact, ornamentation in general requires a light touch. Folk singer and teacher Jeff Warner points out that even thinking about ornaments as ornaments gives them too much weight. "Good traditional singing requires some decoration—traditional singer Bob Copper from Sussex, England, uses the term 'variance'—but not necessarily a lot of ornamentation," he says. Like so much in singing, less is more, and that "less" has to be practiced until it can be integrated seamlessly into what you're doing.

GOING TO THE SOURCE

The best way to understand folk style and ornamentation, of course, is to listen and absorb. Roy Andrade, who heads the old-time music program at East Tennessee State University, says he urges his students to immerse themselves in older artists.

"I try to convince my students that if you spend a month or even just two weeks listening to Roscoe Holcomb every day and trying to sing like him as an exercise, you'll push your voice into different directions, find different ways of enunciating or moving the resonance around inside your head or down in your chest."

He says this strategy is often met with reluctance. "They'll tell me, 'I don't want to sound like that, I can't sound like that, I'm not even a man,' but that's not the point. The point is the process. You learn things. You don't even have to take notes. Just spend some time trying

RUTH CRAWFORD SEEGER'S TIPS

Ruth Crawford Seeger (1901–1953) was a renowned modernist composer who, after meeting and marrying musicologist Charles Seeger, devoted much of her life and musical energy to the study of American traditional music and song. In her "Music Preface" to *Our Singing Country*, the second of the John and Alan Lomax songbook collections, published in 1941, she offers numerous suggestions on how to sing the songs in the collection. Here I've paraphrased a few of her points:

- The songs are best sung in a natural style. Don't try to smooth out your voice; if your voice is reedy or nasal, so much the better.
- Maintain the same degree of loudness or softness throughout the song. Don't *try* to be expressive or make an effort to dramatize the song.
- Keep time with your foot.
- Use slurs. Don't "typewrite out" each tone, and when two or more tones are sung in one syllable, "bind them together."
- Don't make too much of major or minor degrees in songs that contain both. Generally they are "closer to major than minor, or vice versa."
- Don't feel you have to harmonize. Singing in unison or octaves is appropriate.
- When singing without accompaniment, pause between stanzas.
- When singing with accompaniment, choose guitar or banjo, or possibly fiddle, dulcimer, autoharp, or accordion; if you use piano, make sure it doesn't "obtrude," and keep chord progressions simple and spare. In addition, leave space for instrumental "interludes."
- Don't "sing down" to the songs. "Theirs are old traditions, dignified by hundreds of thousands of singers over long periods of time."
- Listen to recordings.

Even though Ruth Seeger wrote these suggestions more than seventy years ago and trends change, for the aspiring American traditional singer their basic ideas hold true.

THE VOWEL CONUNDRUM

Classical singing is all about unifying your resonance to your vowels. Folk singing is more about exploiting the variations of resonance. Teacher and folk singer Emily Eagen explains that in classical singing "you find the perfect *ah* or *oh*—they're rounded and they match. Then you work your vowels together so when you're singing a long stream of vowels they sound like they're being bowed on the same string of a violin. In folk singing that would be robbing you of what you want, really interesting color variations between vowels." In learning to sing, vowels are really important—they carry pitch and resonance—but it's up to you, the self-starting folk singer, to determine how uniform you want them to be.

to inhabit that sound, and then move on to another artist. But that's the way you build style."

Roy continues: "Students say, 'I want my own sound,' and who doesn't want that? But how do you get it? It doesn't come out of nowhere. If you study, if you know great artists or people in your own life, and you find out how the people you appreciate the most learn, it's almost always this way. They learn by trying to make the sounds that inspire them and then at some point all of this stuff synthesizes and you're a mix of all these things. I like to tell them of Einstein's quote: 'The secret to creativity is knowing how to hide your sources.' I didn't get to learn from [primary sources]. I was too late, and many people have died in my lifetime. Recordings, films—this is the closest we can get, and it's not bad. It's definitely not the same thing, but if you put your headphones on and close your eyes, you're going to get something from Almeda Riddle."

DEADPAN SINGING

Americans folk musicians, particularly those who sing Southern styles such as bluegrass, have mastered the art of deadpan singing—finding resonance without seeming to move their faces much at all. If YouTube is handy, check out a short video of Roscoe Holcomb singing "On Top of Old Smokey" in 1961 (he sings after the banjo intro). Not much is happening visually, but there's no doubt about the resonance in his voice. Is it possible to sing like Roscoe? Maybe not, but it's worth spending a bit of time trying to "channel" him. The idea is to aim your sound into your sinuses (taking care not to push or squeeze your throat!). If that seems impossible, try one of teacher Charles Williams's strategies, using a lips-closed *mm-huh* sound (think of the sound you might make for "that's *so* good!"). The *mm* in particular is right up behind your nose, under your eyes, propelled there by a little push from your abdominal muscles. Your throat is not involved at all. As you practice, make that sound before you sing your phrase and then put the phrase in the same place in your voice. It takes a while, but eventually you'll feel the vibrations up where you want them, and you'll have added another color to your sound.

This isn't simply an American phenomenon. British teacher Kate Howard has a lot of experience with the choral traditions from the Caucasus Republic of Georgia. There, she says, "they talk about a cathedral inside your mouth, which is an image I like. It doesn't mean you have a big, wide mouth, but the back of the tongue is out of the way and the tongue is very forward. In contrast, in South African gospel music your mouth is really wide open, really vertical. It's a different sound. But in Georgian and American music, they don't open their mouths much, and they still get a really bright, pingy sound."

SINGER-SONGWRITERS AND THE "HANG"

With singer-songwriters, of course, there are no absolutes about deadpans or really anything else that's specific to folk singing. Folk-based singer-songwriters have the freedom to use (or not use) any of the folk "conventions" we talk about here. As with all of us, their goal is to sing well, and additionally to sing in a way that best communicates their songs. The relationship of any particular singer-songwriter to the folk world is really a matter of self-identification and attitude. Singer Moira Smiley, who has had a foot professionally in both the folk and the indie rock worlds, calls it a difference in the "hang." "The 'hang' is a big part of the business," says Moira. "In indie rock it's all about you the singer and your special skills; in folk music it's about *not* making a big deal out of yourself. I'm naturally drawn to the folk hang because of where I grew up [immersed in the New England folk community]. Everybody's in the band, everyone can make music. Don't make a big deal of yourself, but excel. Push yourself to make good music. You're not special, but maybe you can elevate some of the great things that everyone can do, make *that* special. It's like musically focusing a light on what everyone can do." Singer-songwriters who identify with this "everyman" quality in folk music typically incorporate aspects of various folk styles while maintaining a strong individual style. For an example of a folk-based singer-songwriter who does this, check out Laura Cortese.

A FEW "DON'TS" FOR CLASSICAL SINGERS

Mollie Stone, a director at Chicago Children's Choir, sometimes ventures into folk territory with her singers. For a more folk-based sound, her advice is:

- Don't take out the diphthongs.
- Don't exaggerate pronunciation or accent; don't add an overt "twang."
- Don't pronounce the *r* in that light way you do in classical music. Folk music enjoys the *rrr* sound.

IT TAKES A VILLAGE . . .

Folk singing technique is in many ways uncharted territory. There aren't any real how-to manuals. But there are singers and teachers who, through the course of their substantial work with folk singers, have come to some conclusions about what's involved in singing in folk styles and how a singer aimed in that direction might improve his or her voice. In writing this chapter I consulted several colleagues who I feel are particularly adept at doing this. All have had classical training, all have worked professionally both as singers and teachers, and all have been involved in the folk world to varying degrees. In this chapter I've leaned heavily on their input, which was substantial. Here are their names and a little about the people behind them:

Julie Dean is a singer and voice teacher who counts a number of singer-songwriters among the students at her studio in Charlotte, North Carolina. Julie studied singing at Queens University of Charlotte and Winthrop University, and she has continued to develop her skills as a functional voice teacher through training in Somatic Voicework™, the LoVetri method, Lisa Popeil's Voiceworks® method, and other professional development resources.

Emily Eagen, singer, songwriter, and vocal coach, is a doctor of musical arts candidate in vocal performance at the Graduate Center of the City of New York, a teaching artist and commissioned songwriter through Carnegie Hall's Weill Music Institute, and a two-time world champion whistler. She's also a popular teacher of group harmony classes at music camps and at the Jalopy Theatre and School of Music in Brooklyn. When not wearing her folk hat, Emily sings early and contemporary music.

Kate Howard is a longtime and beloved choir and workshop leader and teacher in Britain, well known for wrestling both teens and adults into becoming their better singing selves. She studied opera before turning to world music. Over the years she has been creating and adapting classical singing techniques and applying them to folk music styles, with the aim of creating an authentic sound while supporting and developing the voice. She lives in southwestern Scotland, where she runs the Cairn Chorus, a community choir.

Jeannette LoVetri, known to her friends as Jeanie, is a veteran (forty-five-plus years) vocal teacher and creator of Somatic Voicework™, her method for teaching "contemporary commercial music," a term she created for singing styles formerly referred to as "nonclassical" (this is where folk music fits in). Besides giving workshops and lectures all over the world, she teaches a full schedule at the Voice Workshop (which she directs) in Manhattan and finds time to perform as well.

Moira Smiley, a singer and composer, grew up in the communal folk-singing communities of New England and went on to study piano and earn a vocal performance degree at Indiana University's Jacobs Music School. An active touring musician (she has a group VOCO and works with a number of other projects), she also gives singing and composing workshops. Moira's recordings feature spare, vocally driven collections of traditional song, original polyphony, and body percussion.

Charles Williams, an internationally acclaimed singer, vocal teacher, and spoken-word artist, is a master teacher at the Levine School of Music in Washington, D.C. In addition to the "opera" side of his life, Charles has been a longtime vocal consultant for the Grammy-award-winning a cappella group Sweet Honey in the Rock. He works regularly with folk singers on a private basis and in workshops across the country, including at Augusta Heritage Center's Vocal Week. His classes fill immediately, which tells you something.

③

SWEET HARMONY

> If you really listen and dial in to your co-singers, you'll sing with a
> sort of gentle clarity that is different than when you're singing alone.
> . . . It's not only rewarding, but your technique can become so much
> better.
>
> —Emily Eagen, singer and teacher, Brooklyn, New York

If you sing folk music, whatever the style, sooner or later you're going
to be called on to sing a harmony line. You might be in a knee-to-knee
session at a festival, or in a studio adding background vocals, or onstage
joining another singer in his or her set. Whatever the setting, the expectation is that you will be able to provide an appropriate harmony, in
style, in tune, and in support of whoever is singing lead, without necessarily having the luxury of rehearsing a part beforehand.

THE LANGUAGE OF FOLK HARMONY

Singing folk harmony is not so much a matter of memorizing a part as it
is speaking or rather singing a harmony language. You learn a harmony
vocabulary, idioms, conventions, and what's expected in a certain genre
or setting. It's different from singing something that has been set down
on a page.

Of course, listening deeply and widely over time improves your harmony vocabulary. It doesn't hurt to know in your bones the actual notes that Maybelle Carter sings to Sara Carter's lead in "Lover's Return," or the cool part A. P. Carter throws in, or how the Wailin' Jennys approach the shape-note song "White," bending the harmonies to create their exquisite "Long Time Traveller." But this being folk music, there can be no expectation that your lead singer will be quoting those performances. Your job is to sing to what's happening at the moment.

How do you do that? Well, if you're like many singers who find themselves in the folk genre, you probably already have an instinctive sense of harmony. When people launch into a song at a beach campfire, you can join in with something that sounds OK. But often there's a gap between that intuitive harmony and what's required to get the job done. Here we'll look at what's involved in becoming a solid—and, we hope, in-demand—harmony singer.

The added benefit in all this is that singing harmony improves your singing in general. New York-based singer and vocal teacher Emily Eagen says, "It was a revelation to me when I started teaching in groups how much your singing as an individual can improve by singing harmony because it calls upon you to use your ears so much more than just singing along with a piano." And what's more, it's really, really fun.

DIFFERENT NOTES FOR DIFFERENT FOLKS

When I sing a harmony I often don't know what I'm doing. It's more intuitive. I love harmony, and I just want to fill it in. But my harmony when I'm singing on an Irish song that wouldn't really have had harmony is very different than what I might come up with for an Appalachian song.

—Singer and teacher Moira Smiley, Los Angeles, California

Folk harmonies differ markedly from the harmony you hear and learn about in classical music. And genres of folk harmonies differ from one another. (If you want to hear some wild harmonies, check out the traditional music from the Caucasus Republic of Georgia.) And among

English-language folk styles, you do different things depending on what you're singing. If you're singing with an American bluegrass group, one person per part, you've generally got a specific role cut out for you, depending on the underlying chords and the part you're singing—tenor or baritone or bass to a lead singer. In England, however, where the harmony tradition and instruments guiding the underlying harmonies are less clear-cut, you've got a bit more freedom; you might double the melody much of the time, for example. In pub sings, which are currently popular in New England, where I live, you might sing melody on the choruses but hit a favorite harmony note at the end, which, says British folk singer Brian Peters, was pretty much what was happening in England in the 1950s, when the folk revival was heating up.

But whatever the style, there are truisms in singing together that allow you to sing *with* rather than merely alongside your singing partner or partners. To accomplish this you have to blend.

THE MYSTERIES OF BLEND

Blend is the process of matching up with another singer on a number of different fronts—phrasing, rhythm, resonance, pronunciation, attack, intonation, volume, and so on. You're creating a unified sound for the listener. And this is largely up to the harmony singer. Whoever is singing lead needs to concentrate on singing the song in the way that he or she can do it best. When you're singing harmony your job is playing second fiddle.

Obviously, to sing harmony you have to listen, and bringing some sort of intelligent focus to the process is important. You're listening to the melody of the song, of course, but also to any other harmonies that are happening, as well as any rhythm and lead instruments that are participating in the musical conversation. Emily Eagen calls it "dialing in" to your co-singers. This sort of listening is the opposite of the figurative finger-in-your-ear approach that some fledgling singers take so that they can stay on their part. It's "listening lightly," and it helps create the right combination of concentration and looseness that you need to be really musical. "You want to have a soft focus" is how Emily describes it. This allows your ear to take control but your intellect to provide direction.

San Francisco-based singer and harmony maven Kate Brislin points out that lead singers aren't off the hook when it comes to achieving blend. "All participants in a harmonized song have to be aware of and attempt to blend or it won't happen," she says. "Sometimes the lead singer just won't do this, and you [the harmony singer] have to be skillful in your singing to make something good. When I coach singers, I try to get everyone on board, picking a different key if that would make it all work better. This is especially necessary with singers of mixed gender. The guys always want to pitch it too low, when in fact, if it were pitched higher, there's maybe only one or two notes he'd have to use falsetto for. That's the other thing about blend—it's not going to happen if the voices are too disparate or quirky, and this includes range."

PITCH AND INTONATION

Knowing what notes to sing and singing them in tune is clearly a big part of creating a harmony line. The note options you choose will depend a lot on style, genre, and circumstance. But to really make those notes into a harmony requires, among other things, tuning—all the time. When you get on a note, you don't just stay there; you adjust so that it's really in tune with your fellow singers. It's a quick, almost imperceptible process, and it's something all harmony singers do. Emily calls it "a sort of slip-and-slide quality."

In folk music, we all have our out-of-tune moments, and generally they're fixable. The previous chapter details some strategies for honing intonation. In terms of musical friendliness and goodwill, it's best to address consistent intonation problems on your own, away from the group harmony setting.

RESONANCE AND VOWELS

Resonance is also a huge factor in singing harmony. Creating a blend ultimately comes down to not only creating your own resonant sound but also matching your sound with the overall sound your lead singer is producing. And that comes down to matching vowels. This involves paying attention on several fronts. You've got to recognize not only the broad variations between, say, British and American vowels, but also the regional differences, where someone is using diphthongs (two vowels sounded in a single syllable), and when the vowels are pure. This is a study in itself, but for harmony purposes the idea is to do whatever the lead singer is doing.

"The simplest thing to think about is the shape of the vowel," says Jeannette LoVetri, longtime voice teacher and creator of Somatic Voicework™. "This means paying attention to the lips, jaw, mouth, tongue, and maybe inside the mouth."

By watching your lead singer's mouth shapes you can get a lot of information about how he or she is making the vowels, and with practice you can even figure out what's happening inside his or her mouth. This will result not only in a better blend but also in your own vocal flexibility and ability to create different sounds.

VOLUME

Creating the appropriate amount of volume is also fundamental to blend. In singing harmony, the issue is to create enough volume that your fellow singers have something to sing with. Once you've got control over your volume, it's a matter of style. If you're meant to be providing a background harmony, giving certain chords and phrases added depth—something you might do for a songwriter's solo album—you'll want to dial down your volume to take a backseat to the lead singer and to blend into whatever other harmony is being provided. But if your harmony is expected to have equal status (in terms of volume and presence) with the melody, as is often the case in people revisiting early American country music, you're going to want to match the volume of your lead singer. It's something to approach case by case.

PRONUNCIATION AND PHRASING

In folk harmony, matching your vowels to your lead singer is only half the battle. You also need to be aware of his or her speech patterns. What syllables are stressed and which ones are swallowed? Are syllables added or dropped? Folk music is vernacular, so you aren't going for some ideal "correct" pronunciation. If your lead singer is singing "gonna" you need to do the same, even if in your own speech you might sing "going to."

Phrasing is also part of the package. Phrasing has to do with the natural inflections your lead singer is using, the rise and fall of the musical sentences, the way he or she comes into or finishes particular phrases or words, the emphasized words, and the words that are almost swallowed. What you want is for the harmony to be exactly in sync at both the beginnings and ends of words and phrases, which takes practice and attention to that specific detail. Coming in late creates a muddy, stutter-like effect at the beginnings of words and phrases, and ending late creates a "blurred" sound, like ink that's smeared at the end of a sentence. Useful strategies include mentally hearing the note you want to sing before you sing it and watching how your lead singer is breathing. In particular, watch for the singer's initial breath, how his or her face changes to form the first syllable in the instant before the voice actually starts.

RHYTHM

Rhythm, important in all aspects of music, is also front and center in singing harmony.

Listen to how your lead singer is approaching the pulse and pace of a melody and make mental notes about what he or she is doing and where. Tap your foot and pay attention to places where what you're inclined to do rhythmically doesn't match what's actually happening. Hesitations and anticipations are tricky spots, as are odd emphases that are musically appropriate but not necessarily what you would emphasize in speech. Some lead singers use irregular phrasing to play off their band's rhythm. Usually a singer who wants harmony backup will make an attempt to sing something the same way each time, but not always. A good harmony singer brings a lot of intuition to the table.

Pulse and pacing can vary wildly between folk genres and of course between singers. A blues singer, for example, might lay back on the beat, while a bluegrass singer might keep way ahead of it. Some singers emphasize the offbeat (the second and fourth beats of a 4/4 measure). As a harmony singer, you're expected to mirror whatever rhythmic bumps are occurring.

VOCAL QUALITY

Vocal quality is something else to recognize. Be aware of registration (chest, head, mix, falsetto), where any shifts are happening and how (smoothly or with an emphasized break), how focused or breathy his or her sound is, how "forward" it is, and how much, if any, vibrato is used. Ideally you'll be able to negotiate these aspects in your own voice with facility, as the material and genre dictate. Note that as a harmony singer you're likely to spend more time at the outer edges of your range, especially if you're of the same gender with a similar range as your lead singer, who will be singing the melody in his or her comfort zone. Likely this is going to push you higher or lower than you ideally would like. It's important to know how to do this gracefully and appropriately.

Vibrato isn't generally something we welcome in folk music, but if your lead singer is using vibrato, you'll need to recognize where and how much, and to make what you're doing blend, so having the singing technique at hand to pull vibrato out when necessary is useful. More important, if you have a vibrato, as many classically trained singers do, and you want to sing harmony with someone who sings with a straight tone, you'll need to develop the vocal control to also sing with a straight tone. Microscopic amounts of vibrato are inevitable and sometimes help the blend, but an obvious vibrato in the harmony isn't going to work.

In short, as a harmony singer you want to match vocal quality as much as possible. If your lead singer has an edgy quality to her voice, you're going to have to match that edginess in your sound. If your lead singer has a smoother, more mellow sound, you want to echo that. The trick is to be able to quickly recognize what's going on and have the vocal flexibility to mirror it—which means you've got to practice.

STRATEGIES FOR PRACTICE

There are several practice strategies that can help you arrive at the point where you can lock on to any singing partner, or at least give it a credible try.

Look at your singing partner. Harmonizing with someone involves mimicry. Watch your singing partner's mouth, posture, breathing, everything that you can take in. However, if looking at your co-singer is simply too distracting, try shutting your eyes. That can have almost the same effect of focusing your attention.

Listen to one part and match up with that. Sometimes there is so much going on in a particular musical moment that it's difficult to find your place in the sound. Try picking one part to home in on. It can even be another harmony part, or perhaps the chords the rhythm guitar is playing. The point is to get your mind and your ears off what you're doing and on to what the people you're making music with are doing. Choir directors sometimes tell their singers, as a focusing technique, to imagine their voice coming out of the mouth of a singer next to them, and that can be a useful image in singing one-on-one as well.

Work in unison. In many ways, singing harmony is singing in unison, only with different notes. Try having your co-singer sing a phrase of a song or even go up and down a chord arpeggio on a single vowel, such as [a] or [i]. Listen first, then sing it with your partner in as close a unison as you can manage, so that every sound is in sync and every space between the sounds is the same. It helps to mimic and match mouth shapes. If you record yourselves, you can hear objectively how close you've come to achieving the one-voice effect. You can also do this on your own, using a recording of a singer you admire, preferably someone of the same gender who sings in a range that works for you. It helps if the song isn't complex or lathered with harmonies, but in any case you'll want to go phrase by phrase.

CHORD-BASED HARMONY

Dig deep enough into American roots music and you'll find examples of some pretty crazy sounds that squeeze under the "harmony" umbrella, from octave singing to meandering lines that seem to bear little relationship to the melody. But as American folk harmony has evolved, principally in the guitar-based "brother duet" years of the first half of the twentieth century, it has become all about the chords. Whether you're listening to the Carter Family, the Blue Sky Boys, the Delmore Brothers, or pretty much any bluegrass band, past or present, what you're hearing is the sound of singers filling in the chords, even if those chords aren't actually being played on an instrument. There are variations and exceptions, such as in shape-note, where a harmony line might seem like an alternate melody line, but most basic American folk harmony these days involves singing chords.

THE NUMBERS GAME

Talking about chords means talking about numbers. The musical numbers game is familiar to musicians, no matter the genre, but it will be helpful to go over the basics here through the lens of folk music.

Folk songs are keyed where the lead singer wants them keyed, so to communicate easily across keys, we tend to describe chords and the notes within the chords in numbers, defining the relationship of chords within the key with Roman numerals (I, IV, V) and the relationship of the notes within the chord in Arabic numbers (1, 3, 5). Using numerals for chords allows musicians to speak the same language even if the guitar player has a capo on and is playing a G chord shape to make an A chord, and it makes hand signals across a stage easier—four fingers tells the bass player that you want a IV chord there. There are dozens of

KEEP IT SIMPLE

If you've had some classical musical training, you might be inclined to use a number system that refers always to the scale degrees of the key you're in, so in thinking of a IV chord you'd think of the notes in it as 4-6-8/1. I know singers who do this, and it works for them, but I prefer to think of each chord as a world unto itself, with its own 1-3-5. It allows me to think more clearly about what's going on with the chords and the melody and harmony and how they overlay each other.

resources to find out more along these lines (you can find free tutorials on music theory online at whatever level you want to tackle this), but to get to the basics of folk harmony what you really need to know is that there are possible underlying chords to any folk melody. What those chords are, or what you choose them to be, plays a large role in dictating what your harmony is.

WADING DEEPER INTO THE NUMBERS POOL

In addition to knowing what the underlying chords are, it's important to hear what's happening (or not happening) within the chords. The notes within a chord are what we're working with when we come up with a harmony, even if we're harmonizing intuitively. Having a grasp on how this all works is the secret to finding an appropriate harmony note when intuition fails and the harmonies we're singing are not producing the sound we want.

It's simplest to talk about a basic major chord—a major triad. To the three notes involved we can assign numbers—1, 3, 5—that describe their relationship within the chord. It's a matter of knowing your musical alphabet and counting. Looking at a C major chord, the 1 is a C and, counting up, the 3 is E and the 5 is G. For the purposes of singing folk harmony we also need to add the next chord note up, which we can call either an 8 or a 1 (I often write this as 8/1). It's the C again, but an octave higher. Thus, if you think of the notes in a major chord by the numbers, you've got 1-3-5-8/1—the slots within the chord. There is, in theory, an infinite continuum of chord slots 1-3-5-1-3-5-1-3-5-1 but practically, to sing harmony, we only need deal with those few chord slots that you would encounter in a given song.

Still Deeper . . .

There's one additional numbers issue to think about—the intervals. Intervals define the spaces spanned by various chord slots. It's helpful if you can check this out on a keyboard, but it's enough to know that the space between the 1 and the 3 in a major chord is a major (wide) third, the space between the 3 and the 5 is a minor (narrow) third, and the space between the 5 and the 1 above is a fourth. These intervals exist whether you're going up or down in pitch within the chord. Take the time to know cold what that string of notes in a major chord sounds like: 1-3-5-8/1-5-3-1. There are many exercises to practice this, but simply singing up and down the notes of a chord, the chord arpeggio, concentrating on landing exactly on each note, is one of the best. You should quickly get to the point that you can pull a note out of the air, make that the 1 of a major chord, and create the arpeggio around it.

Recognizing intervals is a useful tool—both for your own understanding of what's going on musically and for communicating with other musicians. If you don't already have this skill down, there are many mnemonic devices you can use to train your ear. For example, in the song "Row, Row, Row Your Boat," the interval between "row" and "boat" is a major third; for a minor third, you might think of "What Child Is This" (the tune is "Greensleeves"); the first two notes of the song, "What" and "child," make a minor third. The song most often referred to as an illustration of a perfect fourth is "Here Comes the Bride"; the interval between "here" and "comes" is a fourth. Singers often find it difficult to go down a fourth, an interval you need if you want to find the harmony note below the 1. The example I like is the "ding, dang, dong" at the end of "Frere Jacques." The interval between "ding" and "dang" is a descending fourth. And on the children's song theme, the most often used example of a perfect fifth is "Twinkle, Twinkle, Little Star." The interval between the two twinkles is a fifth. If you search online you can find lists of mnemonics for each interval. If you don't recognize the references in one list, try another list. You're bound to find one that works for you.

A Detour around the Numbers

Assigning numbers or letters to notes or chords is just a way of describing the sounds involved. If you're numbers-phobic you might do better to go straight to singing the harmony note (above or below the melody) that comes naturally to you, and then checking that it fits into the chord you've been working from. In my experience, anyone growing up in our Western culture has the sounds of Western chords already implanted in his or her musical brain. Thus your harmony intuition will likely do 80 percent of the work for you. There are trouble spots, such as when

THE HARMONY CONVERSATION

Folk harmony is a response to a melody line. If something doesn't sound right, check that you're actually hearing the melody correctly, as it's being sung at the moment. Often, if you've learned or created a harmony line to a song in the past, your tendency is to sing the harmony you've worked out. If the lead singer has a different idea of what the melody is, or if he or she uses different phrasing and inflections, your preconceived harmony may be in trouble. Harmony singing involves a close interplay between lead and harmony; your first job is to listen carefully and adjust accordingly.

the chords change or the melody leaps down or up, but there are strategies for dealing with these problems. The message here is to not be intimidated by all the numbers talk, as central as it is in the world of folk harmony. The first rule is to sing it, and then, if it doesn't sound right, fix it. The numbers give you a tool to help you do that, but it's just a tool.

CLOSE HARMONY

Armed with knowledge of underlying chords, the notes or chord slots within those chords and the intervals between them, you can figure out a basic workable harmony to any American folk song. It's like a board game. If a melody note occupies one slot, the harmony must find another slot to land on. There are times when singing unison with the melody for a note or phrase is necessary or desirable, but in general, harmony means singing a different note in the chord, and American folk harmony in particular leans toward close harmony—that buzzy sound where it's hard to tease one note from another. And that means sticking to the "closest available" harmony, the chord slot that is directly above or below the slot occupied by the melody note. Thus if the melody is on the 3 of the chord, the harmony options are the 1 and the 5. Going from chord to chord through a song, following the closest available harmony notes over or under the melody, you'll create what's known as a parallel harmony.

THE JOYS OF PARALLEL

Parallel harmony, meaning a harmony that follows the hills and valleys of the melody, has a bad reputation among some singers (mostly
singers not working in the folk genre), but knowing how to create a
parallel harmony is a crucial first step in learning to sing harmony in
any situation you find yourself. Singing parallel involves singing the
closest available chord slot to the melody, staying on one side or the
other. Note that this does not mean singing "in thirds," a common mis-
conception usually used to talk about what people think of as country
harmony. Instead it means that if the melody is on the 5 of your chord
(we're talking about major chords here), the next available chord slot
above will be the 1—and the interval spanned by those two notes is a
fourth, which pretty much takes care of the "all in thirds" idea. And if
you are looking for the lower harmony, the next slot down is the 3—
the interval here is a minor third. This is where knowing the sound of
the notes in a major chord comes in handy. You don't need to know
the number of a note to know instinctively what the next sound up or
down will be.

I've found that in a simple song most singers can find a harmony line
for most of the notes without much of a struggle, and by trying out harmonies you learn to trust your ear and sing against another voice. You
can usually tell what doesn't work, but pay attention to what does work.
Knowing what you get right intuitively is half the battle; everything else
is fixable.

HARMONY ISLANDS

One approach to figuring out a parallel harmony is to look at a song
in terms of the "big" notes—the emphasized or held notes. Often the
first note of a song or the first downbeat note is a big note. There's also
often a big note signaling a chord change, and of course the final note
of a song is typically a big note. With some exceptions these notes tend
to be in the 1-3-5 of the chord. Once you've determined what the big
notes in a song are (and their role in the 1-3-5 scheme of the chord),
you can establish what I call "harmony islands"—points where you can

10 STEPS TO CREATING A PARALLEL HARMONY

Step 1 *Choose a song.* Choose a song with a simple melody (one you know or can sing easily on hearing it a few times). It will have basic chords that change in predictable places (mostly at the start of a measure) and a melody that doesn't push your vocal limits at one end of your range or the other. One of my favorites is "Don't That Road Look Rough and Rocky." It's a traditional lyric that has morphed into a popular bluegrass song, sung famously by Lester Flatt and Earl Scruggs. ♪

Step 2 *Learn the melody.* Sing the song enough so that you really know the melody and can sing it easily and in tune. If there are spots that repeatedly give you trouble, isolate and practice them. Typically, any spot you have trouble singing in the melody will also prove troublesome in the harmony.

Step 3 *Determine the underlying chords.* Figure out the chords you want to use and where they change. Most American folk songs don't get much beyond I, IV, V, but II, III, VI, and VII chords figure in later folk songs as well as minor chords and chords with added color notes (flat 7s, for example). Because the chords dictate the path of your harmony, this is important.

Step 4 *Record yourself singing the song.* The process of learning to sing harmony can be wearing on your singing partners. With the ease of recording at a reasonable quality (a smartphone will do, and there are many apps to help you out), it's not difficult to create a recording of yourself singing the melody that you can use in your harmony practice. I like to slow the tempo down so that I have time to think about what I'm doing as I sing, but if you do this a few times you'll figure out what works best for you.

Step 5 *Determine the first "big" note of the melody and its role in the underlying chord.* The first note to be concerned with in harmonizing will be the first "big" note in the melody, which comes generally on the first downbeat of the first full measure of the song. In the case of "Don't That Road Look Rough and Rocky," the first melody note, "Dar" of "Darling," is on the 1 of the I chord.

Step 6 *Do the harmony math.* If the melody is on the 1 of the chord, the closest available harmony above the melody, the tenor part, will be the next chord slot up—the 3. Thus in the key of C, that would be an E note.

If you want a lower harmony, then look for the chord slot directly below the melody, the baritone part. In this case it would be a 5, or a G note.

Step 7 *Put your instincts to work.* Record yourself singing the melody and try singing along on the harmony, starting on the harmony notes you've worked out. Typically you'll come up with a parallel harmony fairly quickly. If you run into trouble, go phrase by phrase. This is where using a slow tempo will help. Take stock of what you've got right as well as what is giving you trouble. Remember to follow the hills and valleys—to go up when the melody goes up, down when it goes down.

Step 8 *Fix the trouble spots.* The big notes are the key to fixing trouble spots. Go to the big notes that are on or near a trouble spot. Then do the harmony math: What note is the melody on and what is its role in the chord? What then does the harmony note have to be? By determining the harmony notes for each of the big notes you can create a string of harmony "islands." From there it's a matter of hopping to each of them in turn.

Step 9 *Work out the connecting notes.* After you've nailed down your harmony islands, what's left is getting from point A to point B. As a first strategy, create a harmony that follows each movement of the melody—up when the melody goes up, down when it goes down. This is useful if you want a harmony that thickens the sound but doesn't shout out its presence. Another option is to stay on one big note until the next one comes along, allowing the dissonance that the connecting notes will make and creating a "ceiling" harmony. Still another is to go to the note that will become the next big note before the melody gets there, anticipating the coming chord change. This happens in the singing of various older bluegrass groups, such as the Stanley Brothers. But in general, follow the melody.

Step 10 *Practice, practice, practice.* When you've nailed down your harmony islands and know the architecture of your harmony line, take it for a spin against your recorded melody line. Does it work? If you're facile with any of the computer programs that allow you to make tracked recordings, try recording a harmony track over the melody so you can hear where things sound muddy. If you can't make use of tracking, record your harmony line separately and sing your melody with it. This can sometimes highlight trouble spots that weren't apparent as you sang the harmony. Remember, everything that sounds wrong is fixable. Remember also to enjoy what sounds right.

establish the harmony with clarity. Then it's a matter of linking them. At that point, creating the complete parallel harmony line is relatively easy.

There is nothing that says you need to start at the beginning and carry on to the end. You can go all the way to the final chord in the song and get your bearings there first. That's a particularly easy chord to nail down, because the vast majority of folk songs end on the I chord, and the vast majority of melodies resolve on the 1 note in that I chord. Thus, your harmony notes are the 3 and the 5, easy to find from the 1.

All of what we've been talking about thus far is what you do to find the closest available parallel harmony. Of course there are many perfectly lovely harmonies that aren't parallel, but going through the process of learning to find what would be the parallel harmony for any given folk song gives you a place to start, and it's great ear and voice training. It's also useful if you're called on to sing a trio, something that commonly happens at folk events such as festivals and music camps, where performers tend to collaborate without much rehearsal. If you can accurately add a third part to a duo or create a trio on the spur of the moment, you'll have an important tool in your folk singer toolbox.

HARMONY STACKS

Knowing the vocabulary of folk harmony helps in getting a handle on what's going on, whatever genre you're working with. In much American folk harmony, especially if it's at all close to country—and in my world, "country" refers widely to all rural southern American folk-based music—the melody is often called the "lead." Above the lead, in the next available chord slot, is the "tenor," and below the lead, in the next available chord slot, is the "baritone." This is not to be confused with the soprano-alto-tenor-bass of choral music or the idea of tenor and baritone as a particular vocal range. It's just a way of identifying that string of harmony notes in the chord slots immediately above and below a melody line. You can add a "bass" below the baritone that is formed around the 1 and 5 of the chord, but the bass is typically an octave down from the where the close harmony lines are found and isn't usually part of initial harmony considerations.

THE STACKS IN SHORT

The three basic harmony stacks:

- "Sandwich" stack—lead in the middle, tenor on the top, baritone on the bottom.
- "Low lead" stack—lead on bottom, tenor in middle, "high baritone" on top.
- "High lead" stack—lead on top, baritone in middle, "low tenor" on bottom.

The harmony "stack" refers to the arrangement of the parts on top of each other. If you've got more than one harmony part, you've got to consider the stack. Folk groups often make use of a particular stack to stake out a particular sound, something they hope will set them apart and make the best use of the voices involved.

LOW LEAD, HIGH LEAD, AND SANDWICH

The most common way of arranging a harmony stack in American folk music is to have the lead in the middle and the harmonies on either side. I call that a "sandwich" stack. Many bands use this as their core arrangement. But you can also shift the baritone part up an octave, using the same notes, so pitch-wise it is above the tenor. This is what's known as a "high baritone," useful if you have a lead singer with a low voice, and harmony singers who can't comfortably fit below the lead, as is often the case if the lead singer is a man and the harmony singers are women. I call this stack the "low lead" stack. The bluegrass band the Dry Branch Fire Squad used this stack a lot in one of its incarnations, with founder Ron Thomason singing lead, and female bandmates Suzanne Thomas and Mary Jo Leet stacking tenor and high baritone harmonies above him. Conversely, given a lead singer who has a high voice and harmony singers who can't comfortably fit above the lead, you can shift the tenor part down an octave, below the baritone, making it the "low tenor"; I call this stack the "high lead" stack. This is particularly effective if you want to show off a stellar high voice, such as that of Bobby Osborne in the Osborne Brothers. His bandmates often stacked the baritone and low tenor below his high lead to showcase his voice.

Stacks can also evolve out of arranging considerations. If, say, the tenor line is cast basically around one note, then it might work better to stick it below the baritone so that the lead is on top and the low tenor acts more as a drone, assuming the lead singer can jack the key high enough to make that possible.

For duos, the stack really only becomes something to think about if you need to move an established harmony line to a different place in relation to the lead. If, say, the tenor line is too high and you drop it down an octave, making it a low tenor, you've lost the intense, buzzy sound of close harmony because you have a gap where the baritone should be (we're thinking in terms of duos here). Conversely, if you move a baritone harmony up an octave to high baritone, you have a gap where the tenor should be. This can be a valid musical choice, but it does create a different harmony sound, one that in some genres—bluegrass, for example—is often undesirable. However, there are many examples of great duos where the low harmony is actually a low tenor rather than a baritone.

Given the ranges of male and female voices, men will often be drawn to sing what is actually a tenor harmony below a woman singing lead. Because of the different tonal qualities of men and women, it's often difficult for the harmony to sound like harmony, or to create a pleasing blend, especially because there's a gap where the baritone would be.

ON THE VALUE OF WORKING IT OUT . . .

John Roberts, an English traditional singer and longtime singing partner with fellow countryman Tony Barrand, values thought-out harmonies. "If I'm doing more than singing along in the pub, I'm going to work it out," he says. "I'm not going to try to extemporize every time I do it. I work out what sounds good, what's in my range. Usually it's a matter of working with the chords, finding the notes that go between the chords, and trying to make the part interesting."

But again, there are many examples of this working well, so it comes down to taste. But it's good to know what you're doing and what your options are.

ARRANGING 101

Although knowing how to find appropriate harmony notes and create a blend, particularly in ad hoc harmony situations, is the foundation of singing harmony, there's more to consider, especially if you're working with a regular singing partner or partners, where you have the luxury of working out what you want to do. It's fun to experiment with a number of different harmony devices before settling on a particular way to do a song. Experimentation can help you develop your sound as a group and move you away from treating each song with the same arrangement.

A first factor to consider is where you want harmony. Commonly you hear folk songs where harmony is added only to the chorus. There are also songs where harmony traditionally is sung throughout or where there is some line or couplet, perhaps in the bridge, that might benefit from being sung as a solo. Dropping the harmony out can add as much ear interest as adding harmony. It comes down to whatever serves the song best. I'm hearing a number of young folk groups who are developing different harmonies for the various verses and/or choruses of a song. But sometimes simple is best. The listener depends on a certain amount of repetition to relax into a song, and too much change mid-song can cause what I call ear confusion.

In my harmony classes, when singers split into small groups, inevitably there will be singers who want to be singing all the time, and want to chime in with the melody when they're not singing harmony. This is uncharacteristic of much of American folk singing; singing the melody remains the province of the person singing lead. This is not to say that songs can't be sung effectively in unison, but usually when you're called on to sing harmony you're expected to do only that, unless the lead singer invites you to do otherwise. When you're arranging a song you want moments of contrast, and the contrast between a solo voice and harmony is powerful. If a melody line is generally horizontal—no major hills or valleys—it's relatively easy to find a harmony stack that works, whatever key the lead singer chooses. The problems come when the song's hills and valleys are really peaks and gorges. With such a "rangy" song it's often difficult, especially with singing partners of the same gender, to sing the parallel harmony line because there are melody notes that are just too high or too low to afford the harmonies room for their lines.

One simple compromise is for the harmony line to meet the melody in unison for a note or two. This can be very effective, adding drama when the melody and harmony paths diverge again, but there are spots in a song where this won't work well—for example, if the passage that goes quite high in pitch is also the general high point of the song. Having the harmony meet the melody at that point tends to rob the moment of some of its power. A better solution might be for the lead to sing the phrase solo, without harmony. It boils down to what works best for the song.

CEILINGS, DRONES, CROSSING HARMONIES, AND SPLIT LEADS

Sometimes, if a melody has a lot of hills and valleys, it works to run a harmony line across the top, creating a "ceiling" harmony centered on the appropriate chord slot. Where the melody rises it will meet the tenor harmony in unison; in addition, as the melody passes up and down it can create some interesting "crunches." This was a favorite strategy of "brother duets" in the 1930s and 1940s (the Blue Sky Boys and the Louvin Brothers come to mind). That effect can be used below the melody, often to create a mixture of a baritone and a low tenor or bass part.

Sometimes it works to have the harmony lines crisscross the melody so that when the melody is low the harmony is the tenor line and when the melody is high the harmony is the baritone line. This often requires that the harmony be in unison with the melody for a moment on the way up or down. If you and your singing partner have similar ranges, this is one way to handle it. The Carter Family made considerable use of crossing harmonies. Duets are a fertile ground for crossing harmonies, but you'll also find crossing harmonies in trios, especially in instances where the high voice is featured. For example, the high voice might toggle back and forth between singing tenor and high baritone to capitalize on the high sound, while the next harmony voice down might float back and forth across the melody, at times taking the tenor role and at times the baritone role. "Who Will Sing for Me," a bluegrass standard that goes quite low in the melody, is sometimes arranged this way. ♪

Another way to showcase a singer with a particularly effective high voice is to give him or her all the high notes regardless of whether they are melody or harmony, splitting the lead. Conversely, the lower singer or singers might take all the lower notes. This strategy of splitting the lead was also a common device of many of the brother duets. If you listen to the Delmore Brothers' "Blow Your Whistle Freight Train," neither Alton nor Rabon Delmore is singing the melody all the way through. Rather each is singing part of the melody. That, coupled with the blend that often comes in instances of familial ("DNA") harmony, creates a very specific dense sound, where it's difficult to tease out one voice from the other. This can be thrilling to listen to but requires two voices that are closely matched in every way.

BLUE NOTES, SEVENTHS, DISSONANCES

There are times when you hear a harmony that, as British folk singer Brian Peters says, "knocks you sideways." In addition to the larger issues such as stack, harmony crossings, and so on, there are myriad subtle changes you can make that can add ear interest and create tension and dissonance, what in the folk world we call "crunch." For example, if you go to the 7 of a chord (and we're almost always talking about a flat 7 in folk music) instead of the 1, you can create a bluesy feel that's quite different from using the 1. You can also flat the 3 for a similar bluesy feel or toggle between the flatted and true 3. You can also create a minor chord by flatting the 3, particularly if the melody is on the 1, as often happens at the ends of lines. This is sometimes used in ballads, where there are a number of verses. By adding the minor to an ending chord in an important verse, you can in effect underline that part of the plot.

Another device that you hear in bluegrass groups from the mid-twentieth century, such as the Stanley Brothers, is to go to a chord a measure or a few notes before the band plays that chord. If the singers sing a IV chord and the band is still on the I chord, there's a built-in crunch that then resolves when the band moves to the IV chord. If you analyze some of the memorable moments in the "high lonesome sound" that characterized much of rural Southern harmonies, you'll hear that at work.

In short, don't be afraid to experiment with your note choices, but also keep in mind the genre and the singing situation. If you find yourself in a jam where the singers are singing one-on-a-part, covering the chords of a song, they likely won't appreciate your experimentation. It's almost never about how weird and wonderful you can be as a harmony singer, but rather what you can do to support the lead.

Beyond adding color notes, there is the magic of ornamentation—the slips and slides, the grace notes, triplets, vocal rolls, and inflections—that give a singing style its character. In terms of harmony singing, be aware of what your lead is doing ornament-wise so you can support it, either by holding your note steady against the lead's ornament or echoing it (doing a similar ornament directly following the lead). The temptation with harmony is to mirror whatever ornaments the lead singer is doing. While there are spots where this can work, it can have the effect of diluting what the lead singer is doing, eliminating the ear interest that

TAKING IT A STEP FURTHER

If your goal is to become a harmony singer, there's no substitute for listening deeply and widely to all manner of singers, both in the corner of folk music you want to embrace and in the wider world of folk music, past and present. One way to get a deeper grasp of harmony possibilities is to tease apart the harmonies of two or three of your favorite groups and figure out how they get their sound. Where is the lead in their stack? Are they using strict parallel harmonies? Are they switching the lead around in the group (i.e., is one singer taking all the high notes, whether they are melody or harmony?) or crossing their harmony lines? Are they singing a chord before the band is actually playing it, creating a dissonance? Are they using the same harmonies on each pass through the chorus, or are they changing the chords they're singing? When something wakes up your ear, try to figure out what's going on, what the music gains from that strategy. This exercise can develop your own musical flexibility and give you added tools.

a contrast might bring. Like so much of harmony singing, it comes down to taste and what the lead singer prefers.

TROUBLE SPOTS AND HOW TO FIX THEM

For most singers of folk genres, becoming a good harmony singer is a journey. Some lucky singers have sung harmony since childhood, with siblings or parents or cousins, so they might be farther down the road, but we all continue to learn as we sing. We also all encounter harmony problems at some point—harmonies that sound muddy, out of tune, out of sync or unintentionally dissonant, or people we find it difficult to blend with; or places where the harmony we need seems impossible to get to logically. Typically, harmony problems come down to either the notes or the blend, or sometimes a bit of both.

Note Problems

If something just doesn't sound right, it's often a specific note or string of notes that aren't working well together. Your job is to figure out which ones they are and find substitute notes. A common problem is too much gap between melody and harmony. Ideally we want to be a third, fourth, or fifth apart, or sometimes even a second. Larger gaps happen, but the farther away you are, the less the sound is going to sound like harmony. The solution is to check the melody note and then the note you're on and adjust your note.

If you're below the lead, the problem may well be that you're hearing the tenor line down an octave. By working out the melody and the logical harmony notes you can easily clarify where you are and where you need to be. Parallel lines always exist in possibility even if you don't choose to use them for some reason. If you're above the lead, your problem may lie in not following the melody as it takes a dive into lower notes. I call it "getting off the bus too early," and I hear many examples of this among my students. It's not difficult to harmonize with an ascending lead line, but when the melody goes back down, the tendency is to stay up or only come down partway. In a duo you have the freedom to do that, although you're moving away from close harmony, but in a trio you'll find that when you leave your harmony pathway you're doubling the notes that another harmony singer is taking. At that point you'll need to negotiate. If the harmony parts are taking a parallel path alongside the melody, they create their own melody lines, which are pleasing to sing, but if a third part is being added to a well-established duet, you may find yourself jumping around a lot to find unoccupied harmony notes. It's a challenge.

Often harmony problems stem from the harmony singer not actually knowing what the lead singer is singing as the melody. In folk music, harmony is a response to a melody, but it's not necessarily to the melody you have in your head. This is particularly troublesome if you already know a song well and have figured out a harmony for it in the past, in another setting. The tendency is to sing what you already know, and that can lead to a mismatch between lead and harmony. If you find yourself in trouble, it's always a good idea to check on how the lead singer is singing the melody. Usually that is enough to allow you to adjust your harmony to an appropriate note. You can also sing through the song in unison with the lead singer to get a clearer understanding of how he or she perceives the melody.

Sometimes the problem is a difference in how you and the lead singer are hearing the underlying chords, something that will be clear if an instrument is involved. It may be that the guitar player is adding or eliminating chords or changing them in different places than you're used to, all of which will change the harmony.

Blend Issues

The second category of problems lies under the umbrella of blend. Clearly all the things mentioned earlier about blend—resonance, vowels, matching pronunciation, and so on—come under scrutiny when you're trying to fix a harmony problem, but none give singers more grief than intonation.

To fix an intonation trouble spot, isolate the passage. Check the intervals leading up to and away from the note and make them as in tune as you can. Check that you're making the same vowels and diphthongs as your singing partner. Check that you're breathing in such a way that you have sufficient air (lack of air support can cause intonation problems) and that you're switching registers effectively (maneuvering your voice "break" can also cause odd intonation).

If you can't isolate a specific problem note or notes, eliminate the ornaments (scoops and slides) and go interval by interval through the problem area of the song, checking that you're giving each interval its full value. Undershooting ascending thirds is sometimes a problem, as is overshooting a descending fourth. Check fifths as well, and any dissonances. Also try working the lead and harmony lines on a single vowel, to eliminate awkward diphthongs and problematic consonants. If you're working with three or more singers, it's best to work on two voices and get them solidly in tune before adding the third voice. And in terms of general rehearsal etiquette, avoid pointing fingers. As a harmony singer, your focus is on what you can do to make the sound better; you can hope to inspire by example. It's rarely helpful to accuse someone else of singing sharp or flat.

Another blend issue is phrasing. A typical problem is coming in late—a product of mentally waiting to start until you hear the lead singer's note. Watching that person is the best way to come in on time. In particular, watch for the singer's initial breath, how his or her face changes to form the first syllable in the instant before the voice actually starts.

The ends of words and phrases are also trouble spots, and easy to overlook, because often you've mentally gone on to what's happening next and have stopped listening. But endings are critical. If the lead singer has ended a word and you're still trailing on with your harmony note, you're singing a solo. Keeping an eye on your singing partner is the best way to get in sync. But avoid chopping off your sound; that can be as disruptive as letting the sound carry on. Most people allow their singing to trail off a bit. As you get to know your partner's singing, you will learn how he or she begins and ends phrases.

Keep in mind the "speaky" quality of much folk singing. In folk music we tend to keep the singing conversational and avoid holding notes unnecessarily; we also allow space between the words and phrases to let the instruments have a say in the musical conversation.

Sometimes, typically because of issues with resonance and breath support, you just aren't singing loudly enough to create a blend. Beginning singers often think they're singing louder than they are because of

ON THE BRIGHT SIDE

Patty Cuyler, a director of the choral folk program Village Harmony and a longtime leader of folk choirs, talks about singing "on the bright side" of a note, to get singers to tune up to one another. She also tries for different vocal tones, which can alter the way a pitch is sounded. "When I hear off-tuning I'll have the two singers or voice parts sing against each other, and isolate fifths and dissonances," she says. Often this process of isolating typical problem spots is enough to tune up a muddy area.

what they are hearing inside their heads. If the volume between you and your singing partner is off balance and your partner can't hear you, it's tough to get things in tune. If you find you don't have the breath and vocal technique to increase your volume in a natural way, or if you find yourself wanting to shout to increase your volume, it's best to work on these issues away from the harmony setting.

Drifting Too Far

Some people find that they can't sing a harmony against another singer because they always drift to whatever the other singer is singing, especially if it's the melody. To prevent this they figuratively (or literally) stick their fingers in their ears to block the other singer out so they can hang on to their part, which leads to problems with intonation and blend. The opposite approach, listening as completely and openly as possible to your singing partner, is the way to learn to sing another part against them. If you have a consistent problem with drifting onto someone else's part, there are a couple of strategies you can try. One is to work on singing unison until you can sing it exactly and with confidence (you should be able to sing the melody by yourself). Typically, drifting back onto the melody is a confidence issue as well as a listening issue. Becoming totally familiar with a melody builds your confidence in the song and lets you know exactly what you're singing against, and at the same time improves your listening skills. For some singers this makes the jump to singing harmony easier. You can also work on your own, recording a simple song or round ("Row, Row, Row Your Boat" works well) and practicing singing with yourself. It helps if you sing the melody slowly when you record it, so when you're singing harmony you have time to think.

IN THE EAR OF THE BEHOLDER

In folk music, harmony is a marriage of expectation and surprise. Our harmony expectations come from what we've listened to all our lives. If you grew up in the U.S. state of Georgia listening to country and bluegrass, your idea of what is "right" in terms of folk harmony is wildly different than if you grew up in the Caucasus Republic of Georgia, where harmonies can involve entirely different combinations of tones and half tones. The surprise element comes when what you're hearing foils the expectations that you've developed through your listening experiences. Much of what we find interesting and engaging in folk harmonies happens in those surprise moments, but to really set up the surprise, we also need to understand and be able to accomplish the expected harmonies.

Singing intuitive harmonies around a campfire is always fun, but having the skill to blend in with a lead singer, support what he or she is doing, and perhaps offer that element of musical surprise is where many of us find our musical joy.

ACROSS THE POND

Brian Peters, a traditional English folk performer and writer, says British singers take a different approach to harmony from what we see in American close harmony. "I grew up with parents who sang harmony in two parts, so I developed an instinctive sense of harmony," he says. "I would come up with a high harmony or a low harmony to any given line pretty quickly. Quite a lot of [British singers] seem to work on that basis.

"In the pub sings of the 1950s people would join in on a chorus, but in unison. It was rare that you'd hear harmonies, except for maybe the last note. What we have are the Christmas carols that started out as very specific part-singing arrangements that over the years have got a bit broken down, so people might sing a bit of one part one moment and then peel off and sing a bit of another part; it's become more instinctive, but it's based on quite set written arrangements from years ago.

"And we have the Copper Family [Bob and Ron Copper plus various relatives, who sang traditional songs from their hometown, Rottingdean, in Sussex, and whose recordings in the 1960s and 1970s influenced the harmonies of a generation of British folk singers]. When I think about the Coppers' bass harmony, it is usually a low harmony, although in some moments you can hear Ron Copper—on the old recordings with just the two of them together—sing a particular passage merely an octave lower than Bob. He could do that. Ron also quite often would hit the lower fifth, that harmony there. I don't think it was intuitive in that they made it up fresh every time, but even so the bass part wouldn't necessarily have a scientific consistency to it.

"The Watersons [a folk-singing family from Hull who began recording in the 1960s] were very instinctive in their approach. Mike was a natural harmonizer with an ear for some quite unusual sounds, but in the early recordings the other three are often in unison, with occasional bass harmony. Sometimes all four voices were in unison. When Martin Carthy joined, the bass lines got more interesting. Then Norma and Lal started departing occasionally from the melody. Lal's crunching discords were my favorite part of their sound. The other big harmony group of the 1960s was the Young Tradition, who had just three voices and made sure they used them to maximum harmonic effect. Much more chord-based, I would say. After them came the fantastic Swan Arcade, who again had the female-male-male trio format, and worked out their harmonies very carefully to maximum effect. Their bass singer is Jim Boyes, now in Coope Boyes & Simpson.

"What we didn't have here was the link between the old traditional singers and the church and gospel music that you have in the U.S. There's nothing like the evolutionary line that you have through the Louvins to the Everlys, et cetera. Although many of the groups did branch out into U.S. gospel music, English church music was generally considered a bit too sedate. That said, one very vibrant ongoing tradition we have just a few miles from where I live is the pub caroling tradition around Sheffield. The carols are sung in parts, written down years ago in the songbooks of village choirs, though those 'in the know' don't need a book. It's largely taken over by folkies these days, but still an exhilarating experience!"

4

WORKING UP A SONG

My advice is to just sing. There's no reason to stop just because no one wants to hear you. . . . Sing all the time, listen carefully and sing hard.

—Tim Eriksen

Many of us in folk music today can recall the moment we first fell in love with a piece of music, when listening to it just wasn't enough. We had to *do* it. We needed that song, that harmony, that turn of phrase, that chord progression. Then, of course, came the real work.

That is what we're going to talk about here: what's involved in going from that moment of musical true love to making the song something that you really know and want to sing, maybe even perform—and maybe, if you're well along a musical career path, even something you want to perform every night of a tour. It's the process of making the song yours, and it's a well-trodden path. Each singer you talk to has some unique detour, but the work is the same—listening, capturing the words in some way, perhaps hunting down sources and versions, listening more, putting the song in your mouth (playing with keys, tempos, and rhythms), experimenting with instrumentation, and then maybe listening even more to see what you've lost or gained in this "folk process." Then you're off on your own path with the song.

The strategies here apply primarily to songs you're learning from someone else's singing or perhaps from the pages of a song collection, but even if you're working up a song you've written yourself, the process is much the same, once you're into the actual preparation work. But for songs you haven't written, there's usually a falling-in-love process, and it's different for different musicians. Folk musician Jefferson Hamer says he is attracted to the melody first. Then, he says, "certain phrases or aspects of the lyric stay with me. If I hear the song enough times, I start to notice the plot. By that time I'm probably interested enough to want to learn it." For singer Tony Barrand it's the language. "Some songs have wonderful tunes," he says, "but I go for the language first, the combination of words." Ballad singer Elizabeth LaPrelle says it's a combination of words and plot. "I love the storytelling aspect of it," she says. "It sweeps me away. . . . I get excited about the words and what's going to happen next, the poetry of it."

Often the object of our song "crush" is a particular version of a song, and our first impulse is to re-create it exactly. That's a huge and valid part of the folk process. I probably would never have learned to finger-pick the guitar if I had not become smitten (obsessed, actually) by Joan Baez's singing and playing of "Railroad Bill." Eventually, however, you'll find it saves time and musical energy if you can separate the artistry that has been applied to a song—the unusual vocal approach, perhaps, or the dissonant harmony or the complex guitar arrangement—from the song itself. This is where it helps to seek out other versions of a song and also to write out the song words to see if, once you see the words in front of you, the song is still something you want to learn. There have been a number of times where this preliminary process has taken a song off the table for me; I've discovered that I just couldn't sing those particular words, or I've realized that I couldn't really figure out an approach that would do the song justice. In the folk world we all learn by imitation, but eventually, if we're performing a song, we don't want to be copying a particular singer or singers or a particular arrangement unless we're specifically paying homage to that artistry. Singer Ginny Hawker says, "If someone else has done the definitive version of a certain song that I like, I probably won't sing that one. There are many good songs out there for me to sing." But, she adds, "If I just can't get it out of my head, I'll have to do it!" For many of us, the key factor ultimately is whether

GRANNY RIDDLE ON LEARNING SONGS

"When I want to learn a song I just can't do anything else. I can't turn it off.
. . . There will be three or four days or a week where that song and nothing
else will run through my mind. I'll sing it constantly. And though I may forget where I put the dishrag, I never forget a song. I may forget it for a while
but then somebody will sing a word or two of it and it will come back."
   Almeda "Granny" Riddle, from *A Singer and Her Songs.*

we feel we're bringing something of ourselves to the song, something
true or something new—or if, as Ginny describes, we just *have* to do it.

How and how much a singer borrows from a source has a lot to do
with what that source is. If you're listening and learning from a "tradition bearer," someone who can be considered, if not a primary source,
at least a source that epitomizes a time and style, your job is different
than if you're learning from a contemporary musician who is currently
performing a particular song in a particular way. "I'm very skeptical of
'learning' songs from people at festivals and such, since they are often
many steps away from the prime source," Ginny Hawker explains. "We
have many good recordings available today from these prime sources, so
I'd rather listen to them when learning a new song." In addition, your
colleagues in the folk world, however flattering they might find your
rendition of their arrangement of a song, probably would prefer that you
bring your own musical sensibilities to the project. It's clear that if we're
not singing songs we've written, we are going to be singing songs from
other sources, and our musical ideas aren't necessarily unique. It's how
we approach the process that gives it and our singing validity. Elizabeth
LaPrelle says it wisely: "The beauty of folk or traditional music is that
the song outlasts any one singer. Any person you might be able to find
in history was only doing their little part. . . . They might be incredible
musicians who changed the song or made it a certain way, but each one
of us is only handing it on to the next, and only holding it for a short
part of its history."

To be effective carriers of that song, it often helps to find out where
it's been and also to look around you to see where it might be going.

DOING DUE DILIGENCE

I often think of delving into a song's history as doing "due diligence"—taking steps to figure out where a song is from, who wrote it, how it got to where it is today. For many of the singers I know, it can be a passionate and engrossing search. "When I'm attracted to a piece of music, I lunge for it," says Scott Ainslie. "Typically it involves searching for the oldest versions I can find. My strategy, as a musician, has always been to find the oldest people I can who play the music I am interested in and put myself in front of them." Physically getting in front of older singers can be problematic, of course; many of the old masters, and even their protégés, have died or are no longer available for would-be apprentices. That's where online research comes in. The Internet and YouTube, although not as helpful as one-on-one contact with a musician, have opened up access to an increasing number of archival films and audio recordings, and archived collections are continually being digitized and made available online.

My strategy, when I'm first working on a song, is to find as many recordings of the song as possible, and in particular, if the writer of a song has recorded it, to include that original version among those I'm listening to. Often I make a playlist of my favorite versions to play when I'm driving or doing the dishes or am otherwise occupied, to allow the song in question to sink in a bit before I actually sit down to learn it. Other singers have different strategies. Elizabeth LaPrelle finds that multiple versions of a song can be overwhelming. "Usually I get really attracted to one person's rendition of a song, their singing of it and their particular words," she says. "I'll go really deep, listening and listening. And because I've learned it from that one person I'll be really excited about who that person was, where they got that version, why they sang it just that way." It also means, she says, a lot of repeated listening and a lot of practice.

For Jefferson Hamer, the research process is not so much about amassing historical facts as connecting to the content—the notes and the words—in a convincing way. "It doesn't matter how much you know about the history of a song," he says, "as long as people believe you when they hear you sing it. From an educational perspective, of course, it's useful to know as much as possible about the origin of the song and who sang it before. It helps put the song in a broader context of material that someone who would be drawn to that kind of song might also be drawn to. It also adds value to you, the singer and storyteller, because you're then in a position to offer your audience, class or campfire more than just a single performance; you're in a position to offer them a backstory and a history lesson and another song thematically related to that last one. But producing a 'good' rendition of a folk song doesn't mean you have to go deep into the history of the song."

So it's a balance you'll have to create between listening and singing and researching.

Doing research involves keeping a level head about what you read and hear. Inaccuracies abound. Online lyric sites are notoriously wrong, and errors tend to get repeated across numerous sites. In addition, many sites simply credit a song to whatever popular singer sang it last rather than listing the actual songwriter or lyricist and composer. Wikipedia, even with its "reader beware" warnings and calls for further citations, is also far from definitive. And you'll find even your fellow folk singers will offer up some bit of information about a song that proves on further examination to be more good story than fact.

With time you'll know when you've done enough research. For me the basics are to know who the songwriter is, if there is one; to have listened to the original version, if such can be found, along with other important versions; and to write out the words, from the songwriter's

SINGERS ON SINGING

"There are lots of different reasons why I learn songs . . . because I think they'll be fun to play or an interesting challenge, because a particular lyric or melody grabs me, or because I think it will make a good dance tune. I don't often learn anything 'cold' . . . that is to say, I usually learn a song if I've heard it somewhere and one or two lines stuck in my head long enough that I want to get the rest of it. This might take years or just a few days. Sometimes I have an idea for an arrangement and I learn the song in order to see if it will work, and sometimes I just get excited about the song itself and try to figure out some way I can make it work for me."

Jesse Milnes

"In my family we didn't listen to the field recordings because they were old and authentic; we listened to them because we felt these were some of the greatest musicians we'd ever heard. I don't love Dock Boggs because he sounds old; I love Dock Boggs because he's a master musician."

Sam Amidon

"I just love the history of a song. I love a song that has a historical basis. I love it when the tune and the text hang in the balance. I love it when you get a wonderful text and an exquisite tune, where you can take away the text and are left with an exquisite tune and you can do the reverse . . . you're left with a truly wonderful set of images and words and you can remove the tune and still have sheer poetry. I gravitate to that sort of thing, to a lot of old Appalachian songs that don't resolve, for example. I love that about them."

Sara Grey

"There's that moment where you say, 'Oh, I really like that song'—that's when you start learning it. Bits of it get stuck in your head and you think, 'Oh, what is that second verse, because I want to keep singing this,' or 'I want to keep working with this melody' or 'Oh, the way she swoops that note, I really want to do that, that's really cool.'"

Elizabeth LaPrelle

recording if possible. I find it useful also to check out iTunes, YouTube, Spotify, or Pandora to find out what's happening with the song today. Songs trend, and if you've embarked on learning one that twenty-three people have just recorded and scores of others are putting up on YouTube, consider setting it on the back burner for a while, unless it's really in the "have to do it" category for you. It's tough to bring something new to such a well-used song.

GETTING DOWN TO IT

So there's a new song that you're excited about. You've done some background research, you've listened a lot, perhaps you've written out the words. The next step is to get it into your voice, to actually start to sing it. There are many approaches to this process.

One strategy is to work on singing the song exactly as the singer you're listening to does it. You have probably sung along with the singer already, and that's partly what drew you to the song—that it works in your voice. But in this sort of singing along you're looking to mimic everything you can, from phrasing to ornaments to anticipations and lags, so that it's a perfect fit. You won't ultimately sing the song this way, but it will allow you to really know it and at the same time give you insight into the singing choices your model singer is making. If the singer is singing in a key that doesn't work for you, there are a number of apps that allow you to change the song's pitch as well as to slow it down (or speed it up) so that you're well matched. I use Amazing Slow Downer for this, but applications come and go. The important thing is to have an aural reference that works with your voice. Jeff Davis, a longtime singer of traditional songs, uses a variation on this technique when he teaches traditional singing. His strategy is to have students pick one verse of a song from a singer they admire and learn it exactly as the singer has recorded it. "It improves their singing dramatically to go at a particular ornament or where the breath falls or whatever it might be," he says. "People often don't know how to listen or what to listen for, so it's a process of guiding them through it step by step." It's also an excellent way to absorb a style.

Another strategy is to follow your initial bout of listening to a song with several sessions of casually singing through it until you've loosely arrived at a key and a feel for the song and how you might want to do it. "One of the best exercises for this is to record yourself playing or singing and just see what it sounds like," says Jesse Milnes, a musician, singer, and teacher. "Does it sound the way you want? If not, why not? Listen closely to the people you want to sound like and see what's different. It all boils down to close listening and lots of practice." I use the recording process quite a lot in working up a song, as it provides me with something I can listen to and shows me immediately where something is or isn't working. I often wait a day or for my next practice session to listen to the recording, since with the passage of time I hear things differently and can be more objective. In addition, I often go back and listen again to the original recording to ensure that in my work on the song I haven't lost what I originally liked about it.

Still another strategy is just to start singing a song and see where it takes you, without worrying about how close you are to any other person's singing of it. I know a number of singers who consciously distance themselves from any particular version of a song early on in order to develop their own musical voice and put their own stamp on it. This is a more useful approach if you've already developed a style vocabulary and a voice of your own and you've got a number of songs under your belt. The danger for people new to the folk world is that the "folk" part of it is as much about how a song is sung as it is about the song itself. If you're not grounded in a folk style and have grown up listening to Western popular music, there's a great likelihood that you'll end up creating a pop song. Folk music is a language that's best learned by listening and repeating what you hear.

For my part, I agree with Roy Andrade, who heads the old-time music program at East Tennessee State University. "I tend to take a slow, analytical approach to any piece of music I'm going to do," he says, "and then at some point I let that all go, switch over to art mode. It makes all the sense in the world to me." It does to me too. The careful, almost scientific approach gives you a firm base for the art that is to come.

SOUND ADVICE

"Listen a lot to music that you like, immerse yourself in it, and then try to make a lot of music that seems like music you'd like if you were listening to it."

Emily Miller

"The hardest thing to do is piece together a new lyrical setting of a song, because nobody is there to tell you if you're making good or bad choices. Unless you have a partner, which can be really helpful. Like a cowriter in songwriting. You can steal bits from other songs, make up new bits, listen to different versions of the same song sung by different people and combine it all together. The challenge is getting something that you want to sing in the end. Something you believe in without flinching. If you believe in it, there's a good chance somebody listening will too."

Jefferson Hamer

CONSIDERATIONS AND MORE CONSIDERATIONS

Considerations quickly mount up when you begin working on a song. To keep things at their most basic, singer Jeff Warner counsels his students to first sing the song unaccompanied. "Whether or not you end up accompanying a song, be able to get it across without an instrument," he says. Additionally, singing unaccompanied allows you to avoid getting locked into a specific chord pattern or rhythm, keeping the song as flexible as possible for as long as possible. That's a useful strategy, but because I'm a longtime guitar player and harmony singer I often need to work with some very simple guitar backup in order to feel the movement of the chords I'm inevitably hearing—often it's the chord sequence that has attracted me to the song in the first place—and of course to see where the song falls key-wise. "Keying" a song is a critical step as it has everything to do with where the song falls in your voice. Much of American roots music is keyed so that the bulk of a song falls toward the top of a singer's chest range; if you're singing roots music, that's where you'll likely want to be. Celtic-inspired folk singers, wherever they are, tend to sing more in their head voices. Singer-songwriters sing where they enjoy it, although to keep under the "folk-based" umbrella they likely want to work within the parameters of a folk voice. Most singers, when keying a song, look at the most extreme pitches—how high or low a song goes—as well as the skill level of accompanying musicians. For example, fiddlers don't use capos or any sort of easy key-shifting device, and many aren't at their best playing in "difficult" keys (keys with a lot of sharps or flats) such as C♯ or A♭. If you have a folk fiddler in your band, know his or her parameters and key your songs accordingly. Most fiddlers who play regularly with singers can handle A, B♭, B, C, D, E♭, E, F, and G. Mandolin players and bass players tend to play more by repeating patterns on the neck of their instrument rather than specific notes, so are more key-ambidextrous, but beginning and even intermediate players are often stuck in first position, which limits key options. Another consideration is harmony. Depending on how you plan to stack harmony onto a song, you'll need to key it so that the bulk of what your harmony singers have to sing is in a comfortable or at least doable range. Of course, as a lead singer you need to sing in a key that allows you to sing freely and with strength, but if you sing with a band some ability to compromise is expected.

At some point in working up a song, the arrangement you're going for also becomes a consideration. This is another argument for singing a song unaccompanied for a while. "Learning a song without any chords present kind of leaves space for you to let it sit and find out what you might want to try with it," Elizabeth LaPrelle says. "You think maybe this part has guitar or maybe it feels like it can be performed quickly or maybe it has a banjo with it, maybe it would sound better if there were harmony on this little part." If you've been recording yourself, you might arrive at a conclusion about timing or cadence or general approach to the song. Singer and multi-instrumentalist Jesse Milnes describes his process: "My main technique for arranging a song is to play it in the morning while I'm drinking coffee and just fool around until I find something I like. I might change the rhythm, make it swing or not, make it fast or slow, et cetera. I try it in different keys; I try it with fingerpicks and with a flatpick. I might try singing it in an out-of-time a cappella style, or accompanying myself with the fiddle instead of the guitar. I might try adding some passing chords or chord substitutions. I might pick out the melody or a bass line instead of playing chords. Basically I'm just trying to find something that feels right to me. There are no rules to what is good or bad; you just know it when you hear it."

For some musicians this path involves altering a song a little or even a lot, for aesthetic reasons or to find workarounds for vocal or instrumental trouble spots. "There are shortcuts and tricks for just about any problem," counsels singer Kate Brislin. "Don't sing that high note that you can't hit; change the melody for just that note if you just can't make it sound good." For example, I've changed a line of the melody of "Remember Me," a song by Scotty Wiseman that I've sung over the years, because it didn't work well with a harmony line a band member was singing. It's a matter of taste. "I'm not so precious about a song that I can't add to it myself or enhance it or change the melody or add a verse to make the story make more sense or cut out some verses that make it fall together in a more cohesive way," says singer Lissa Schneckenburger. "I'm looking for songs that appeal to me lyrically and melodically, but I'm also happy to tinker with things, make them more appealing to me."

STYLE

"In my twenties I would try to help kids sing. I would say 'sing with your own voice' because what I was hearing was replication of their stars. They were white, middle-class kids from Long Island trying to sound like a black Texas pop star. It wasn't happening for them, but I couldn't seem to convey that. They didn't know what I was talking about. . . .

"I was talking about style, and they weren't separating it out from the song."

Jeff Warner

But before you start changing songs willy-nilly, take singer Scott Ainslie's advice to heart: "You should allow the music to change you before you change it."

THE INSTRUMENT REQUIREMENT

A fantasy that many beginning folk singers have is that they will find a band eager to back them up, giving them a musical home and people to perform with. The reality is that this happens only rarely, usually to already-known singers who can headline a group and help them get jobs. You can sometimes find yourself on the ground floor of a band that's starting up, but typically folk bands evolve, and they evolve around instruments. In the folk realm, the finances of touring are such that no one can really be "just a singer"; you've pretty much got to do double duty—as a fiddler/singer, say, or a bass player/singer. A band much on the folk scene these days is Laura Cortese & the Dance Cards, a group of four women who all sing but who are also virtuosos on their various stringed instruments, and that instrumental expertise is a critical factor. Performing-level competence on your instrument is vital. A stellar singer might be able to get by with playing guitar in the "just OK" category, but there are simply too many folks out there playing and singing at a high level to ignore this very real aspect of folk music performance. "It's enormously important to be able to play an instrument well," says

FIDDLES AND UKULELES

The usefulness of instrumental expertise is not limited to the American scene. In Britain, reports folk musician Brian Peters, there's a trend these days of singers accompanying themselves on fiddle. There's even a term for it—"fiddle singing." Brian points out that many young singers play two or three instruments. "And they play them well too," he says. "They're not just bluffing it." Time to get practicing.

Interestingly, in the United States, many singing students who hear me out on the importance of playing an instrument turn up next with a brand-new ukulele. The ukulele is an admirable and lovely instrument in the hands of musicians who play it well, and I know many who do. And learning ukulele can be a benefit to singers who don't play an instrument in that it teaches you to hear chord changes and also to accomplish the tricky coordination involved in singing and playing an instrument at the same time. But ukulele is not a substitute for guitar, and for many bands, if it comes down to a choice between adding a singer with a ukulele or a singer with a guitar, they'll go with the singer/guitar combo unless one singer is critically better than the other. Obviously there are musical styles where the ukulele is paramount (Hawaiian music comes to mind) but the uke is often viewed as a novelty instrument. These days, if you're serious about singing folk music professionally you're better off knuckling down and learning guitar.

singer Suzy Thompson, who has made excellent use of her topnotch fiddle and guitar skills. "It gives you a lot of cred and makes your show better, more fun to watch. It doesn't mean you have to play fancy, but you have to play strong, with good rhythm. And you have to know how to get your instrument really in tune." That, she explains, means making appropriate adjustments beyond what an electronic tuner tells you, and checking your tuning regularly.

SETTING THE GROOVE

For lead singers, guitar expertise is particularly useful in establishing the rhythmical "groove" of a song. "Even if you're doing a boom-chuck rhythm, there are a lot of different ways to place those beats," says singer Emily Miller. "You can be moving along with a front-of-the-beat BOOM-chuck rhythm and the band will follow you with that or you can be more laid back, with a boom-CHIKa rhythm, and the band will follow you with that. If you're not playing guitar, the band will fall into its own determination of what the groove for the song should be, and you may or may not like it."

You can make the groove happen on instruments besides the guitar, however. Emily continues: "I've recently thought the best instrument for leading a song in a band is mandolin because you can play rhythm and you can play lead. When my husband Jesse and I play, Jesse really doesn't like to lead a song without playing the guitar, and I often feel like that, too, but I feel comfortable with Jesse playing guitar. We don't do two guitars, and if we want him to play lead guitar, then he plays guitar. Generally, though, if I'm leading something, I prefer to play guitar. There are so many subtleties about how to back up a song on guitar, there are so many cues you can give a band, and so if you can do that, everything is going to be tighter and better."

The ability to play lead is useful, too. "It makes you a more rounded musician," Emily says. "I play fiddle and guitar. I use guitar mostly when I'm singing and fiddle for playing tunes and sometimes accompanying songs. The more you work on your musicianship the better you'll be."

As with everything involved with music, there's a learning curve. If you're an inexperienced guitar player, playing is going to make you less free with your singing until you get better at doing both at once. It takes time and practice.

Aoife O'Donovan, a stellar singer in the folk realm, talks about the process in a video interview for *Acoustic Guitar Magazine*. "Playing guitar while singing took a lot of getting used to," she said in the interview. "In Crooked Still [a past band] I played guitar . . . but I was definitely not a competent guitar player in any way. . . . Then the Punch Brothers asked me to go on tour with them and I had about two months to get ready. I practiced guitar for, like, six hours a day, working on just being able to accompany myself, to be able to still sing with the freedom I had without the guitar and to work on my guitar style, a two-finger fingerpicking pattern. I practiced a ton with a metronome to get those fast fingerpicking rhythms locked in. In my singing I prefer to be kind of floating over the beat, to really hang back or really push over a steady rhythm section, which I was used to with the band, but on my own I had to *be* the steady rhythm section." It's well worth taking a moment to check out Aoife's playing and singing on YouTube. If you're on the fence about dedicating time to an instrument, her obvious prowess should inspire you. And if you need still more persuading, listen to what musician Keith Murphy has to say. "There's barely a way to sing traditional music in any professional setting, but as an unaccompanied singer it's an even harder road," he says. "In the professional world, in all aspects of traditional music, including songs, it's more about the arrangement than the material. I don't see many young traditional singers singing in the old ways; they're doing it in bands with slick arrangements, and they're motivated to try to wow a lot of people quickly. That's harder to do when you're doing it in the more restrained, hardcore way." And it's harder still for the unaccompanied singer.

FINDING A SONG

Sometimes a song finds you. You hear it and fall in love. At other times you have to go on a hunt for a song that you feel like singing. In the past I would go to libraries to check out books and recordings. These days I tend to "troll" online for material that interests me. I do listen regularly to what other contemporary singers are doing, but generally, when I'm looking for a song, I go to the websites where various collections of re-cordings of older singers are gathered, such as the Library of Congress or the Max Hunter Folk Song Collection.

"The availability of material is staggering," says Keith Murphy, who sings traditional New England and Canadian material. "[In the past] I might have spent months tracking down the words of the song, but now you have it within seconds. And in terms of performance there's so much amazing stuff online, both audio and video. You have access to a tremendous amount of material." So it's important to work out how to use these resources and keep abreast of what's being done.

In any case, wherever you turn up a song, it might not be love at first listen. It's useful to make playlists of possible songs to listen to while you're driving or are otherwise occupied, so that the music comes in side-ways. I always have "to-learn" playlists, without expecting to learn all the song. When you find yourself humming a song, that's a good indication that it's time to start learning it. Conversely, if you find yourself quickly wanting to skip a particular track, that song probably isn't for you.

"HER BRIGHT SMILE HAUNTS ME STILL" ♪

"Her Bright Smile Haunts Me Still" is an example of a song that has caught the attention of many folk musicians. It made an entrance into the current folk world in 2000 as part of a compilation CD by that title featuring field recordings collected by American collectors Frank and Anne Warner. In their travels in the summer of 1951, the Warners visited Eleazar Tillett on the Outer Banks of North Carolina, who sang the song for them, joined by her sister Martha Etheridge. The song, plainly sung, is stunning and easy to fall in love with. But should you work it up to perform? Clearly many singers have said "yes"; a quick check on iTunes shows some thirty different versions including recordings by Elizabeth LaPrelle, Matt Brown, Eric Merrill, the duo Eamon O'Leary and Jefferson Hamer, the duo Eric Brace and Peter Cooper, and the bands Cordelia's Dad and John Reischman and the Jaybirds. There's even a version in Japanese by Kenji Yamamoto. The Tillett-Etheridge version is unaccompanied and unharmonized and uses a loose 3/2 rhythm, but if you preview the listings you'll quickly see that there are other directions to go in that involve changing rhythm and adding accompaniment and harmony.

You'll also get a glimpse into the pre-folk version of the song, as recorded in 1919 by Edward Johnson, who treats it as an art song and a vehicle for his rich classical tenor. What's important about that 1919 recording is that it points to an earlier history of the song. A bit more digging online turns up various renditions of the sheet music, including one from 1860. W. T. Wrighton is credited as the composer, and J. E. Carpenter is credited as the lyricist. Various publishers have published the song in various incarnations at various times, but the earliest seems to be the 1860 version. The Library of Congress lists it as a Civil War song connected with the Confederate side. But on a completely different tangent, it also turns up in Selkirk, Scotland, as part of the annual procession known as the Selkirk Common Riding. Apparently it's a song sung as the riders return to the town square, and the people of Selkirk view it as a song of exile that lauds the beauty of the city of Selkirk.

ACTIVE LISTENING

> For me the goal [in learning a song] is to evoke the emotion of the
> original but without duplicating the original, which would be impos-
> sible. That said, there are almost always little details in the original
> that are part of what makes it have the effect that it does, so very close
> listening is very important.
>
> Suzy Thompson

> The thing about listening and learning and performing [is that] it's
> really about listening. And practice . . . really carefully attending to
> what you're hearing, doing it over and over again."
>
> Jeff Davis

Listening is an ongoing theme in this book. Of course, it is key to any musical genre or style, but with folk music, where so much isn't written down
and where what is written down is often a mere shadow of the music it is
referencing, listening takes an even greater role, and nowhere is this more
evident than in working up a song. "You can't possibly sing traditional songs
without listening to traditional singers," says singer Jeff Warner, who grew
up listening to the music collected by his parents, Frank and Anne Warner,
and the musicians who made the music. Much of our access to traditional
singers comes from archival recordings that are far from easy listening, but
practice helps. "There's a value in allowing yourself an apprenticeship period where you give yourself a goal of getting inside that kind of sound," says
Mark Simos, a teacher at Berklee College of Music in Boston, who spends
considerable time in his classes playing old recordings for his students.

   I call this kind of attention "active listening." It's listening where you're
not just hearing the wash of the music but paying attention to all the
choices the singer is making in all facets of the song, from the lyrics to
instrumentation to rhythm and timing to ornamentation and phrasing—
everything. "When you hear, watch a singer do something you like, take
notes," says Jeff Warner. "Be observant, analyze it."

How much of this do you need to know as you work up the song?
It really depends on you, the singer. As a folk musician, you have a responsibility to the material, so even if you love and want to emulate the
version the Jaybirds do, you should be listening to various sources and
deciding how you yourself might like to do the song. I find that knowing

how a song has grown, and even some of the song's mysteries (Did the song really come from Scotland? Or was it somehow an outgrowth of partings and lost loves rampant in the Civil War?) helps me find a way to approach the song in a way that is unique to me, despite the many other renditions that are out there. It's a clear benefit.

STEP BY STEP

"If I'm going to learn a song," says singer Emily Miller, "I listen and write out the words by hand or on the computer, then get out the guitar, learn the details, go back, listen again to see if I've departed too far from the original. I don't necessarily like just the source recording, but I do want to know how the song goes. I want to make sure that if I'm making changes to a melody or the lyrics that it's a conscious choice, not just a mistake, and even if it was originally a mistake, I know what I'm changing it from. If it was a song somebody wrote or a traditional song from a specific source, I would like to have a good base of knowledge of the song. If it's a song I've heard from other sources I have an idea about it, but if it's a more rare song I try to learn about the song, where it came from, so when people ask I can tell them. I want to be a good bearer of tradition."

SIX STEPS IN WORKING UP A SONG

- Listen to various versions. This can mean listening to two or three versions in your music library or running down the "preview" list in iTunes to hear how a wide variety of singers have approached the song. The process of learning a song explicitly from one singer, and learning it in every detail, is extremely valuable as you develop as a folk singer, but if you plan to perform the song, your reach should be broader than a single singer, unless the singer is the person who wrote the song. My strategy is to create a playlist that includes the songwriter's rendition if possible and any other seminal recordings, plus other renditions that seem to add something to the song.
- Capture the words. This can mean hunting down the lyrics online or copying them from your primary source, but most singers agree that writing them out yourself is an important step in making the

song yours. Many singers have notebooks of songs (I have some that date back to the 1960s). Remember that online lyric websites are notorious for word errors and inaccuracies about such things as who wrote the song.

- Try the song in a variety of keys to figure out what feels good in your voice. Don't worry at the outset about making the song band- or harmony-friendly. That comes in the arranging of the song. First just sing it a lot.

- Try the song with and without accompaniment. Usually a guitar or banjo or other rhythm instrument will box the song into a specific meter, so if the song is typically sung as an unaccompanied ballad, you'll need to figure out what to add or subtract and whether that will affect the song adversely.

- Record yourself singing the song. Check for anything that seems odd—the beginnings and ends of phrases, where you're taking a

A WORD ABOUT CHANGING SONG WORDS

While many singers performing today regularly add to songs (traditional and otherwise) with new and rewritten verses or recast less easily understood language, in my view this practice is best postponed until experience can offer some guidance. The wiser strategy for a beginning folk singer would be to locate the most credible version of a lyric, for example the version that the songwriter sings, and use that as a base. It's generally OK to remove the odd word, such as eliminating the "well" in front of a phrase, but if you feel the need to rewrite major portions of a lyric you might consider moving on to a different song until you have a better handle on what can be changed and what can't. This is particularly true if the song in question is contemporary and the songwriter is performing it. Most songwriters feel understandably possessive about their work and want to have some control over how it's disseminated. A friend of mine ran into trouble with a songwriter when she rewrote a verse of a song, which she then recorded. Even though appropriate accreditation had been given and royalties paid, the songwriter was extremely unhappy about the rewrite, and my friend had to pull the recording, an expensive solution, or risk a potentially more expensive legal tangle.

breath, any intonation trouble spots or fuzzy ornaments. Are you building in spaces (keeping it conversational)? What about rhythm and tempo? If rhythm is central to the song, do you have the beat emphasis in the right place, on the offbeat for example? Are you making use of anticipations and lags appropriate to the song and style? Are you getting the plot of the song across, and if not, how might you do it better? Are you managing the emotion of the song?

- Let the song rest for a week or so and then go back to the original to see what you might have overlooked or lost in your efforts. Often this is where you'll notice an important chord change that you missed initially or a melodic phrase that you've made less interesting.

GETTING INTO THE FIELD

"I think you learn best from an actual person, as opposed to a recording or book," says singer Jefferson Hamer. "There's something really valuable about having a teacher or mentor and learning music from them. If they happen to live in a cave in the mountains or a holler in hills or a ramshackle shack somewhere, all the better, because people love that kind of story. It's like the ancient Greeks going to see the oracle."

In the not-too-distant past it was relatively easy to go out into various communities and find "tradition bearers"—singers and musicians such as Ozark singer Almeda "Granny" Riddle and Adirondack singer "Yankee John" Galusha, who represented a tradition that stretched back into another century, who had learned in that tradition and exemplified it.

Singer Sara Grey recalls singing a number of songs from her collecting trips into the logging camps of the Northeast in the 1960s for college music students. One student wanted her to teach him all the songs so he could do them for a recital. "It wasn't that I didn't want him to have these songs," she recalls. "But I told him, 'If you really care about these songs and you want to know what makes them tick and what makes the singers tick, you need to spend some time with the singers who are singing these songs. It's the last generation, but you might just get in on the tail end.'

"He did, and when he got back he called me. 'Oh my god, what a difference that made,' he said. 'I would never have understood these songs; I didn't understand the placement of them, the background. All I would have done would have been to grab them from you. I am so glad I went.' And from that point onward he made a point of seeking out the source whenever he could.

"It's true that it's difficult to find the sources anymore, but it's important to do the work when you can," Sara continues. "It makes your understanding of the songs so much better. You have to understand, for example, that the Irish were poor, there was no place for them to go, so they ended up in the logging camps where they were quite literally starving, hence the expression 'He was so thin he could slip through a straw.' Men were starving in these camps, and the songs were tied up with the history of the people. You can't separate it out. The history, the background, the roots, it's all inextricably tied together.'"

ONE SINGER'S APPROACH

"I think about each song I work up through the lens of the modern folk performance aesthetic," says singer Lissa Schneckenburger. "There are a lot of really amazing and inspiring musicians that are playing and recording traditional music today here and around the world, and I've been inspired by a lot of peers to, say, make arrangements a certain way or come up with instrumentation or production things in recording. There are a lot of little subtle things that you can layer into a song, make it come alive, give it a certain personality on top of the bare bones, and that keeps it feeling contemporary in whatever we are experiencing as a contemporary folk world. That's something I think about a lot with each song: What's a way of making this feel fresh and current to the contemporary folk audience, whether it's a certain production thing or a certain arrangement or certain chord changes or any number of things?

"There are so many, many different people out there performing and many who inspire me. I really enjoy Kate Rusby who has done a lot of recording with contemporary brass brands [on YouTube, check out Kate Rusby's "My Young Man," which she does with the Grimethorpe Colliery Band], or Sam Amidon's recording that he did with some orchestral parts that were very tasteful and at the same time musically interesting and unusual. I'm inspired by those kinds of things—people bringing a broader palette of sounds and textures into a song to orchestrate the emotion behind a story. I think that's really cool."

THE FINE ART OF INTERPRETATION

At East Tennessee State University, Roy Andrade, who heads the old-time music program, says he talks to his students a lot about the art of interpretation. "That's the great challenge for a traditional musician," he says. "You want to say something new, something different, something original. You want to find your unique voice, but at the same time you need to be thinking about style and building style. I try to not say 'This is the way,' but rather 'One way is through imitation.' There are other ways.

"Art is a murky word, but the art in [performing traditional music] is the interpretation. What are the choices you're making at each step of the way? Why? I make my students articulate: Why this song? Why this key? Why this approach? Why do we want to add another chorus at the end? Just to make it longer? Why do we need to make it longer? They know they need to have thought through these things because I'm probably going to ask them.

"If I can help them to think about things, if they can come out of this program with some sense of what it means to interpret traditional music, some sense of the repertoire, some sense of the vastness of it all, and some sense of being empowered, I'll feel great."

Most folk musicians, particularly singers of old songs, have grappled with the "art versus tradition" issue. Singer Jeff Davis, a great proponent of learning everything you can from a source singer, points out, "Even if you do a perfect rendition you're still going to sound like yourself. But there's a point to going through the process."

And for many musicians, therein lies the art. "I do not believe that a tradition should not change," says Scott Ainslie. "I do believe that statically embedding a piece of music or a tradition in amber will prevent it being a living part of our cultural and artistic life.

"I think one of the more authentic things I do is continually change things," he says. "This is much more authentic and much more in the folk tradition of America; it's much more traditional to change things."

For singer Jefferson Hamer, it's about connection. "You have to connect to the content—the notes and words—in a convincing way," he says, "in your own style. How you come up with your own style is a different question. I'd say by learning as many different songs as possible."

FOLK SINGERS AND SINGER-SONGWRITERS

There has been in recent years something of a dividing line between folk singers who consider themselves "traditional" singers or singers of old songs or even of newer songs that can be gathered under a folk umbrella, and people who sing their own songs—the singer-songwriters. Today that line is blurring, and most young musicians who call themselves folk musicians prefer to see the genre as something more inclusive. Jefferson Hamer, whose work ranges from ballads from the Francis Child collection (exquisitely rendered on a must-have CD, *Child Ballads*, with Anaïs Mitchell) to original songs, is in this camp. He uses the term "folk" to talk about what he does because, he says, it's the broadest possible category. "It can mean traditional, contemporary, acoustic, and electric—both music with words and instrumental music," he says. "I like all those kinds of music." And indeed if you look at the work he's currently doing, it reflects his eclectic tastes. So it is with many of the artists you'll see featured on lists of top folk albums or doing showcases at the Folk Alliance or IBMA (the International Bluegrass Music Association) or taking the stage at the Newport Folk Festival or on *A Prairie Home Companion*.

In short, there is a huge value to listening and learning from the folk music of our past, but then there's that next step—making it yours. The more you learn and the more you do, the easier this is and the deeper and the more artful your music becomes.

SONGWRITING

"There are many definitions of folk music," Pete Seeger wrote in 1967, "but the one that makes the most sense to me is the one that says it is not simply a group of old songs. Rather it is a process that has been going on for thousands of years in which ordinary people continually recreate the old music, changing it a little here and there as their lives change. Now that our lives are changing so rapidly, obviously there will be a lot of new songs."

There *are* a lot of new songs in the "folk" genre, and many of them sound as if they've tumbled through the folk process for decades.

Sometimes the songs are inspired by something old—Joe Newberry's "I Know Whose Tears" harks back to Rudyard Kipling's poem "Mother o' Mine," about a mother's love, and Tim Eriksen's "I Wish the Wars Were All Over" was fashioned from writings in the prison diary of a Yankee imprisoned in England for privateering during the American Revolution. "He wrote down lyrics from some of the popular songs of the day, but he didn't write down the music," Tim says. "I thought it was interesting, so I made up a tune for it."

The how-to of songwriting is a huge topic, on which many books are available, but a useful strategy, particularly if you're interested in the folk genre, is to work from a model, says Mark Simos, associate professor of songwriting at the Berklee College of Music and author of *Songwriting Strategies: A 360° Approach*. "It's empowering to go back and listen to traditional material with a songwriter's ear, thinking, 'What would it have been like to have actually written that song?'" he says.

"It's hard to do that with really traditional material because it sounds like no one wrote it, that it fell out of the sky or grew out of the stones. But I believe someone did write it, and chances are they wrote it by building on earlier models and transforming them. I call that technique 'stealing fire.' For me it's about diving deep into a source song and really studying it, seeing the way it's put together compositionally and then finding some aspect of that model that you want to try to incorporate into your own work. It doesn't mean imitating every aspect of that song—otherwise it will feel like you're just rewriting the song—but the rhyme scheme or the way the refrain works or something about the melody, and use that as a springboard for your own work. That is a less scary step if you're just getting into writing your own stuff than, say, just writing something that's new and never heard before. It's trying to understand traditional material from the writer's side and not just the performer's side.

"The key is to start with material that you genuinely love, a model that's touched you as a listener," Mark says. "That's what makes it transformational. Ask yourself, 'How did that piece create that magical effect?'"

Mark also advises gathering song "seeds"—song themes and fragments to have available so that when you do sit down to write you have something to work from. "It's like gathering nuts for the winter," he says. From there it's a matter of writing a lot, and perhaps taking a workshop or joining a songwriter's circle or listening to local singer-songwriters.

AN INTERVIEW WITH WEST VIRGINIA
SONGWRITER JESSE MILNES

**Can you describe your process in writing a song? Do you start
with a phrase, a chord progression, a snatch of a tune, an image?**

"I find that the best melodies come to me when I don't have an instrument in my hands. If I'm playing chords while I'm working on a song, the melody is usually not as creative, although occasionally I'll think of an interesting chord progression and write a melody to match it. I guess I usually start with a lyric that I like—just a line or a phrase. I'll sing it in any melody that seems to suit it, and I try to flesh that out into a whole verse or chorus before I try to find the chords. I'm not at all averse to borrowing a melody and then reworking it.

"Sometimes I start working on a song with just a rhythmic feel that I want to capture. I think it's very important to sing songs out loud and in time as you write them. Otherwise it's easy to write things that are impossible to sing.

"Sometimes I try to speak the lyrics that I'm writing as if they were prose, to make sure that the accents are falling in natural places. I used to write lyrics that filled in every available beat with a syllable, but the more I write the more I value lyrics that leave a little bit of space."

**How do you know when a song is "done"? Does the editing
process go on after you start performing a song?**

"Some songs come out more or less in one piece and are done. Other songs I cobble together out of pieces that I might have written years ago that never really went anywhere. I pretty much reserve the right to change any song at any time, though, even one that I or someone else has recorded. A song has to clear a certain threshold of quality for me to want to play it in public or show it to someone. Some songs seem really promising but aren't working, so I guess I consider them not done, because I plan to come back and do the work to get them right.

"I have dozens of songs sitting around that will never see the light of day because they're just not good enough. I like to keep track of them, though, because sometimes I'll need a verse for another song and I'll find a song I wrote that didn't work out but has a verse or two I can steal."

Any advice to beginning songwriters?

"Write as much as possible. For a while I had a job where my coworkers and I would amuse each other by making up parodies of well-known songs with lyrics about people we knew or anything we were talking about at work. The parodies were juvenile, but it was great practice. I spent hours each day mentally working lyrics into rigid meters and rhyme schemes—you can't really add a beat to "I Walk the Line" or "Home on the Range," or people will notice—and forgetting them almost as soon as they were done. Without ever meaning to, I got pretty good at saying whatever I wanted within a structure. When you know what you want to say and exactly how many syllables you have to say it, it's like solving a puzzle, finding just the right words in the right order. Sometimes the structure of a verse will lead you to say something you weren't planning. Don't be afraid of a happy accident. Ask yourself what you like in a song, what grabs you. Ask yourself what kinds of songs you enjoy singing."

How important is it to get someone else to sing your songs? Do you write with a particular band or singer in mind?

"I started writing songs in earnest because I was playing with a great band [The Sweetback Sisters], and I thought that anything I could get them to sing would sound amazing. It did! I don't particularly enjoy singing my own songs, but it's a real thrill to hear someone else sing them. I think it can be good to write songs with other people in mind—it might make you think a little bit differently. I find that frequently a song I write for a particular singer's style ends up not sounding like something they would do, but maybe the value is that it makes you imagine yourself as the audience, not as the singer."

AN INTERVIEW WITH NORTH CAROLINA SONGWRITER JOE NEWBERRY

Can you describe your process in writing a song? Do you start with a phrase, a chord progression, a snatch of a tune, an image?

Each song that I write has a slightly different birth. Sometimes the words for an entire verse will come as a piece. Other times I will hear or think of a phrase that would make a good hook for a chorus, and so I will start there. I rarely think of a stand-alone melody that later has words added to it, but from time to time the words and melody come at the same time. That is when I say to myself that really all I am doing is taking dictation."

How do you know when a song is "done"? Does the editing process go on after you start performing a song?

"I tend to write and revise before I start performing a song, but occasionally an even better word will come after I have lived with a song for a while."

Any advice to beginning songwriters?

"I tell students in my songwriting classes to always remember that a song will have more impact with its listeners if it is a 'true song.' That doesn't mean that it has to be true, but it does have to be true to life. An exercise that I often use is to have folks take a pen and a piece of paper and write as fast as they can for ten minutes without lifting the pen from the page except to turn it. I give them the topic of what they did and felt the previous day. Not lifting the pen and writing fast bypasses the 'edit' function in their brain, and usually the truth of something comes out. When people revise as they write, they will often not tell the whole truth—people even lie to themselves in their diaries. When I ask folks to read back to themselves what they have written, I will often hear a little gasp. When I ask why they gasped, I already know the answer—they have written down something that they didn't mean to utter out loud. That is usually the basis for a true song."

How important is it to get someone else to sing your songs? Do you write with a particular band or singer in mind?

"I have written with people in mind, and it is always gratifying to hear someone's recording of a piece using the voice you heard in your head. I find it helpful to know the singer or the band, because it makes it easier to get your material in front of them. Plus, your songs are like your children. It is very gratifying to give them wings and see where they go. All that said, I write songs that might never see the light of day, because that is how my brain works. I also write in lots of different genres, because I like a lot of different kinds of music."

An added note: Joe's song "Singing as We Rise," recorded by the Gibson Brothers with Ricky Skaggs, was named the International Bluegrass Music Association's Gospel Recorded Performance of the Year for 2012.

"TWILIGHT IS STEALING": A CASE STUDY ♪

Recently I was recruited to sing harmony on a lovely old song, "Twilight Is Stealing," for a concert at a summer music camp. Although I didn't know the song, I recognized it from recordings I'd heard in the past—in particular Doc Watson and Almeda Riddle—and had even included it on at least one "to-learn" playlist in past years. After the concert the song kept edging into my consciousness. It had an engaging chorus (that included the wonderful word "gleameth"; I'm always attracted to interesting song words) and despite having the feeling of a Victorian parlor song it was in 4/4 time rather than the typical 3/4 meter and it moved along with a pulse. Additionally, although the song clearly referenced heaven it wasn't overtly religious, which can be a consideration.

Fast-forward to my next stint at home when I started some initial song investigation. My first stops were iTunes and YouTube, where it turned out that although people had recorded the song regularly over the years, the song didn't appear to be on the Top Ten of the Americana hit parade.

The next thing was to find out everything I could about the song. A Google search turned up lyrics from various artists who had recorded the song and assorted YouTube renditions, but importantly it showed an "origin request" entry on the Mudcat Café site (mudcat.org), a forum where folk musicians and scholars share information about folk songs. Clicking through, I found that people had been asking about and commenting on "Twilight Is Stealing" and offering various versions of the lyric and title since around 1997. I learned also that the song had various titles (often it's called "Twilight Is Falling"), that it's considered a hymn, and, at least among the folks who commented in the Mudcat site, that the song was popular a few generations back.

More sleuthing turned up Aldine Sillman Kieffer (1840–1904) as the lyricist and Benjamin Carl Unseld (1843–1923) as the composer. In addition I found the song as the final entry on a list of public domain songs for 1877. Another site, hymnary.org, listed the song as "Twilight Is Falling," which seems to have been the original title, and showed page scans of several published versions, including one from *The Song Victor: For the Sunday School and Public School Use* (1878) p. 47." With still more sleuthing I found that the author, Kieffer, was the principal of the Virginia Normal Music School, the first school for rural singing teachers in the South, established in Newmarket, Virginia, in 1874. He founded *The Musical Million*, a monthly musical periodical devoted to rural music, and he became a staunch advocate of shape-note music. Both he and Unseld were prolific writers. Among the songs in Kieffer's legacy are "Grave on a Green Hillside" and "My Mountain Home." All of this gave me a bit more of a feeling for the world from which "Twilight" emerged.

The next step was, of course, to listen to the song. Again, YouTube and iTunes proved useful. Here I found, among more recent recordings, one from Jody Stecher and Kate Brislin on their 1993 album *Our Town*. This tender, slow rendition featured mandolin and guitar. Kate (whom I've interviewed in these pages) provided a tenor harmony throughout. I also found a recording by Missouri singer and fiddler Betse Ellis on her 2013 album *High Moon Order*. Betse played tenor guitar and Roy Andrade (another contributor to this book) played banjo and added a baritone vocal harmony on the chorus. This version had a spare quality and was compelling in a different way; I added it to my growing playlist.

There were a number of recent renditions of the song that I passed over because they weren't, to my ear, particularly compelling; in some instances the singing had moved into a pop realm, in others the arrangement or changes to melody and harmony seemed jarring. But by listening to a variety of arrangements I could solidify what I liked about the song and what I want to preserve.

As always, it was the renditions by older singers that I was drawn to. I was already familiar with Almeda Riddle's version (she sang it on her album *How Firm a Foundation*, released in 1985). Granny Riddle, as she was known, used a slightly different tune than the written versions I was turning up, but her version echoed recordings of other singers of her generation; clearly among singers who learned by ear, the song was taking a path that diverged from the written music. She also had some odd word choices—"lea" instead of "sea," for example. I would have to be making decisions soon about both words and tune.

My research eventually included checking liner notes and books and various digital archives such as the Max Hunter Folk Song Collection to hear if and when this song had been collected and the path it had taken from its nineteenth-century roots. There was an up-tempo country version that Lee and Juanita Moore sang on the radio in Wheeling, West Virginia, in 1957; there was also a version by popular radio duo Lulu Belle & Scotty in 1950 (with a whistling introduction), and a priceless string band version by the Dykes Magic City Trio, who traveled from Virginia to New York City in 1927 to record this and a handful of other songs. Their rendition of "Twilight" featured fiddle, guitar, and a high melody "octaving" the lead on the chorus, added by the band's auto-harpist, Myrtle Vermillion. By now my playlist had grown to include eleven tracks, and I also had two musical scores and a handful of texts that I could consult for word choices. And, importantly, I now knew the song in a way I didn't before the hunt began. I could begin to put it into my voice.

I needed to decide on a set of words that made sense to me, seemed close to Kieffer's original lyric, and were comfortable to sing. Here's what I settled on:

> Twilight is stealing over the sea,
> Shadows are falling dark on the lea,
> Borne on the night wind, voices of yore,
> Come from a far-off shore
>
> Far away, beyond the starlit skies,
> Where the love light never, never dies
> Gleameth a mansion filled with delight,
> Sweet happy home so bright
>
> Voices of loved ones, songs of the past,
> Still linger round me while life shall last,
> Lonely I wander, sadly I roam,
> Seeking that far-off home
>
> Come in the twilight, come, come to me,
> Bringing some message over the sea
> Cheering my pathway while here I roam
> Seeking that far-off home

From there I could begin singing along with my playlist. This is always illuminating. For one thing, even though this song was written down, there were significant variations in melody (and harmony) choices among the various singers. No one was doing it exactly like the written music. Almeda Riddle's was the version that worked the best for me, mostly because I'd heard it a lot, so I decided to start there.

Because the song has a definite pulse, I put a guitar with it right away, a simple boom-chuck rhythm augmented by flat-picked melodic phrases and something more developed for a break. The chords (only I and V) and the key choice (A) were simple, but now, as I take the song into the next phase, "singing it in," I know I want to experiment with various tempos, phrasing, and vocal quality as well as dynamics. There may be places where I want to be softer, or perhaps edgier. It's the sort of song that's often best served by keeping things simple, so I know I'm not going for heavy ornamentation or a lot of word yodels, which can augment the emotion of the song. Over time I'll record it and think about what I might want a fellow musician to do in terms of harmony or accompaniment. But I'm well on the way to making this song a part of my repertoire. Elizabeth LaPrelle talks about each singer being only a conduit. "Each of us has our own gifts, our own interpretations that we might bring to a song," she says. I'll be conduit for this song for a while.

5

PUTTING IT OUT THERE

I view music as a way to connect with people on an elemental and primary level. It is a responsibility and an honor.

—Joe Newberry

You've worked on your singing. You've worked on your songs. You've worked on your accompaniment and you've rehearsed up your band. Now you feel you're ready for that next step: an audience.

In the folk world, "performing" can range from a slot at an open mike to a set at the local library or nursing home to a steady gig at a bar in the next town, on up to festivals and concert halls and venues of increasing size and stature. The audiences and ambience might change, but many of the considerations are the same.

PERFORMANCE-READY

The first thing, clearly, is to be performance-ready, and there are a number of different levels. There's the part that has to do with knowing the lyrics of a song cold and being able to manage instrumental responsibilities automatically—being on top of chords and breaks and fills (melodic lines between phrases) and the musical conversation between voice and instrument so that the music flows easily. It's here that you'll want to include workarounds for any vocal trouble spots or rethink that complicated guitar run you repeatedly flub in practice. There's also the issue of delivering the lyric believably, working on dynamics and finding different voice qualities to enhance the song. And then there's the more ephemeral part of singing, the emotion.

For most of us in folk music, being "emotive" means presenting emotion purely through the voice, rather than employing the sort of body movements you might find in other genres. Emily Miller, singer and coach for the Davis & Elkins College Appalachian Ensemble, explains: "I want the performance to look intentional, but I don't want it to look forced. One can stand perfectly still and sing with a lot of emotion, and I encourage that. I want a completely vocal approach to the song." For an excellent example of emotive singing without any extra body language, check out the numerous online videos of Ralph Stanley. He exemplifies a strong tradition in American folk singing: standing behind the song.

Ballad singer Almeda Riddle talks about this practice in her 1970 book, *A Singer and Her Songs*. "I'm not an entertainer and never have been," she said. "My songs may entertain, but I'm not an entertainer. The ballads I do, you're not supposed to perform them. You have to put yourself *behind* the song. By that I mean get out of the way of it. *Present* your story, don't *perform* it. Let's get the picture of Mary Hamilton [a character in one of the ballads Almeda sings], the weeping, betrayed girl, before the public. If your ballad is good enough, it'll hold them. You don't have to put any tricks to your voice or anything else, if you sing it with feeling."

Delivering that feeling is of course the responsibility of anyone singing solo, but it's also true in a band context for whoever is the lead singer. "When you're singing lead you're in charge of delivering the song in the best way possible," Emily says. "For someone who's very skilled and who can do a ton of things with their voice, sometimes delivering a song is deciding to *not* do some of that stuff. Sometimes your decisions involve thinking, 'OK, I'm going to do this really simply.' It's figuring out the best way for your voice to deliver the message of the song, and that's different for each person."

SINGERS TALK ABOUT THE MUSIC

"With traditional music, the point is that you're singing songs that have been sung by many people before you, and you can assume that the song's been sung better than you're doing it right now, but you are bringing your joy of that song and of traditional music to your audience."

Emily Miller

"It has always served me well to remember that there is always a better musician, songwriter, and singer right around the corner, which is a great way to keep yourself humble. (The old joke is that I have a lot to be humble about.)"

Joe Newberry

"If you have a vision, don't let how other people are fulfilling their goals sway you. Really believe in your sense of what feels authentic. Don't act in a way that doesn't feel authentic."

Laura Cortese

There are deliberate ways of emphasizing the emotive aspect of a song, via vocal ornaments such as voice breaks at the beginnings of lines or on significant words or through shifts in volume, variations in phrasing, or changes in vocal quality, but it takes considerable practice to fold them seamlessly into your singing. If you're moving a song toward performance, it's wise to incorporate new vocal techniques sparingly, getting one technique or ornament to where you feel natural doing it before adding another. Student singers who have just figured out, for example, how to do word yodels or sliding dissonances or feathering at the ends of words are often tempted to lather their songs with these techniques, and they end up sounding artificial and self-conscious. Be sparing. Sounding natural is a big part of folk music.

Songs, Sets, and Shows

How many songs do you need? Figuring this out is part and parcel of going onstage. Although single songs are sometimes called for, it's much more common to do two or three songs at an open mike, or a ten-to-twelve song set in a concert involving multiple acts. If you're doing the entire evening you can expect two sets or more, although lately I've seen a number of performers do a single long set. When I was starting out playing old-time country music, my band was hired as a house band at a bluegrass club in San Francisco. The gig involved four fifty-minute sets a night, two nights a week. Even if we repeated material from night to night we were looking at a repertory of more than fifty songs—a huge amount of material for us to get together at that point in our careers.

A tried-and-tested method of amassing material is simply to work up songs you love until you have enough for whatever you have in mind, with of course some extras thrown in for flexibility. Performing songs you love works, particularly if you can find a way to help the audience understand what it is you love about each one and make connections between them.

Working with a theme is another useful strategy. You can gather together railroad songs or songs from camp meetings or around a particular season or holiday or even a state of mind. I once worked up a set under the umbrella "Songs of Desperate Love." The title was evocative, there were many wonderful songs to draw from, and the subject matter was something everyone could relate to.

You can also develop an entire show, the approach taken by the performing duo Anna & Elizabeth (Anna Roberts-Gevalt and Elizabeth LaPrelle). Impressive singers and musicians, they have coupled their deep love of traditional music with theater skills and artistic talents to put together shows that involve not only their stunning music but also storytelling and elements such as crankies—illustrated scrolls that are cranked between two spools and backlit. The crankies give their audiences a visual way to experience long, sometimes difficult-to-follow ballads.

"We both like the story part, like the challenge of taking a traditional song and bringing it to the stage in a way that also incorporates the context," Anna says, in talking about how their shows develop. "Often when you do traditional music on the stage it doesn't have the things that make the music fun in the living room. If you do an unaccompanied song in a living room it works, but when you put it on the stage it sort of asks too much of the song. We want people who have never heard a ballad to have some entry point into it." The crankies and the storytelling help with this. At the time of this writing the two were immersed in putting together a new show that explores what they call "the connections between place and tradition" and involves ballad singers of the 1930s and 1940s in Vermont and Virginia, the states where they grew up.

And There You Are . . .

All the preparation is done and there you are, onstage, and for the next little while you have two main responsibilities: to the music (singing and playing to the best of your ability) and to the performance (sharing that music with the audience).

The hope is, of course, that before you step onstage you're practiced up and musically confident. In any folk musician's life there will be times when one or both of those elements are missing, but the idea is that your musical abilities are solid before you perform. The rest is about connecting with the audience. A good connection with the audience will make you, the performer, more relaxed, clearing the way for your music to be as good as it can be. Most of the "don'ts" you hear from seasoned performers have evolved because if you *do* those don'ts you risk breaking that connection.

Your first opportunity to connect with the audience is when you walk onstage. This is where you show your warmth for the audience, your pleasure at the prospect of sharing your music with them. This doesn't mean that you have to be artificially sparkly (audiences can always tell if you're insincere), but do look at them, show them that you're happy to be there, and let them glimpse who you are. This doesn't necessarily mean talking, although that's what I do, but acknowledging the audience is the best icebreaker.

"Everyone wants to feel like you want to be there," says Emily Miller. "No one wants to come to a show and feel like they've inconvenienced you." A particular trap for road-weary musicians is to believe that because an audience is small, insufficiently appreciative, or the wrong demographic ("gray-topped," say, rather than a hip young folk crowd), it isn't worth their best musical efforts. Audiences sense this, and the connection is broken. What's more, you've missed the opportunity to be musical, and the more you create music in a performance setting the freer and better your music becomes.

SINGERS TALK ABOUT PERFORMING

"A constant in my performing life is that I feel like my preacher grand-father. I don't worry about the size of the crowd. . . . I preach the same sermon to one or one hundred."

Joe Newberry

"For me, getting behind the song is the A-number-one thing—making the performance important but secondary to the song. It's a combination of stage presence and being in the song. I'll be in the song for two or three beats and come back out and realize I'm in an auditorium and pay homage to my audience, then drop back in."

Jeff Warner

"When I bring a song to the stage I know that if it fits in my mouth, if I can honestly sing or perform it, then it is a legitimate expression of my musicality, which is deeply based on and informed by the traditions I carry within me."

Scott Ainslie

"In performance, I often close my eyes so that I can really go into the music. This keeps me from getting distracted and helps me to imagine the place that the song is coming from. That place might be an emotion, or it might be the physical place I was when I heard it first, or someplace it reminds me of, or something that it evokes."

Suzy Thompson

"My father [folk musician and collector Frank Warner] used to say that he'd sing to a single person [in the audience], but I couldn't do that. I try to look at the middle distance beyond the last row so I'm not singling anybody out."

Jeff Warner

"If you look comfortable and in control, the audience will relax. They won't notice small mistakes if you don't look flustered. And try to really enjoy what you're doing, or at least look like you do. It will be infectious."

Kate Brislin

"I generally prefer to stand when I perform because it feels like I'm taking it seriously. I think you can sit and perform, but standing feels like a respect thing. I wouldn't judge someone for sitting, but you still have to be very engaged. You don't want to sit back and cross your legs and be passive. If you're sitting you should sit forward and be active."

Emily Miller

"Sometimes with the Sweetback Sisters we'll play a concert and in the first half I'll feel like I'm not really getting anything back from the audience, and it will make me feel self-conscious," Emily says. "Then I'll go out and sell CDs at the break and I'll hear 'You guys are amazing, I haven't heard music like this since I was a kid!' I'll always feel better after that. I'll understand that they're just not particularly effusive, and that's OK. So I think sometimes if you engage more, your fears will be assuaged. Manning the CD table, introducing songs, that's all part of the experience. You're spending these few hours together with the audience, so you might as well make it fun for everyone."

Along these lines, it's always useful to know your audience. Find out who you're playing for. I recall being in the crowd when a young singer announced she was going to sing something from "an old group called the Carter Family." At least a quarter of the audience were musicians or had some relationship to early country music, and many had likely been playing and singing Carter Family songs since before this singer was born. Her remark, and her clear assumption that she was giving us new information, created a disconnect, and she never quite got back the ground she lost.

Different singers have different ways of "holding the stage," keeping the attention of the audience. Mostly it boils down to where you, the performer, put your focus. Focus is compelling: your focus is inevitably your audience's focus. If you're engaged internally with the song you're singing, picturing the images and hearing the song as you sing it, your audience will be with you. You don't have to feel every emotion the song talks about, and indeed you can't expect to, but you have to recognize the song's emotional content, the truth of it. Even if you're a shy performer and feel more comfortable singing than talking, your focus will compel your audience's focus and give your listeners a place to be. It's key for a solo performer, but it's also critical in a band context. The difference is that you have each other to focus on, and that's an audience grabber. "I think it's more interesting to watch a good band," Emily says, "because music is such a social thing. It's all about personal interaction. Even a duo is many times more interesting than a solo performance because then you get to see interaction between the musicians, hear some harmony, or hear them playing off of each other. Up to a certain point, the more people there are in the band, the more interaction there is, until you get to the point of so many people that no one is interacting with anyone. A band of four to six people is very exciting to watch."

Performing "Dos"

- Be yourself.
- Come to the stage with a positive attitude and a willingness to engage your audience.
- Keep instrument tuning to a minimum, especially while you're playing. If your guitar is far enough out of tune that you feel you have to repeatedly try to tune it while you're singing, it's probably best to stop, tune, and start again.
- Keep your focus where it needs to be—on the song or on the player taking the break, wherever you want your audience to focus. Avoid checking the set list or looking at your watch or getting annoyed with that guy over by the exit door who's looking at his iPhone.
- Banter with band members if that's something you can do spontaneously, as long as you keep the audience in the conversation. You're inviting the audience to get to know you a bit. But avoid "in" jokes and endless stories of how hard life on the road is.

TO TALK OR NOT TO TALK

"I'm not always in favor of lots of talking and exposition before, and especially after, playing a song, but if there's a lot of complicated plot detail, it can help to give the audience a little primer before launching into twenty verses of something. It feels generous, and it helps them stay with you."

Jefferson Hamer

- Assume your audience is as smart and savvy as you are, and talk to them as you would to anyone you respect. Avoid making disparaging remarks about their town, the size of the turnout, and so on.

Keeping Time

One important performing skill is timekeeping. Get to your gigs (and sound checks) on time, start on time, end on time, and exit the venue in a timely fashion. Allow plenty of time for loading in and packing up so that neither you nor the staff at the venue feel rushed. Be tuned up and ready to go when required, and keep to the schedule. If an organizer asks for a twenty-minute set on a festival stage, that includes walking on, walking off, and everything in between: setup, tuning, song introductions, and whoops and hollers from the audience. Plan accordingly. If things are running behind, check with the organizer about whether he or she wants you to shorten your set. Doing three songs instead of four won't matter hugely to the audience (or will leave them wanting more), and you'll be doing your part in helping the stage schedule to get back on track and the whole event to run more smoothly. That sort of thing generates far more goodwill than the missing song would have. I generally figure five minutes per song for the typical three-verse song and relaxed between-song patter—more if there's going to be a long song or story in there. I usually have a song or two in reserve in the event that things go more quickly than I expected, so I can fill out the set. But less is always more. It's much better to leave the audience looking at the festival schedule for where else they can catch you or heading for the CD table than to squeeze in every second of music you can, and a spacious set is easier on the ears. And of course be especially vigilant if you're an opening act. Running over your allotted time as an opening act is never OK.

BEFORE ALL THAT . . .

The really tough phase is where you kind of know a song but you haven't taken the shrink-wrap off it yet. You need to sing a song in front of somebody to figure out if you really know it.

Jefferson Hamer

Performing seems like the goal when you're practicing your musical skills, but for many folk singers the real challenge comes in negotiating the stretch of time between woodshedding the music and playing that first gig. It can seem endless and discouraging and fraught with unknowns. The biggest issue is that you're no longer in control of your musical experience. You can decide what song to work on and how and whether to practice your guitar. But then you get to a point where it takes other people to make the magic happen. Your musical joy is dependent on finding people to jam with, people to work up song arrangements with, people to perform with, people who will give you gigs, come to your shows, buy your CDs, and help you along a professional musical path in all the necessary ways. Everyone from your parents to the local guitar teacher to your quarterly folk magazine confirms the reality of the situation: The competition is fierce, the performing venues (at least for beginning performers) are limited, the money is terrible, and it's really tough to keep a band together. But many people are doing it, even if it means living out of a van or couch-surfing for months (or years). Like so many tangles of seemingly insoluble problems, the problems facing a professional folk singer can be dealt with if you tease them out one by one. But first there's the issue of getting out of your practice room and into the real world.

For folk singers who are just looking to do more singing with other people, there are a growing number of choir-type opportunities—shape-note singing sessions that you can drop in on and community folk and hospice choirs that require a specific time commitment for a given season. These will answer the immediate question of "Who can I sing with?"

Finding more intimate groups of musicians is less straightforward, but it gets easier the better you become as a musician. Excellence attracts. If you continue to work on your craft it will show. Jam sessions are a good way to show what you can do and to hear what other people are doing. In my area several local bars host "old-time" jams, which aren't great venues for singing, since they mostly involve fiddlers and banjo players playing fiddle tunes. But there are also "pub sings," which *are* great venues for singing. "The pub sings fill a need for a place for people to come and just sing by themselves," says singer Tony Barrand. And indeed you don't need a band or an instrument or much of anything but a song or two—preferably something with a chorus that is relatively short and easy to pick up. It's best if you know the words and know how to start the song, and where you want to put it pitch-wise. You don't need to teach the song at all—and it works best if you don't try. People will pick it up on the fly. If it's too complex to be picked up easily, it's likely not right for the session. In the pub sings where I live, unaccompanied songs are the rule, although someone may occasionally pull out a concertina. The convention is usually to let the song leader sing the verses on his or her own, and then everyone joins in on the chorus. Spur-of-the-moment harmonies are usually welcome. If you're coming to a particular pub sing for the first time, get there at the beginning so you can see who's doing what (you don't want to sing a song that someone already sang). Also, there are usually fewer people at the beginning, so this is a good time to exchange names with a person or two.

In many areas there are also bluegrass jams and honky-tonk sessions, and these tend to have different conventions. Watch and learn. One big difference is whether and how you jump in on a song. Typically, in sessions with skilled musicians, both leads and harmonies in songs are limited to one voice on a part. It's not a "singalong." You don't "double" the lead unless others are already doing it. It's the same with the harmonies, which are usually of the parallel variety—one part above the melody (tenor) and one below (baritone). If someone takes the tenor harmony and you can come up with an accurate baritone part, go for it, but if that's taken too, then listen and wait for another opportunity. It's a lot like waiting to turn across traffic. Eventually there will be clear space and your turn will come.

As in any new social situation, if you go in with nothing to prove and are willing to listen and join in appropriately, things will go well for you, and you just might find that elusive "someone to play with." Be realistic in your goals, however. What you're looking for is someone who's at your general level.

Small-Group Jamming

If you do meet that someone and you get together, there are ways to make the meeting of your musical minds a smooth experience. First, come prepared with a few things you can sing without needing to look at the lyrics—know the songs you're leading. It's friendly to have a personal song binder on hand to share songs, but remember you're also sharing musical ideas, which means allowing your friend to bring his or her musical sensibilities to the table. There's a time and place for re-creating exactly what Gillian Welch and David Rawlings did on "By the Mark," but most musicians find it very frustrating to be constantly told how they should or shouldn't do something, and they need the freedom to work things out for themselves, which may take two or three passes. If you jump in right away to offer corrections, you're short-circuiting the musical process. Allow the music to develop. Also go easy on trotting out your homemade songs. One song that you've written is probably fine, especially if it's easy to follow in terms of chords and harmony, but un-less it's a situation where you're all sharing songs you've written or there is a real clamor for more, take it slow. There's always another time.

Folk music camps offer an ideal setting for meeting musicians and making connections. Typically these camps offer instruction (I teach at many of them), jamming opportunities, and student showcases where you can perform. They're highly social and they're fun. Often you'll see listings and advertisements in folk magazines such as the *Old-Time Herald* or *Sing Out!* Folk festivals sometimes give you an opportunity to make connections, especially if there are workshops or campground jamming, but these days the larger festivals are typically geared specifi-cally toward a listening audience.

Getting Those First Gigs

If you do find a like-minded group of musicians and you're all getting along well musically and otherwise, eventually someone is going to bring up the notion of getting a gig. The typical first option is to try a local "open mike"—a night put on at a bar or coffeehouse that allows you to sign up to do a specific number of songs or play for a certain number of minutes. Because the setup at open mikes changes dramatically from one to another, your best bet is to go to the ones in your area to see how they're run, the level of musicianship, the length of the spots, what you have to do to get on the evening's roster, the microphone situation, and anything else that seems a mystery to you. But be appropriate. If your local open mike seems to feature singer-songwriters, set aside your thirty-verse Child ballad for another time or venue.

Nursing homes are typically brought up as potential gig opportunities for beginning performers. My feeling is that playing in nursing homes is fine, as long as you give such jobs the same effort and practice that you would any music job and that you choose your material with your audience in mind. If you make an effort to include songs that featured in their lives, your efforts will be greatly appreciated. Many private events (weddings, for example) will want to have some say in what you sing and play and when, so you should have flexibility and a varied repertoire before going in that direction.

The point is to get out there with your music and keep your ears open for opportunities. Sometimes a local small event such as a street fair is looking for local performers. There are eating establishments that have music for, say, a Sunday brunch or a Mother's Day lunch or a Wednesday night series. You may have a folk club in your community that features local performers, sometimes as opening acts for touring groups. Coffeehouses used to be prime spots to play but now, if they have good Wi-Fi, they are likely to be filled with people hunched over their computers and not particularly receptive to live music. House concerts, however, seem to have taken their place, and house concerts are put on in most areas. But again, competition is fierce and house concert series get booked up rapidly, months in advance. To get a foot in the door, suggests musician Suzy Thompson, join Folk Alliance International (previously the North American Folk Music and Dance Alliance), a nonprofit organization that produces an annual conference that is reportedly the world's largest gathering of the folk music industry and community. The Folk Alliance has five regional organizations, in the Midwest, the West, the Northeast, the Southeast, and the Southwest, all of which have conferences. "A lot of the people who book the house concert circuit go to those conferences," she explains. The downside to house concerts is that they are private events, usually with very limited seating, and the audience has heard about the concert through word of mouth or an e-mail notice. "So there's no longer the possibility of someone just wandering in off the street and having their mind blown by your music," she says. "They would never find out about the concert."

Some bar gigs still exist for acoustic music. "Those gigs have a low cover charge, so that's where you get people in off the street," says Suzy. Sometimes there will be a venue that's looking for a singer or a duo or a band to fill a slot every week or every month. Keep on the lookout for local places that do that, and if your music seems appropriate to their needs, let them know of your availability. Usually they'll need to be able to hear you, so be prepared to tell them where you're playing and have a good-quality demo CD or video on hand to give them.

Of course, the Internet offers you opportunities to get your music in front of people without leaving your living room, through YouTube, Concert Window, and other online concert venues. The digital landscape, as we know, is constantly changing, and folk musicians are taking advantage of it.

Overall, when you're setting out to play music professionally there are a lot of little steps, and the adage "don't quit your day job" applies. Suzy offers this advice: "Look for regional gigs. Team up with another act and do a double bill. Get as good as you can, and don't try to put yourself out there until you're ready, because first impressions are critical—there are no do-overs. And don't worry about whether it goes anywhere. Enjoy the music for the music's sake—that's really important."

Quitting Your Day Job: Touring and More

So at what point do you take your folk music career full-time? There's no one right answer, but typically it's when prospects look good, you can afford it, and your life situation supports it. Singer and musician Joe Newberry left his day job at age fifty-eight, after many years of playing gigs in and around his job responsibilities. "The previous year, a friend of mine asked me if I wanted to do music full-time," Joe says. "When I said 'yes,' he said, 'You should do it now, because you have a great future behind you.' That resonated with me, because my sun is closer to the horizon than that of younger players. When I got a call to be a featured singer on the Transatlantic Sessions tour in January and February of 2016, I was able to make that transition."

The ability to tour is crucial. "You can sit at home and make albums," says musician and folk publicist Sabra Guzman, "but if you're going to go out and be something, touring's the way to go." But that doesn't just mean getting in your car and hitting the road. There's a lot to think about: the vehicle (and its roadworthiness); tour management; where you're going to stay; whether you need to hire other people to come along, such as a bass player or a drummer; and what you're going to pay them. "In the beginning it's going to be rough," Sabra says. "You're not going to get those guarantees that you think you should get and probably deserve, and there's so much hard work in the beginning, but it pays off, especially if you hold yourself in such a way that you're not getting drunk at the end of gigs and you're not pissing off promoters. You're actually starting to make connections and you're reaching out to radio stations—'Hey, we're this band coming in, we're playing such and such, and we'd like to get on the air; how do we do that?' You have to book far in advance, and you have to talk to radio stations and the press far in advance. Having a four-month calendar is your best friend. Learning how to be organized is also going to be key." In other words, you have to look at touring as a business, which is how most touring musicians see it.

"About 75 percent of my income comes from touring," says Emily Miller, who lives with her husband Jesse Milnes in West Virginia and tours all over the country. "At a minimum it's about 50 percent, which I augment with teaching. Most of my performance income is from playing elsewhere, but when Jesse and I do our duo act, we get hired a fair amount around West Virginia. We don't play a ton in our town, but we do play around the state fairly frequently." Ruth Ungar Merenda and Mike Merenda, of the duo Mike & Ruthy, look at it in terms of time on the road versus time at home. "We're on tour a little more than we're home," Ruthy says. They've been touring for sixteen years, and at this point their touring involves taking their two children with them whenever possible. Nearby grandparents are available as well. Laura Cortese, who has a band, Laura Cortese & the Dance Cards, says she usually does 130 to 150 dates a year with the band and 100 more with other projects. "I'm trying to concentrate more on the band, pull it back closer to 30 or 50 with other people," she says.

The folk duo Ordinary Elephant (Crystal Hariu-Damore and Pete Damore) spend all their time on the road, since they live in their motorhome, "Millie," which they use to travel to various places where they play. Living on the road and managing a folk music career has its challenges, but it also provides some really beautiful spots to call home, as a video of the couple at an Oregon campground shows, but it means that your organization and management have to be exemplary. And you need to have a recording.

ADVICE FROM A ROAD WARRIOR

Sabra Guzman, publicist with Bird's Word PR and veteran of a number of touring bands, offers this advice: "Get ready to wear all the different hats that you might have to do for your band. If you really want to take it seriously, if you want to make it more of a profession with some actual income being garnered to help you out in your life, you really have to look at it as a business. Of course focus on your music, that's the soul of it; make sure your band is who you want to be playing with and the material you're doing is something that you love . . . that it's coming from you. But there's going to be a lot of dirty work; there's going to be a lot of time in front of the laptop, and it's a dream if a band gets picked up. Even when I was touring full-time with a band that was doing well, Old Sledge, and we were playing a lot of festivals and were at a good point to start looking for agents, it was really hard even to get booking agents. They wanted to see more work done; they weren't looking for this sort of band yet. It was hard. Booking agents don't come easy; labels don't come easy. Maybe I wasn't what they wanted—that's also a cold hard fact you have to swallow—but at the same time, it doesn't mean that a band shouldn't go forth. At the same time, you have to become computer-savvy; you have to learn how to write e-mails well, and you have know how to book yourself in such a way that you come across as a smart, business-savvy individual."

RECORDING

Despite the doomsayers' predictions of the death of the compact disc, CDs are still relevant in folk music, if the pile I came back with from a summer's work is any indication. "The CD is still essential," says Laura Cortese. "You may have more young people listening on Spotify, but people buy CDs and they listen to them. The volume may change—you may print 10,000 instead of 20,000—but CDs are still a calling card in the folk world. I sold more of my recent album than I did prior albums."

Making a professional recording is a valuable (albeit often humbling) experience for many musical reasons, not least is that you can really hear yourself and assess how you sound. "There's nothing like the recording process to really get to know a song and arrangement," says singer Jefferson Hamer. But these days it's also an expensive business. And it *is* changing, even if the changes tend to be slower in folk music than in other music streams. There are few absolutes. When I first made an album (vinyl) with my band, Any Old Time, the Arhoolie label hired us, provided the studio, and covered the expenses of recording, production, cover art, promotion, and everything else. We purchased our albums from the label to sell at our gigs. Now folk artists are pretty much expected to fund recordings themselves, and with the considerable outlay of money involved—it can easily be upward of $10,000 for a professionally produced CD, and that's before you get to associated costs such as publicity—there is the question of whether one should be making a CD at all. Indeed, by the time you read this, artists may only be making recordings for digital download.

If you do decide to go into the studio, you need to have clear goals. You should have thought about why you want to make the recording, how much money you're prepared to put into it, what you expect to get out of it and, importantly, how you plan to promote the recording. Are you going to tour? Hire a publicist? The more professional your recording is and the better you plan the business end of things, the more use it will be to you. Home recordings or recordings made by your buddy in his basement don't do well on radio, because their sound quality just doesn't stand up to a professionally produced sound. Also, do your homework. Talk to local musicians who have made recordings you enjoy. What studio did they use? Did they have a producer? Who was the engineer? Who mastered the album? What about distribution? PR? What did it all cost? Basically, you want to go for the highest quality you can afford. If you plan to make folk music your profession, your recording should reflect that.

Increasingly these days you also need video.

"We're a video culture," says Ruthy. "It's hard to have enough video content to keep up. I always wish we had more, whether it's a live video from a show or us sitting around doing a song or a really produced music video. That's how people are experiencing a new piece of music—they're watching it. I like the idea of every once in a while releasing a new song with a video to it. It keeps people interested, and it's a great way for people to hear your new songs." Still, Mike & Ruthy produce a new CD every two years or so. "We like to play shows," Ruthy says. "That's when we sell CDs. Our two sources of income are CD sales and gig pay."

You can't talk about recording without talking about record labels. Sabra Guzman was a director of Rebel Records, a bluegrass label in Virginia, for several years. "What I see in the music industry at large is that labels are shrinking because people don't buy albums, although that's a big source of income for touring bands," she says. "People don't necessarily want some type of physical product. Labels are shrinking their size. They used to have in-house people to do publicity and to help out with managing the bands and so on, but now the labels can do so little. They don't have the money to put out the albums; the artists have to pay for it themselves. And bands can't shop their record around, go into Capitol Records and say 'Listen to our record,' and that's especially true of folk music bands."

SINGERS TALK ABOUT THE BUSINESS

"I have to say, for me it's been all about touring and the slow build. My friend Ward Stout (a bluegrass fiddle player) told me this adage when I first moved to Nashville: How do you make fans? One at a time."

Nora Jane Struthers

"You want to be positive and collaborative. People want to work together and they want it to be fun. The person [they'll hire] is the one that's the most collaborative, the most positive."

Ruthy Ungar

"I show up, I bring a consistent sound, and I'm flexible—I will bend to [the situation]. That's been a big part of my being able to make my living doing this."

Moira Smiley

"I think that like any business, you have to be prepared to take advantage of an unexpected turn of events. Also, like any business, you have to be scrupulous with your word. I have learned over the years to ask for what you want. If you believe in what you are doing and your worth as an artist, you should never apologize for that. In negotiations, start high. You can always come down on a quote, but it is darned near impossible to go up."

Joe Newberry

On the West Coast, Suzy Thompson says the same thing. "Hardly anybody is making records for record companies," she says. "Almost everybody is putting out their own records. And in general, the ante on what
you have to spend in terms of time and especially money to get something going now is way off the charts. It's not uncommon for people to
spend thousands of dollars on marketing." This is where, increasingly,
Kickstarter, GoFundMe, and other crowd-funding campaigns come
in. Nashville singer-songwriter Nora Jane Struthers reports running
Kickstarter campaigns for her two most recent albums, raising $20,000
in 2012 for the first and $50,000 in 2014 for the second. "My small but
mighty fan base has lifted me up and empowered me to have a career in
music without a label," she says, but she adds that she would still like to
find the right label partner. "I would value having the infrastructure and
industry relationships of a team of people who believe in my music. If I
can find that, I will go for it. If I cannot, I will likely self-release again."
And increasingly, musicians who are self-releasing their CDs are turning
to folk-oriented PR companies to take up the publicity slack.

GETTING THE WORD OUT

Publicity, or PR, or whatever you want to call it, is now a reality in
the folk music business. "It's not that it's going to make you a star,
but it's part of the larger engine," says Sabra Guzman, who is part of
Bird's Word PR, a Louisiana-based publicity company that specializes
in "American traditional music for a digital age." "If you're trying to
promote your band, promote your album, promote your music, get out
there, be heard, have your name dropped, publicity is this really important part of that, but not necessarily through a label, since the resources
of labels are so restricted now."

Ruthy of Mike & Ruthy says that they spend "frightening amounts
of money" on PR when they make a recording. "If we don't spend it,
it's like a tree falling in the woods," she says. "Why did we put all this
effort and heart and soul into making the record?" The money doesn't
necessarily go to a multifaceted firm like Sabra's. There might be a radio
publicist who does radio promotion and a press publicist who's working
with a string of release dates. "On this tour [I was talking to Ruthy on the

phone while she was between restaurant and motel] we hired a publicist just to work four shows, the club dates. We don't always feel like we can afford it, but right now we're touring in states that we haven't played with the new record, so we feel like it is still part of the record push. It really just depends on what you're trying to do."

Laura Cortese says similar things. "When I released my album in 2006 I asked people I trusted, asked venues, asked record labels that I had no hope of being on, where was the best place to put my energy, and pretty much the universal answer was 'publicity'; whether it's grass-roots publicity or paid publicity or a combination of both, that's the first step, people actually hearing your music. I hired a print and radio publicist—at that point we weren't quite in the world of social media. I gave my CD to a lot of people, and that got me on folk radio and reviews in various folk magazines.

"Now to publicize an album I hire one or two people to do print me-dia, blogs, and radio; you can hire people to focus on social media, but so far I've done that on my own."

Sabra and her colleagues provide folk musicians with a one-stop shop for PR. They work on radio publicity, craft bios, negotiate premieres, and oversee press publicity. "Before an album is released we reach out to cer-tain outlets, press, or media, and try to get them to premiere the album," Sabra explains. Premiering an album means giving a particular blog or media first dibs on something new that's coming out. "It's not only good for the artist to get on the blog but also for the blog to get possible new readers. The artist and PR company and label are using this website link."

Like Ruthy, Sabra stresses the importance of having a good video. "What better way to draw an audience who doesn't know you from jack than a great-looking video that sounds great and puts you out on a good foot?" she says. "Some people don't have the equipment to do it, or the funds, but maybe you're near a university and they have an art depart-ment and they have a student who is interested in doing videos and is willing to do it for free or for a few drinks or something like that."

Social Media

A given in all this is that you'll use social media as part of whatever promotion you do. There's no way to manage a career in folk music these days without it. "It's huge," says Ruthy Ungar. "And it takes a huge amount of time—Facebook, Twitter, Instagram. You can spend $20 or $40 on a Facebook ad and they are able to direct it to people who like the kind of stuff you do, who live in the vicinity where you're playing. I've had presenters, when we're booking a show, say, 'And we'll split the cost of a $40 Facebook ad.' The reason they do it is because that's what actually works. People are addicted to their devices, constantly checking, getting information. That's how I know who's playing where; it's coming into this little device in my hand. It's a complex tool, but the technology is there. We might as well be using it to drive people to our events."

Publicist Sabra Guzman agrees. "It's a changing landscape," she says. "There are so many different outlets and attitudes about how to go about getting music out there, but I would definitely say for a band that, as much as they might hate it, some type of social media helps. There are a lot of creative ways, with your iPhone, Instagram, or Vine. There are ways to get new fans and to keep your band in the ether, but that's also why people go for publicity help. It's hard to make all those contacts, to know where to put your stuff out at, and it's time-consuming."

Even if you don't use social media to full advantage, it's a tool you can't ignore. "It's easier to spread the word about gigs through e-mail and social media," says Emily Miller of the Sweetback Sisters. "We have an e-mail list that's geographical. We do a monthly e-mail to our entire list, and if we hear that tickets aren't selling well in a particular town we'll do a geographic blast." Anna & Elizabeth used social media to get to know their online fans and supporters a bit better. "We posted a note saying 'We'd like to know who you are; why don't you send us a postcard?'" They received a lot of postcards and cemented a lot of friendships in the process, friendships that will ultimately result in ticket and CD sales, even though that wasn't the intent of the exercise.

That sense of creativity and play is important, says singer Laura Cortese. "If you aren't able to bring the same creativity to your self-promotion that you are to your art, it's going to be really difficult. Think of social media as another way to be creative and really try to bring joy and the idea of experimentation to it. If you can bring a sense of play to your social media, you're going to have a lot more energy for it." Part of the social media dance, of course, is keeping up with the constant changes. "Whatever I tell you today about Facebook, by the time the book is printed something will have changed," Laura says. "There are many articles out there about how to use Facebook effectively. It's important to actually study that on a regular basis, study how things are changing. When you notice something different, figure out what has changed about this platform so that you can be on the front edge of it. Make it feel like an adventure rather than this annoying thing that you have to do. Try to think what would be fun. How do I connect with and engage the people who like my music? What I've learned over and over again is some of my first fans, the people who saw me play five or six years ago, are actually my best advocates. They will repost my posts on social media and tell their friends verbally when they see them because they're on my e-mail list, so every post that I make I want them to be part of the conversation."

THEN AND NOW

There's no doubt that folk music as a business has undergone dramatic changes since the "revival" days of the 1960s. In her decades-long career, Suzy Thompson has witnessed many of those changes. "The whole scene is much, much bigger and more competitive," she says. "Now we're at the point where a lot of it is blended with mainstream popular music. It's harder to find a niche. Music used to be purely regional and you could market yourself as representing a region of music or a genre of music. It's much harder to do that now because of the Internet. Everything is available to everybody, so it's less meaningful. The whole question of authenticity is more tricky now."

"I've seen it change in the forty years I've been around," says singer-songwriter Ruthy Ungar (of Mike & Ruthy), who, though only forty, is daughter of musicians Jay Ungar and Lyn Hardy. "My dad and mom were of an era where folk music was just something you would do. There wasn't all this marketing, and the traditional musicians you would hear didn't do it all the time. It wasn't a job. When my dad was hearing the Balfa Brothers at Newport [the Newport Folk Festival], they weren't on some sort of world tour.

"Now you can't really do both—a steady job and a life on the road. Newport isn't going to book anyone anymore who does that. Some great banjo player from the backwoods, he's never going to get looked at. If there's somebody willing to put money behind it, maybe we'll hear it." Suzy points out another big difference: the necessity now to look good. "It was always important how you look, but now, because of YouTube, the visual part of it is much more important. You can no longer just send a promo photo. You have to be on YouTube. If you're not on YouTube, you're not considered to be legitimate. It's upped the ante."

KEEPING IT FUN

What you've undoubtedly gathered is that folk music, like every other area of music, is highly competitive and must be approached as a business. But at the same time you want to keep the joy of it alive. For Emily Miller, this means going to a festival where there's a lot of jamming. "That's the most rejuvenating thing for me," she says. "If I'm in a lull where I'm not feeling inspired about music, all I have to do is to go make music with people for fun and I'm totally inspired again—to write songs and learn new tunes and songs and practice more." Ruthy Ungar says she's careful to take gigs that "feed your soul" as well as ones "that pay great but aren't all that much fun." Folk musician Lissa Schneckenburger finds her sustenance in her community and family. "I truly love music, and I truly love performing and touring, and obviously you have to do what you love," she says. "But I see how you really can't get anywhere in the music business and in the folk world without family and community support."

This chapter has been a speed-walk through what it's like to be in professional folk music today. We haven't touched on many aspects of the business, such as agents and managers, booking and bookkeeping, what to charge and when to do freebies, finding a label, and much more, but those issues take us even farther from the actual singing, which is at the core of what we want to do. If you need guidance on these other subjects, talk to people around you who are successfully doing what you want to do, and do your homework.

Taken as a whole, the folk music business can seem fraught with insurmountable problems, but the music is out there and people are

playing it and negotiating the business and making a go of it. The main
thing, if you love singing folk music, is just to keep singing it, find places
to do it and people to do it with. If a career path unfolds that puts you
on the road and into the venues you hope to play in, great! But keep
the joy of singing close at hand. Suzy Thompson puts it frankly: "To be
a success nowadays you have to be driven," she says. "You have to have
an enormous amount of energy and a really thick skin and be willing to
keep at it, even if you never get the success you're looking for. That's
why it's important that it's still fun, because if it isn't, what's the point?"

SCHOOLS, COLLEGES, AND CAMPS

The educational side of folk music, both traditional and modern, is thriving
in the United States. There are classes and workshops and instructors just
about anyplace you go. Schools that specialize in folk music continue to crop
up. The venerable Old Town School of Folk Music in Chicago is a prime
example, with classes and teachers numbering in the hundreds and students
in the thousands. Smaller schools offer an excellent if less varied roster,
including the Summit School in Montpelier, Vermont, the Acadia School
of Traditional Music & Arts in Bar Harbor, Maine, the Calliope School of
Folk Music in Pittsburgh, Pennsylvania, and the Jalopy Theatre & School
of Music in Brooklyn, New York, where I teach. Classes for guitar, fiddle,
banjo, and so on are clearly in the majority, but more and more singing or
harmony-singing classes are being included. If there isn't a specific singing
class listed at the folk school in your area, request one. Usually it's a matter
of demand, and demand for singing classes seems to be on the rise.

Increasingly, young musicians are seeking college-level degree courses
at places such as the Berklee College of Music in Boston and East
Tennessee State University in Johnson City, which has both bluegrass
and old-time programs that include vocal and instrumental instruction.
There are also numerous minor or non-degree programs. Although the
descriptions vary, the emphasis tends to be on old-time or Southern Appalachian music or bluegrass. Warren Wilson College in Asheville, North
Carolina, in its Appalachian music program, offers a "concentration in
traditional music" that includes ensembles and classes. The University of
California at Los Angeles, through its ethnomusicology department, sup-

ports an Old-Time String Band Ensemble, under the direction of multi-instrumentalist David Bragger. The Florida State University College of Music in Tallahassee has a number of folk-based ensembles, including an Old Time Ensemble. At Brown University in Providence, Rhode Island, there is an ongoing, non-performance-oriented Old Time String Band Class. The emphasis in most such programs is typically on instruments, and a level of proficiency is usually required; the amount of vocal instruction varies from school to school. The Appalachian Ensemble at Davis & Elkins College in Elkins, West Virginia, features singing as well as instrumental music. Students are recruited from around the country for their instrumental skills (playing fiddle, guitar, banjo, mandolin, or bass), but ensemble string band director Emily Miller says, "I also look for students who are decent singers and have some base knowledge of singing, because I work with them a lot on singing." For a more comprehensive listing of college-level programs see the adjunct material for this book on the NATS website. ♪

Music camps are perhaps the best way to get concentrated instruction, meet like-minded people, and have a lot of fun as well. The Ashokan Music and Dance Camp in New York state, Pinewoods Camp in Massachusetts, the Augusta Heritage Center and Allegheny Echoes in West Virginia, the Swannanoa Gathering in North Carolina, Voice Works and the Puget Sound Guitar Workshop in Washington state, and the California Coast Music Camp all offer various weeks and sometimes weekend events specializing in particular styles of music or instruments, and most have a vocal component. They are worth checking out. ♪

6

SINGING AND VOICE SCIENCE

Scott McCoy

This chapter presents a concise overview of how the voice functions as a biomechanical, acoustic instrument. We will be dealing with elements of anatomy, physiology, acoustics, and resonance. But don't panic: the things you need to know are easily accessible, even if it has been many years since you last set foot in a science or math class!

All musical instruments, including the human voice, have at least four things in common, consisting of a *power source, sound source* (vibrator), *resonator*, and a system for *articulation*. In most cases, the person who plays the instrument provides power by pressing a key, plucking a string, or blowing into a horn. This power is used to set the sound source in motion, which creates vibrations in the air that we perceive as sound. Musical vibrators come in many forms, including strings, reeds, and human lips. The sound produced by the vibrator, however, needs a lot of help before it becomes beautiful music—we might think of it as raw material, like a lump of clay that a potter turns into a vase. Musical instruments use resonance to enhance and strengthen the sound of the vibrator, transforming it into sounds we identify as a piano, trumpet, or guitar. Finally, instruments must have a means of articulation to create the nuanced sounds of music. Let's see how these four elements are used to create the sounds of singing.

PULMONARY SYSTEM: THE POWER SOURCE OF YOUR VOICE

The human voice has a lot in common with a trumpet: both use flaps of tissue as a sound source, both use hollow tubes as resonators, and both rely on the respiratory (pulmonary) system for power. If you stop to think about it, you quickly realize why breathing is so important for singing. First and foremost, it keeps us alive through the exchange of blood gases—oxygen in, carbon dioxide out. But it also serves as the storage depot for the air we use to produce sound. Most singers rarely encounter situations in which these two functions are in conflict, but if you are required to sustain an extremely long phrase, you could find yourself in need of fresh oxygen before your lungs are totally empty.

Misconceptions about breathing for singing are rampant. Fortunately, most are easily dispelled. We must start with a brief foray into the world of physics in the guise of *Boyle's Law*. Some of you no doubt remember this principle: the pressure of a gas within a container changes inversely with changes of volume. If the quantity of a gas is constant and its container is made smaller, pressure rises. But if we make the container get bigger, pressure goes down. Boyle's law explains everything that happens when we breathe, especially when we combine it with another physical law: *nature abhors a vacuum*. If one location has reduced pressure, air flows from an area of higher pressure to equalize the two, and vice versa. So if we can create a zone of reduced air pressure by expanding our lungs, air automatically flows in to restore balance. When air pressure in the lungs is increased, it has no choice but to flow outward.

As we all know, the air we breathe goes in and out of our lungs. Each lung contains millions and millions of tiny air sacs called *alveoli*, where gasses are exchanged. The alveoli also function like ultra-miniature versions of the bladder for a bag pipe, storing the air that will be used to set the vocal folds into vibration. To get the air in and out of them, all we need to do is make the lungs larger for inhalation and smaller for exhalation. Always remember this relationship between cause and effect during breathing: we inhale because we make ourselves larger; we exhale because we make ourselves smaller. Unfortunately, the lungs are organs, not muscles, and have no ability on their own to accomplish this feat. For this reason, your bodies came from the factory with special muscles designed to enlarge and compress your entire thorax (ribcage), while simultaneously moving your lungs. We can classify these muscles in two main categories: any muscle that has the ability to increase the volume capacity of the thorax serves an *inspiratory* function; any muscle that has the ability to decrease the volume capacity of the thorax serves an *expiratory* function.

Your largest muscle of inspiration is called the *diaphragm* (figure 6.1). This dome shaped muscle originates from the bottom of your sternum (breastbone), and completely fills the area from that point around your ribs to your spine. It's the second largest muscle in your body, but you probably have no conscious awareness of it or ability to directly control

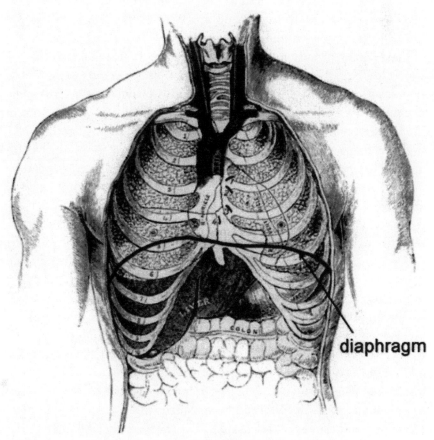

Figure 6.1. Location of diaphragm. *Courtesy of Scott McCoy*

it. When we take a deep breath, the diaphragm contracts and the central portion flattens out and drops downward a couple inches into your abdomen, pressing against all of your internal organs. If you release tension from your abdominal muscles as you inhale, you will feel a gentle bulge in your upper or lower belly, or perhaps in your back, resulting from the displacement of your innards by the diaphragm. This is a good thing and can be used to let you know you have taken a good inhalation.

The diaphragm is important, but we must remember that it cannot function in isolation. After you inhale, it relaxes and gently returns to its resting position through an action called *elastic recoil*. This movement, however, is entirely passive and makes no significant contribution to generating the pressure required to sustain phonation. Therefore, it makes no sense at all to try to "sing from your diaphragm"—unless you intend to sing while you inhale, not exhale!

Eleven pairs of muscles assist the diaphragm in its inhalatory efforts, which are called the *external intercostal* muscles (figure 6.2). These muscles start from ribs one through eleven and connect at a slight angle downward to ribs two through twelve. When they contract, the entire thorax moves up and out, somewhat like moving a bucket handle. With the diaphragm and intercostals working together, you are able to increase the capacity of your lungs by about three to six liters, depending on your gender and overall physical stature; thus, we have quite a lot of air available to power our voices.

Eleven additional pairs of muscles are located directly under the external intercostals, which, not surprisingly, are called the *internal intercostals* (figure 6.2). These muscles start from ribs two through twelve and connect upward to ribs one through eleven. When they contract, they induce the opposite action of their external partners: the thorax is made smaller, inducing exhalation. Four additional pairs of expiratory muscles are located in the abdomen, beginning with the *rectus* (figure 6.2). The two rectus abdominis muscles run from your pubic bone to your sternum and are divided into four separate portions, called *bellies* of the muscle (lots of muscles have multiple bellies; it is coincidental that the bellies of the rectus are found in the location we colloquially refer to as our belly). Definition of these bellies results in the so-called ripped abdomen or six-pack of body builders and others who are especially fit.

The largest muscles of the abdomen are called the *external obliques* (figure 6.3), which run at a downward angle from the sides of the rec-

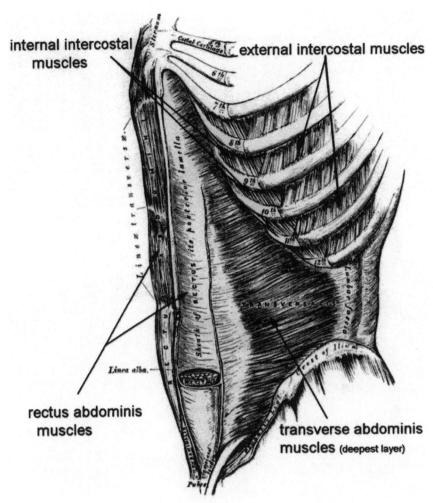

internal intercostal muscles

external intercostal muscles

rectus abdominis muscles

transverse abdominis muscles (deepest layer)

Figure 6.2. Intercostal and abdominal muscles. *Courtesy of Scott McCoy*

tus, covering the lower portion of the thorax, and extend all the way to the spine. The *internal obliques* lie immediately below, oriented at an angle that crisscrosses the external muscles. They are slightly smaller, beginning at the bottom of the thorax, rather than extending over it. The deepest muscle layer is the *transverse abdominis* (figure 6.3), which is oriented with fibers that run horizontally. These four muscle pairs completely encase the abdominal region, holding your organs and digestive system in place while simultaneously helping you breathe.

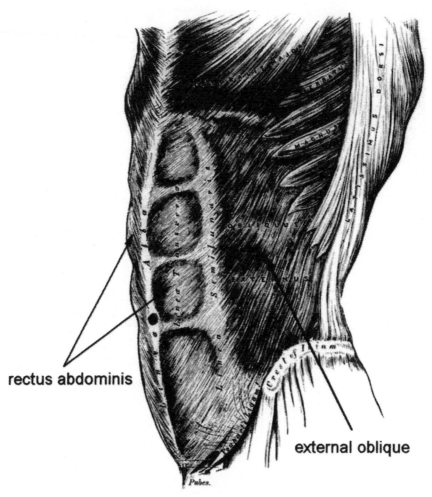

rectus abdominis

external oblique

Figure 6.3. External oblique and rectus abdominis muscles. *Courtesy of Scott McCoy*

Your expiratory muscles are quite large and can produce a great deal of pulmonary, or air, pressure. In fact, they easily can overpower the larynx. Healthy adults generally can generate more than twice the pressure that is required to produce even the loudest sounds; therefore, singers must develop a system for moderating and controlling airflow and breath pressure. This practice goes by many names, including breath support, breath control, and breath management, all of which rely on the principle of *muscular antagonism*. Muscles are said to have an antagonistic relationship when they work in opposing directions, usually pulling on a common point of attachment, for the sake of increasing stability or motor control. You can see a clear example of muscular antagonism in the relationship between your biceps (flexors) and triceps (extensors) when you hold out your arm. In breathing for singing, we activate inspiratory muscles (e.g., diaphragm and external intercostals) during exhalation to help control respiratory pressure and the rate at which air is expelled from the lungs.

One of the things you will notice when watching a variety of singers is that they tend to breathe in many different ways. You might think that voice teachers and scientists, who have been teaching and studying singing for hundreds, if not thousands of years, would have come to agreement on the best possible breathing technique. But for many reasons, this is not the case. For one, different musical and vocal styles place varying demands on breathing. For another, humans have a huge variety of body types, sizes, and morphologies. A breathing strategy that is successful for a tall, slender woman might be completely ineffective in a short, robust man. Our bodies actually contain a large number of muscles beyond those we've already discussed that are capable of assisting with respiration. For an example, consider your *latissimi dorsi* muscles. These large muscles of the arm enable us to do pull ups (or pull downs, depending on which exercise you perform) at the fitness center. But because they wrap around a large portion of the thorax, they also exert an expiratory force. We have at least two dozen such muscles that have secondary respiratory functions, some for exhalation and some for inhalation. When we consider all these possibilities, it is no surprise at all that there are many ways to breathe that can produce beautiful singing. Just remember to practice some muscular antagonism—maintaining a degree of inhalation posture during exhalation—and you should do well.

LARYNX: THE VIBRATOR OF YOUR VOICE

The larynx, sometimes known as the voice box or Adam's apple, is a complex physiologic structure made of cartilage, muscle, and tissue. Biologically, it serves as a sphincter valve, closing off the airway to prevent foreign objects from entering the lungs. When firmly closed, it also is used to increase abdominal pressure to assist with lifting heavy objects, childbirth, and defecation. But if we gently close this valve while we exhale, tissue in the larynx begins to vibrate and produce the sounds that become speech and singing.

The human larynx is a remarkably small instrument, typically ranging from the size of a pecan to a walnut for women and men, respectively. Sound is produced at a location called the *glottis*, which is formed by two flaps of tissue called the *vocal folds* (aka *vocal cords*). In women, the glottis is about the size of a dime; in men, it can approach the diameter of a quarter. The two folds are always attached together at their front point, but open in the shape of the letter V during normal breathing, an action called *abduction*. To phonate, we must close the V while we exhale, an action called *adduction* (just like the machines you use at the fitness center to exercise your thigh and chest muscles).

Phonation only is possible because of the unique multilayer structure of the vocal folds (figure 6.4). The core of each fold is formed by muscle, which is surrounded by a layer of gelatinous material called the *lamina propria*. The *vocal ligament* also runs through the lamina propria, which helps to prevent injury by limiting how far the folds can be stretched for

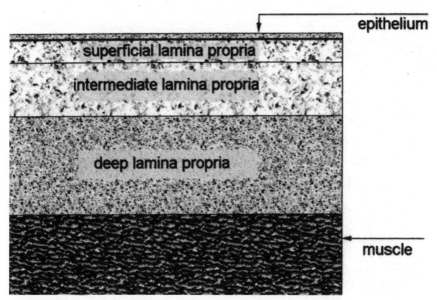

Figure 6.4. Layered structure of the vocal fold. *Courtesy of Scott McCoy*

high pitches. A thin, hairless epithelial layer that is constantly kept moist with mucus secreted by the throat, larynx, and trachea surrounds all of this. During phonation, the outer layer of the fold glides independently over the inner layer in a wavelike motion, without which phonation is impossible.

We can use a simple demonstration to better understand the independence of the inner and outer portions of the folds. Explore the palm of your hand with your other index finger. Note that the skin is attached quite firmly to the flesh beneath it. If you poke at your palm, that flesh acts as padding, protecting the underlying bone. Now explore the back of your hand. You will observe that the skin is attached quite loosely— you easily can move it around with your finger. And if you poke at the back of your hand, it is likely to hurt; there is very little padding between the skin and your bones. Your vocal folds combine the best attributes of both sides of your hand. They provide sufficient padding to help reduce impact stress, while permitting the outer layer to slip like the skin on the back of your hand, enabling phonation to occur. When you are sick with laryngitis and lose your voice (a condition called *aphonia*), inflammation in the vocal folds couples the layers of the folds tightly together. The outer layer no longer can move independently over the inner and phonation becomes difficult or impossible.

The vocal folds are located within the five cartilaginous structures of the larynx (figure 6.5). The largest is called the *thyroid cartilage*, which is shaped like a small shield. The thyroid connects to the *cricoid* cartilage below it, which is shaped like a signet ring—broad in the back and narrow in the front. Two cartilages that are shaped like squashed pyramids sit atop the cricoid, called the *arytenoids*. Each vocal fold runs from the thyroid cartilage in front to one of the arytenoids at the back. Finally, the *epiglottis* is located at the top of the larynx, flipping backward each time we swallow to prevent food and liquid from entering our lungs. Muscles connect between the various cartilages to open and close the glottis and to lengthen and shorten the vocal folds for ascending and descending pitch, respectively. Because they sometimes are used to identify vocal function, it is a good idea to know the names of the muscles that control the length of the folds. We've already mentioned that a muscle forms the core of each fold. Because it runs between the thyroid cartilage and an arytenoid, it is named the *thyroarytenoid* muscle (formerly known as the

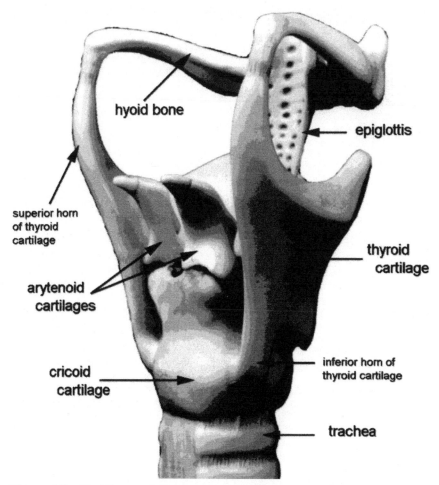

Figure 6.5. Cartilages of the larynx, viewed at an angle from the back. *Courtesy of Scott McCoy*

vocalis muscle). When the thyroarytenoid, or TA, muscle contracts, the fold is shortened and pitch goes down. The folds are elongated through the action of the *cricothyroid*, or CT muscles, which run from the thyroid to cricoid cartilage.

Vocal color (timbre) is created by the combined effects of the sound produced by the vocal folds and the resonance provided by the vocal tract. While these elements can never be completely separated, it is useful to consider the two primary modes of vocal fold vibration and their resulting sound qualities. The main differences are related to the relative thickness of the folds and their cross-sectional shape (figure 6.6). The first option depends on short, thick folds that come together with nearly square-shaped edges. Vibration in this configuration is given a variety of names, including *Mode 1, thyroarytenoid* (TA) *dominant, chest mode,* or *modal voice.* The alternate configuration uses longer, thinner folds that only make contact at their upper margins. Common names include *Mode 2, cricothyroid* (CT) *dominant, falsetto mode,* or *loft voice.* Singers vary the vibrational mode of the folds according to the quality of sound they wish to produce.

Before we move on to a discussion of resonance, we must consider the quality of the sound that is produced by the larynx. At the level of the glottis, we create a sound not unlike the annoying buzz of a duck call. That buzz, however, contains all the raw material we need to create speech and singing. Vocal or glottal sound is considered to be *complex,* meaning it consists of many simultaneously sounding frequencies (pitches). The lowest frequency within any tone is called the *fundamental,* which corresponds to its named pitch in the musical scale. Orchestras tune to a pitch called A-440, which means it has a frequency of 440 vibrations per second, or 440 *Hertz* (abbreviated Hz). Additional frequencies are included above the fundamental, which are called *overtones.* Overtones in the glottal sound are quieter than the fundamental. In voices, the overtones usually are whole number multiples of the fundamental, creating a pattern called the *harmonic series* (e.g., 100 Hz, 200 Hz, 300 Hz, 400 Hz, 500 Hz, etc., or G2, G3, D4, G4, B4; note that pitches are named by the international system in which the lowest C of the piano keyboard is C1. Middle-C therefore becomes C4, the fourth C of the keyboard.) (figure 6.7).

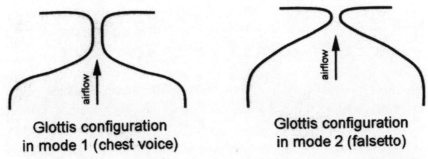

Glottis configuration
in mode 1 (chest voice)

Glottis configuration
in mode 2 (falsetto)

Figure 6.6. Primary modes of vocal fold vibration. *Courtesy of Scott McCoy*

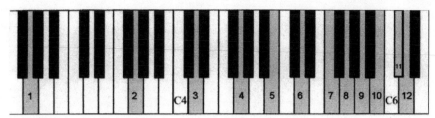

Figure 6.7. Natural harmonic series, beginning at G2. *Courtesy of Scott McCoy*

Singers who choose to make coarse or rough sounds as might be appropriate for rock or blues, often add overtones that are *inharmonic*, or not part of the standard numerical sequence. Inharmonic overtones also are common in singers with damaged or pathological voices.

Under most circumstances, we are completely unaware of the presence of overtones—they simply contribute to the overall timbre of a voice. In some vocal styles, however, harmonics become a dominant feature. This is especially true in *throat singing* or *overtone singing*, as is found in places like Tuva. Throat singers tune their vocal tracts so precisely that single harmonics are highlighted within the harmonic spectrum as a separate, whistle-like tone. These singers sustain a low-pitched drone and then create a melody by moving from tone to tone within the natural harmonic series. You can learn to do this too. Sustain a comfortable pitch in your range and slowly morph between the vowels [i] and [u]. If you listen carefully, you will hear individual harmonics pop out of your sound.

The mode of vocal fold vibration has a strong impact on the overtones that are produced. In mode 1, high-frequency harmonics are relatively strong; in mode 2, they are much weaker. As a result, mode 1 tends to yield a much brighter, brassier sound.

VOCAL TRACT: YOUR SOURCE OF RESONANCE

Resonance typically is defined as the amplification and enhancement (or enrichment) of musical sound through *supplemental vibration*. What does this really mean? In layman's terms, we could say that resonance makes instruments louder and more beautiful by reinforcing the original vibrations of the sound source. This enhancement occurs in two primary ways, which are known as forced and free resonance (there is nothing pejorative in these terms: free resonance is not superior to forced resonance). Any object that is physically connected to a vibrator can serve as a forced resonator. For a piano, the resonator is the soundboard (on the underside of a grand or on the back of an upright); the vibrations of the strings are transmitted directly to the soundboard through a structure known as the bridge, which also is found on violins and guitars. Forced resonance also plays a role in voice production. Place your hand on your chest and say [a] at a low pitch. You almost certainly felt the vibrations of forced resonance. In singing, this might best be considered your *private* resonance; you can feel it and it might impact your self-perception of sound, but nobody else can hear it. To understand why this is true, imagine what a violin would sound like if it were encased in a thick layer of foam rubber. The vibrations of the string would be damped out, muting the instrument. Your skin, muscles, and other tissues do the same thing to the vibrations of your vocal folds.

By contrast, free resonance occurs when sound travels through a hollow space, such as the inside of a trumpet, an organ pipe, or your vocal tract, which consists of the pharynx (throat), oral cavity (mouth), and nasal cavity (nose). As sound travels through these regions, a complex pattern of echoes is created; every time sound encounters a change in the shape of the vocal tract, some of its energy is reflected backward, much like an echo in a canyon. If these echoes arrive back at the glottis at the precise moment a new pulse of sound is created, the two elements synchronize, resulting in a significant increase in intensity. All of this happens very quickly—remember that sound is traveling through your vocal tract at over 700 miles per hour.

Whenever this synchronization of the vocal tract and sound source occurs, we say that the system is *in resonance*. The phenomenon occurs at specific frequencies (pitches), which can be varied by changing the position of the tongue, lips, jaw, palate, and larynx. These resonant frequencies, or areas in which strong amplification occurs, are called *formants*. Formants provide the specific amplification that changes the raw, buzzing sound produced by your vocal folds into speech and singing. The vocal tract is capable of producing many formants, which are labeled sequentially by ascending pitch. The first two, F1 and F2, are used to create vowels; higher formants contribute to the overall timbre and individual characteristics of a voice. In some singers, especially those who train to sing in opera, formants three through five are clustered together to form a super formant, eponymously called the *singer's formant*, which creates a ringing sound and enables a voice to be heard in a large theater without electronic amplification.

Formants are vitally important in singing, but they can be a bit intimidating to understand. An analogy that works really well for me is to think of formants like the wind. You cannot see the wind, but you know it is present when you see leaves rustling in a tree or feel a breeze on your face. Formants work in the same manner. They are completely invisible and directly inaudible. But just as we see the rustling leaf, we can hear, and perhaps even feel, the action of formants through how they change our sound. Try a little experiment. Sing an ascending scale beginning at B♭3, sustaining the vowel [i]. As you approach the D♮ or E♭ of the scale, you likely will feel (and hear) that your sound becomes a bit stronger and easier to produce. This occurs because the scale tone and formant are on the same pitch, providing additional amplification. If you change to an [u] vowel, you will feel the same thing at about the same place in the scale. If you sing to an [o] or [e] and continue up the scale, you'll feel a bloom in the sound somewhere around C5 (an octave above middle C). [a] is likely to come into its best focus at about G5.

To remember the approximate pitches of the first formants for the main vowels, [i]-[e]-[a]-[o]-[u], just think of a C-Major triad in first inversion, open position, starting at E4: [i] = E4, [e] = C5, [a] = G5, [o] = C5, and [u] = E4 (figure 6.8). If your music theory isn't strong, you

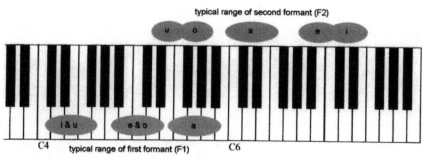

Figure 6.8. Typical range of first and second formants for primary vowels. Courtesy of Scott McCoy

could use the mnemonic "every child gets candy eagerly." These pitches might vary by as much as a minor third higher and lower, but no farther: once a formant changes by more than that interval, the vowel that is produced *must* change.

Formants have absolutely no preference for what they amplify—they are indiscriminate lovers, just as happy to bond with the first harmonic as the fifth. When men or women sing low pitches, there almost always will be at least one harmonic that comes close enough to a formant to produce a clear vowel sound. The same is not true for women with high voices, especially sopranos, who routinely must sing pitches that have a fundamental frequency *higher* than the first formant of many vowels. Imagine what happens if she must sing the phrase "and I'll leave you forever," with the word "leave" set on a very high, climactic note. The audience won't be able to tell if she is singing *leave* or *love* forever; the two will sound identical. This happens because the formant that is required to identify the vowel [i] is too far below the pitch being sung. Even if she tries to sing *leave*, the sound that comes out of her mouth will be heard as some variation of [a].

Fortunately, this kind of mismatch between formants and musical pitches rarely causes problems for anyone but opera singers, choir sopranos, and perhaps ingénues in classic music theater shows. Almost everyone else generally sings low enough in their respective voice ranges to produce easily identifiable vowels.

Second formants also can be important, but more so for opera singers than everyone else. They are much higher in pitch, tracking the pattern [u] = E5, [o] = G5, [a] = D6, [e] = B6, [i] = D7 (you can use the mnemonic "every good dad buys diapers" to remember these pitches) (figure 6.8). Because they can extend so high, into the top octave of the piano keyboard for [i], they interact primarily with higher tones in the natural harmonic series. Unless you are striving to produce the loudest unamplified sound possible, you probably never need to worry about the second formant; it will steadfastly do its job of helping to produce vowel sounds without any conscious thought or manipulation on your part.

If you are interested in discovering more about resonance and how it impacts your voice, you might want to install a spectrum analyzer on your computer. Free (or inexpensive) programs are readily available for download over the Internet that will work with either a PC or Mac computer. You don't need any specialized hardware—if you can use Skype or Facetime, you already have everything you need. Once you've installed something, simply start playing with it. Experiment with your voice to see exactly how the analysis signal changes when you change the way your voice sounds. You'll be able to see how harmonics change in intensity as they interact with your formants. If you sing with vibrato, you'll see how consistently you produce your variations in pitch and amplitude. You'll even be able to see if your tone is excessively nasal for the kind of singing you want to do. Other programs are available that will help you improve your intonation (how well you sing in tune) or to enhance your basic musicianship skills. Technology truly has advanced sufficiently to help us sing more beautifully.

MOUTH, LIPS, AND TONGUE: YOUR ARTICULATORS

The articulatory life of a singer is not easy, especially when compared to the demands placed on other musicians. Like a pianist or brass player, we must be able to produce the entire spectrum of musical articulation, including dynamic levels from hushed pianissimos to thunderous fortes, short notes, long notes, accents, crescendos, diminuendos, and so on. We produce most of these articulations the same way instrumentalists do, which is by varying our power supply. But singers have another layer of articulation that makes everything much more complicated; we must produce these musical gestures while simultaneously singing words.

As we learned in our brief examination of formants, altering the resonance characteristics of the vocal tract creates the vowel sounds of language. We do this by changing the position of our tongue, jaw, lips, and sometimes palate. Slowly say the vowel pattern [i]-[e]-[a]-[o]-[u]. Can you feel how your tongue moves in your mouth? For [i], it is high in the front and low in the back, but it takes the opposite position for [u]. Now slowly say the word *Tuesday*, noting all the places your tongue comes into contact with your teeth and palate, and how it changes shape as you produce the vowels and diphthongs. There is a lot going on in there—no wonder it takes so long for babies to learn to speak!

Our articulatory anatomy is extraordinarily complex, in large part because our bodies use the same passageway for food, water, air, and sound. As a result, our tongue, larynx, throat, jaw, and palate are all interconnected with common physical and neurologic points of attachment. Our anatomical *Union Station* in this regard is a small structure called the *hyoid bone*. The hyoid is one of only three bones in your entire body that do not connect to other bones via a joint (the other two are your *patellae*, or kneecaps). This little bone is suspended below your jaw, freely floating up and down every time you swallow. It is a busy place, serving as the upper suspension point for the larynx, the connection for the root of the tongue, and the primary location of the muscles that open your mouth by dropping your jaw.

Good singing—in any genre—requires a high degree of independence in all these articulatory structures. Unfortunately, nature conspires against us to make this difficult to accomplish. From the time we were born, our bodies have relied on a reflex reaction to elevate the palate and raise the larynx each time we swallow. This action becomes habitual: palate goes up, larynx also lifts. But depending on the style of music we are singing, we might need to keep the larynx down while the palate goes up (opera and classical), or palate down with the larynx up (country and bluegrass). As we all know, habits can be very hard to change, which is one of the reasons that it can take a lot of study and practice to become an excellent singer. Understanding your body's natural reflexive habits can make some of this work a bit easier.

There is one more significant pitfall to the close proximity of all these articulators: tension in one area is easily passed along to another. If your jaw muscles are too tight while you sing, that hyperactivity will likely be transferred to the larynx and tongue—remember, they all are interconnected through the hyoid bone. It can be tricky to determine the primary offender in this kind of chain reaction of tension. A tight tongue could just as easily be making your jaw stiff, or an elevated, rigid larynx could make both tongue and jaw suffer.

Neurology complicates matters even further. You have sixteen muscles in your tongue, fourteen in your larynx, twenty-two in your throat and palate, and another sixteen that control your jaw. Many of these are very small and lie directly adjacent to each other, and you often are required to contract one quite strongly while its next-door neighbor must remain totally relaxed. Our brains need to develop laser-like control, sending signals at the right moment with the right intensity to the precise spot where they are needed. When we first start singing, these brain signals come more like a blast from a shotgun, spreading the neurologic impulse over a broad area to multiple muscles, not all of which are the intended target. Again, with practice and training we learn to refine our control, enabling us to use only those muscles that will help, while disengaging those that would get in the way of our best singing.

FINAL THOUGHTS

This brief chapter has only scratched the surface of the huge field of voice science. To learn more, you might visit the websites of the National Association of Teachers of Singing, The Voice Foundation, or The National Center for Voice and Speech. You can easily locate the appropriate addresses through any Internet search engine. Remember: knowledge is power. Occasionally, people are afraid that if they know more about the science of how they sing, they will become so analytical that all spontaneity is lost or that they will become paralyzed by too much information and thought. In my forty-plus years as a singer and teacher, I've never encountered somebody who actually suffered this fate. To the contrary, the more we know, the easier—and more joyful—singing becomes.

7

VOCAL HEALTH AND THE SINGER OF FOLK MUSIC

Wendy LeBorgne

GENERAL PHYSICAL WELL-BEING

All singers, regardless of genre, should consider themselves as "vocal athletes." The physical, emotional, and performance demands required for optimal output require that the artist consider training and maintaining their instrument as an athlete trains for an event. With increased vocal and performance demands, it is unlikely that a vocal athlete will have an entire performing career completely injury free. This may not be the fault of the singer, as many injuries occur due to circumstances beyond the singer's control, such as singing through an illness or being on a new medication seemingly unrelated to the voice.

Vocal injury has often been considered taboo to talk about in the performing world as it has been considered to be the result of faulty technique or poor vocal habits. In actuality, the majority of vocal injuries presenting in the elite performing population tend to be overuse and/or acute injury. From a clinical perspective over the last seventeen years, younger, less experienced singers with fewer years of training (who tend to be quite talented) generally are the ones who present with issues related to technique or phonotrauma (nodules, edema, contact ulcers), while more mature singers with professional performing careers tend to present with acute injuries (hemorrhage) or overuse and misuse injuries (muscle tension dysphonia, edema, GERD), or injuries following an illness. There are no current studies documenting use and training in correlation to laryngeal pathologies. However, there are studies that document that somewhere between 35 percent and 100 percent of professional vocal athletes have abnormal vocal fold findings on stroboscopic evaluation. Many times these "abnormalities" are in singers who have no vocal complaints or symptoms of vocal problems. From a performance perspective, uniqueness in vocal quality often gets hired and perhaps a slight aberration in the way a given larynx functions may become quite marketable. Regardless of what the vocal folds may look like, the most integral part of performance is that the singer must maintain agility, flexibility, stamina, power, and inherent beauty (genre appropriate) for their current level of performance taking into account physical, vocal, and emotional demands.

Unlike sports medicine and the exercise physiology literature, where much is known about the types and nature of given sports injuries, there is no common parallel for the vocal athlete model. However, because the vocal athlete utilizes the body systems of alignment, respiration, phonation, and resonance with some similarities to physical athletes, a parallel protocol for vocal wellness may be implemented/considered for vocal athletes to maximize injury prevention knowledge for both the singer and teacher. This chapter aims to provide information on vocal wellness and injury prevention for the vocal athlete.

CONSIDERATIONS FOR WHOLE BODY WELLNESS

Nutrition

You have no doubt heard the saying "You are what you eat." Eating is a social and psychological event. For many people, food associations and eating have an emotional basis resulting in either overeating or being malnourished. Eating disorders in performers and body image issues may have major implications and consequences for the performer on both ends of the spectrum (obesity and anorexia). Singers should be encouraged to reprogram the brain and body to consider food as fuel. You want to use high-octane gas in your engine, as pouring water in your car's gas tank won't get you very far. Eating a poor diet or a diet that lacks appropriate nutritional value will have negative physical and vocal effects on the singer. Effects of poor dietary choices for the vocal athlete may result in physical and vocal effects ranging from fatigue to life-threatening disease over the course of a lifetime. Encouraging and engaging in healthy eating habits from a young age will potentially prevent long-term negative effects from poor nutritional choices. It is beyond the scope of this chapter to provide a complete overview of all the dietary guidelines for pediatrics, adolescents, adults, and the mature adult; however, a listing of additional references to help guide your food and beverage choices for making good nutritional choices can be found online at websites such as Dietary Guidelines for Americans, Nutrition.gov Guidelines for Tweens and Teens, and Fruits and Veggies Matter. See the online companion Web page on the NATS website for links to these and other resources.

Hydration

"Sing wet, pee pale." This phrase was echoed in the studio of Van Lawrence regarding how his students would know if they were well hydrated. Generally, this rule of pale urine during your waking hours is a good indicator that you are well hydrated. Medications, vitamins, and certain foods may alter urine color despite adequate hydration. Due to the varying levels of physical and vocal activity of many performers, in order to maintain adequate oral hydration, the use of a hydration calculator based on activity level may be a better choice. These hydration calculators are easily accessible online and take into account the amount and level of activity the performer engages in on a daily basis. In a recent study of the vocal habits of musical theater performers, one of the findings indicated a significantly underhydrated group of performers.[1]

Laryngeal and pharyngeal dryness as well as "thick, sticky, mucus" are often complaints of singers. Combating these concerns and maintaining an adequate viscosity of mucus for performance has resulted in some research. As a reminder of laryngeal and swallowing anatomy, nothing that is swallowed (or gargled) goes over or touches the vocal folds directly (or one would choke). Therefore, nothing that a singer eats or drinks ever touches the vocal folds, and in order to adequately hydrate the mucus membranes of the vocal folds, one must consume enough fluids for the body to produce a thin mucus. Therefore, any "vocal" effects from swallowed products are limited to potential pharyngeal and oral changes, not the vocal folds themselves.

The effects of systemic hydration are well documented in the literature. There is evidence to suggest that adequate hydration will provide some protection of the laryngeal mucosal membranes when they are placed under increased collision forces as well as reduce the amount of effort (phonation threshold pressure) to produce voice. This is important for the singer because it means that with adequate hydration and consistency of mucus, the effort to produce voice is less and your vocal folds are better protected from injury. Imagine the friction and heat produced when two dry hands rub together and then what happens if you put lotion on your hands. The mechanisms in the larynx to provide appropriate mucus production are not fully understood, but there is enough evidence at this time to support oral hydration as a vital component of every singer's vocal health regime to maintain appropriate mucosal viscosity.

Although very rare, overhydration (hyperhidrosis) can result in dehydration and even illness or death. An overindulgence of fluids essentially makes the kidneys work "overtime" and flushes too much water out of the body. This excessive fluid loss in a rapid manner can be detrimental to the body.

In addition to drinking water to systemically monitor hydration, there are many nonregulated products on the market for performers that lay claim to improving the laryngeal environment (e.g., Entertainer's Secret, Throat Coat Tea, Greathers Pastilles, slippery elm, etc.). Although there may be little detriment in using these products, quantitative research documenting change in laryngeal mucosa is sparse. One study suggests that the use of Throat Coat when compared to a placebo treatment for pharyngitis did show a significant difference in decreasing the perception of sore throat.[2] Another study compared the use of Entertainer's Secret to two other nebulized agents and its effect on phonation threshold pressure (PTP).[3] There was no positive benefit in decreasing PTP with Entertainer's Secret.

Many singers use personal steam inhalers and/or room humidification to supplement oral hydration and aid in combating laryngeal dryness. There are several considerations for singers who choose to use external means of adding moisture to the air they breathe. Personal steam inhalers are portable and can often be used backstage or in the hotel room for the traveling performer. Typically, water is placed in the steamer and the face is placed over the steam for inhalation. Because the mucus membranes of the larynx are composed of a saltwater solution, one study looked at the use of nebulized saline in comparison to plain water and its potential effects on effort or ease to sound production in classically trained sopranos.[4] Data suggested that perceived effort to produce voice was less in the saline group than the plain water group. This indicated that the singers who used the saltwater solution reported less effort to sing after breathing in the saltwater than singers who used plain water. The researchers hypothesized that because the body's mucus is not plain water (rather it is a saltwater solution—think about your tears), when you use plain water for steam inhalation, it may actually draw the salt from your own saliva, resulting in a dehydrating effect.

In addition to personal steamers, other options for air humidification come in varying sizes of humidifiers from room size to whole-house humidifiers. When choosing between a warm air or cool mist humidifier, considerations include both personal preference and needs. One of the primary reasons warm mist humidifiers are not recommended for young children is due to the risk of burns from the heating element. Both the warm mist and cool air humidifiers act similarly in adding moisture to the environmental air. External air humidification may be beneficial and provide a level of comfort for many singers. Regular cleaning of the humidifier is vital to prevent bacteria and mold buildup. Also, depending on the hardness of the water, it is important to avoid mineral buildup on the device, and distilled water may be recommended for some humidifiers.

For traveling performers who often stay in hotels, fly on airplanes, or are generally exposed to other dry-air environments, there are products on the market designed to help minimize drying effects. One such device is called a Humidiflyer, which is a facemask designed with a filter to recycle the moisture in a person's own breath and replenish moisture on each breath cycle.

For dry nasal passages or to clear sinuses, many singers use Neti pots. Many singers use this homeopathic flushing of the nasal passages regularly. Research supports the use of a Neti pot as a part of allergy relief and chronic rhinosinusitis control when used properly, sometimes in combination with medical management.[5] Conversely, long-term use of nasal irrigation (without taking intermittent breaks from daily use), may result in washing out the "good" mucus of the nasal passages, which naturally help to rid the nose of infections. A study presented at the 2009 American College of Allergy, Asthma, and Immunology (ACAAI), annual scientific meeting reported that when a group of individuals who were using twice-daily nasal irrigation for one year discontinued using it, they had an increase in acute rhinosinusitis.[6]

Tea, Honey, and Gargle to Keep the Throat Healthy

Regarding the use of general teas (which many singers combine with honey or lemon), there is likely no harm in the use of decaffeinated tea (caffeine may cause systemic dryness). The warmth of the tea may provide a soothing sensation to the pharynx and the act of swallowing can be relaxing for the muscles of the throat. Honey has shown promising results as an effective cough suppressant in the pediatric population.[7] The dose of honey given to the children in the study was two teaspoons. Gargling with salt or apple cider vinegar and water are also popular home remedies for many singers with the uses being from soothing the throat to curing reflux. Gargling plain water has been shown to be efficacious in reducing the risk of contracting upper respiratory infections. I suggest that when gargling, the singer only "bubble" the water with air and avoid engaging the vocal folds in sound production. Saltwater as a gargle has long been touted as a sore throat remedy and can be traced back to 2700 BCE in China for treating gum disease. The science behind a saltwater rinse for everything from oral hygiene to sore throat is that salt (sodium chloride) may act as a natural analgesic (pain killer) and may also kill bacteria. Similar to the effects that not enough salt in the water may have on drawing the salt out of the tissue in the steam inhalation, if you oversaturate the water solution with excess salt and gargle it, it may act to draw water out of the oral mucosa, thus reducing inflammation.

Another popular home remedy reported by singers is the use of apple cider vinegar to help with everything from acid reflux to sore throats. Dating back to 3300 BCE apple cider vinegar was reported as a medicinal remedy, and it became popular in the 1970s as a weight loss diet cocktail. Popular media reports apple cider vinegar can improve conditions from acne and arthritis to nosebleeds and varicose veins. Specific efficacy data regarding the beneficial nature of apple cider vinegar for the purpose of sore throat, pharyngeal inflammation, and/or reflux has not been reported in the literature at this time. Of the peer-reviewed studies found in the literature, one discussed possible esophageal erosion and inconsistency of actual product in tablet form.[8] Therefore, at this time, strong evidence supporting the use of apple cider vinegar is not published.

Medications and the Voice

Medications (over the counter, prescription, and herbal) may have resultant drying effects on the body and often the laryngeal mucosa. General classes of drugs with potential drying effects include: antidepressants, antihypertensives, diuretics, ADD/ADHD medications, some oral acne medications, hormones, allergy drugs, and vitamin C in high doses. The National Center for Voice and Speech (NCVS) provides a listing of some common medications with potential voice side effects including laryngeal dryness. This listing does not take into account all medications, so singers should always ask their pharmacist about the potential side effects of a given medication. Due to the significant number of drugs on the market, it is safe to say that most pharmacists will not be acutely aware of "vocal side effects," but if dryness is listed as a potential side effect of the drug, you may assume that all body systems could be affected. Under no circumstances should you stop taking a prescribed medication without consulting your physician first. As every person has a different body chemistry and reaction to medication, just because a medication lists dryness as a potential side effect, it does not necessarily mean you will experience that side effect. Conversely, if you begin a new medication and notice physical or vocal changes that are unexpected, you should consult with your physician. Ultimately, the goal of medical management for any condition is to achieve the most benefits with the least side effects. Please see the companion page on the NATS website for a list of possible resources for the singer regarding prescription drugs and herbs.

In contrast to medications that tend to dry, there are medications formulated to increase saliva production or alter the viscosity of mucus. Medically, these drugs are often used to treat patients who have had a loss of saliva production due to surgery or radiation. Mucolytic agents are used to thin secretions as needed. As a singer, if you feel that you need to use a mucolytic agent on a consistent basis, it may be worth considering getting to the root of the laryngeal dryness symptom and seeking a professional opinion by an otolaryngologist.

Reflux and the Voice

Gastroesophageal reflux disease (GERD) and/or laryngopharyngeal reflux (LPR) can have a devastating impact on the singer if not recognized and treated appropriately. Although GERD and LPR are related, they are considered as slightly different diseases. GERD (Latin root meaning "flowing back") is the reflux of digestive enzymes, acids, and other stomach contents into the esophagus (food pipe). If this backflow is propelled through the upper esophagus and into the throat (larynx and pharynx) it is referred to as LPR. It is not uncommon to have both GERD and LPR, but they can occur independently.

More frequently, people with GERD have decreased esophageal clearing. Esophagitis, or inflammation of the esophagus, is also associated with GERD. People with GERD often feel heartburn. LPR symptoms are often "silent" and do not include heartburn. Specific symptoms of LPR may include some or all of the following: lump in the throat sensation, feeling of constant need to clear the throat/postnasal drip, longer vocal warm-up time, quicker vocal fatigue, loss of high frequency range, worse voice in the morning, sore throat, bitter/raw/brackish taste in the mouth. If you experience these symptoms on a regular basis, it is advised that you consider a medical consultation for your symptoms. Prolonged, untreated GERD or LPR can lead to permanent changes in both the esophagus and/or larynx. Untreated LPR also provides a laryngeal environment that is conducive for vocal fold lesions to occur as it inhibits normal healing mechanisms.

Treatments of LPR and GERD generally include both dietary and lifestyle modifications in addition to medical management. Some of the dietary recommendations include: elimination of caffeinated and carbonated beverages; smoking cessation; no alcohol use; and limiting tomatoes, acidic foods and drinks, and raw onions or peppers, to name a few. Also, avoidance of high-fat foods is recommended. From a lifestyle perspective, suggested changes include not eating within three hours of lying down, eating small meals frequently (instead of large meals), elevating the head of your bed, avoiding tight clothing around the belly, and not bending over or exercising too soon after you eat.

Reflux medications fall in three general categories: antacids, H2 blockers, and proton-pump inhibitors (PPI). There are now combination drugs that include both an H2 blocker and a proton pump inhibitor. Every medication has both associated risks and benefits, and singers should be aware of the possible benefits and side effects of the medications they take. In general terms, antacids (e.g., Tums, Mylanta, Gaviscon) neutralize stomach acid. H2 (histamine) blockers, such as Axid (nizatidine),Tagamet (cimetidine), Pepcid (famotidine), and Zantac (ranitidine), work to decrease acid production in the stomach by preventing histamine from triggering the H2 receptors to produce more acid. Then there are the PPIs: Nexium (esomeprazole), Prevacid (lansoprazole), Protonix (pantoprazole), AcipHex (rabeprazole), Prilosec (omeprazole), and Dexilant (dexlansoprazole). PPIs act as a last line of defense to decrease acid production by blocking the last step in gastric juice secretion. Some of the most recent drugs to combat GERD/LPR are combination drugs (e.g., Zegrid [sodium bicarbonate plus omeprazole]), which provide a short-acting response (sodium bicarbonate) and a long release (omeprazole). Because some singers prefer a holistic approach to reflux management, strict dietary and lifestyle compliance is recommended and consultation with both your primary care physician and naturopath is warranted in that situation. Efficacy data on non-regulated herbs, vitamins, and supplements are limited, but some data do exist.

Physical Exercise

Vocal athletes, like other physical athletes, should consider how and what they do to maintain both cardiovascular fitness and muscular strength. In today's performance culture, it is rare that a performer stands still and sings, unless in a recital or choral setting. The range of physical activity can vary from light movement to high-intensity choreography with acrobatics. As performers are being required to increase their on-stage physical activity level from the operatic stage to the pop-star arena, overall physical fitness is imperative to avoid compromise in the vocal system. Breathlessness will result in compensation by the larynx, which is now attempting to regulate the air. Compensatory vocal behaviors over time may result in a change in vocal performance. The health benefits of both cardiovascular training and strength training are well documented for physical athletes but relatively rare in the literature for vocal performers.

Mental Wellness

Vocal performers must maintain a mental focus during performance and a mental toughness during auditioning and training. Rarely during vocal performance training programs is this important aspect of performance addressed, and it is often left to the individual performer to develop their own strategy or coping mechanism. Yet, many performers are on antianxiety or antidepressant drugs (which may be the direct result of performance-related issues). If the sports world is again used as a parallel for mental toughness, there are no elite-level athletes (and few junior-level athletes) who don't utilize the services of a performance/sports psychologist to maximize focus and performance. I recommend that performers consider the potential benefits of a performance psychologist to help maximize vocal performance. Several references that may be of interest to the singer include: Joanna Cazden's *Visualization for Singers* (Joanna Cazden, 1992) and Shirlee Emmons and Alma Thomas's *Power Performance for Singers: Transcending the Barriers* (Oxford, 1998).

Unlike instrumentalists, whose performance is dependent on accurate playing of an external musical instrument, the singer's instrument is uniquely intact and subject to the emotional confines of the brain and body in which it is housed. Musical performance anxiety (MPA) can be career threatening for all musicians, but perhaps the vocal athlete is more severely impacted. The majority of literature on MPA is dedicated to instrumentalists, but the basis of definition, performance effects, and treatment options can be considered for vocal athletes. Fear is a natural reaction to a stressful situation, and there is a fine line between emotional excitation and perceived threat (real or imagined). The job of a performer is to convey to an audience through vocal production, physical gestures, and facial expression a most heightened state of emotion. Otherwise, why would audience members pay top dollar to sit for two or three hours for a mundane experience? Not only is there the emotional conveyance of the performance but also the internal turmoil often experienced by singers themselves in preparation for elite performances. It is well documented in the literature that even the most elite performers have experienced debilitating performance anxiety. MPA is defined on a continuum with anxiety levels ranging from low to high and has been reported to comprise four distinct components: affect, cognition, behavior, and physiology. Affect comprises feelings (e.g., doom, panic, anxiety). Affected cognition will result in altered levels of concentration, while the behavior component results in postural shifts, quivering, and trembling. Finally physiologically the body's autonomic nervous system (ANS) will activate, resulting in the "fight or flight" response.

In recent years, researchers have been able to define two distinct neurological pathways for MPA. The first pathway happens quickly and without conscious input (ANS), resulting in the same fear stimulus as if a person were put into an emergent, life-threatening situation. In those situations, the brain releases adrenaline, resulting in physical changes of increased heart rate, increased respiration, shaking, pale skin, dilated pupils, slowed digestion, bladder relaxation, dry mouth, and dry eyes, all of which severely affect vocal performance. The second pathway that has been identified results in a conscious identification of the fear/threat and a much slower physiologic response. With the second neuromotor response, the performer has a chance to recognize the fear, process how to deal with the fear, and respond accordingly.

Treatment modalities to address MPA include psycho-behavioral therapy (including biofeedback) and drug therapies. Elite physical performance athletes have been shown to benefit from visualization techniques and psychological readiness training, yet within the performing arts community, stage fright may be considered a weakness or character flaw precluding readiness for professional performance. On the contrary, vocal athletes, like physical athletes, should mentally prepare themselves for optimal competition (auditions) and performance.

Learning to convey emotion without eliciting an internal emotional response by the vocal athlete may take the skill of an experienced psychologist to help change ingrained neural pathways. Ultimately, control and understanding of MPA will enhance performance and prepare the vocal athlete for the most intense performance demands without vocal compromise.

VOCAL WELLNESS: INJURY PREVENTION

In order to prevent vocal injury and understand vocal wellness in the singer, general knowledge of common causes of voice disorders is imperative. One common cause of voice disorders is vocally abusive behaviors or misuse of the voice to include phonotraumatic behaviors such as yelling, screaming, loud talking, talking over noise, throat clearing, coughing, harsh sneezing, and boisterous laughing. Chronic or less than optimal vocal properties such as poor breathing techniques, inappropriate phonatory habits during conversational speech (glottal fry, hard glottal attacks), inapt pitch, loudness, rate of speech, and/or hyperfunctional laryngeal-area muscle tone may also negatively impact vocal function. Medically related etiologies, which also have the potential to impact vocal function, range from untreated chronic allergies and sinusitis to endocrine dysfunction and hormonal imbalance. Direct trauma, such as a blow to the neck or the risk of vocal fold damage during intubation, can impact optimal performance in vocal athletes depending on the nature and extent of the trauma. Finally, external irritants ranging from cigarette smoke to reflux directly impact the laryngeal mucosa and ultimately can lead to laryngeal pathology.

Vocal hygiene education and compliance may be one of the primary essential components for maintaining the voice throughout a career. This section will provide the singer with information on prevention of vocal injury. However, just like a professional sports athlete, it is unlikely that a professional vocal athlete will go through an entire career without some compromise in vocal function. This may be a common upper respiratory infection that creates vocal fold swelling for a short time, or it may be a "vocal accident" that is career threatening. Regardless, the knowledge of how to take care of your voice is essential for any vocal athlete.

Train Like an Athlete for Vocal Longevity

Performers seek instant gratification in performance sometimes at the cost of gradual vocal building for a lifetime of healthy singing. Historically, voice pedagogues required their students to perform vocalise exclusively for up to two years before beginning any song literature. Singers gradually built their voice by ingraining appropriate muscle memory and neuromotor patterns through development of aesthetically pleasing tones, onsets, breath management, and support. There was an intensive master-apprentice relationship and rigorous vocal guidelines to maintain a place within a given studio. Time off was taken if a vocal injury ensued or careers potentially were ended, and students were asked to leave a given singing studio if their voice was unable to withstand the rigors of training. Training vocal athletes today has evolved and appears driven to create a "product" quickly, perhaps at the expense of the longevity of the singer. Pop stars emerging well before puberty are doing international concert tours, yet many young artist programs in the classical arena do not consider singers for their programs until they are in their mid- to late twenties.

Each vocal genre presents with different standards and vocal demands. Therefore, the amount and degree of vocal training is varied. Some would argue that performing extensively without adequate vocal training and development is ill-advised, yet singers today are thrust onto the stage at very young ages. Dancers, instrumentalists, and physical athletes all spend many hours per day developing muscle strength, memory, and proper technique for their craft. The more advanced the artist or athlete, generally the more specific the training protocol becomes. Consideration of training vocal athletes in this same fashion is recommended. One would generally not begin a young, inexperienced singer on a Wagner aria without previous vocal training. Similarly, in nonclassical vocal music, there are easy, moderate, and difficult pieces to consider pending level of vocal development and training.

Basic pedagogical training of alignment, breathing, voice production, and resonance are essential building blocks for development of good voice production. Muscle memory and development of appropriate muscle patterns happen slowly over time with appropriate repetitive practice. Doing too much, too soon for any athlete (physical or vocal) will result in an increased risk for injury. When the singer is being asked to do "vocal gymnastics," they must be sure to have a solid basis of strength and stamina in the appropriate muscle groups to perform consistently with minimal risk of injury.

Vocal Fitness Program

One generally does not get out of bed first thing in the morning and try to do a split. Yet, many singers go directly into a practice session or audition without proper warm-up. Think of your larynx like your knee, made up of cartilages, ligaments, and muscles. Vocal health is dependent upon appropriate warm-ups (to get things moving), drills for technique, and then cool-downs (at the end of your day). Consider vocal warm-ups a "gentle stretch." Depending on the needs of the singer, warm-ups should include physical stretching; postural alignment self-checks; breathing exercises to promote rib cage, abdominal, and back expansion; vocal stretches (glides up to stretch the vocal folds and glides down to contract the vocal folds); articulatory stretches (yawning, facial stretches); and mental warm-ups (to provide focus for the task at hand). Vocalises, in my opinion, are designed as exercises to go beyond warm-ups and prepare the body and voice for the technical and vocal challenges of the music they sing. They are varied and address the technical level and genre of the singer to maximize performance and vocal growth. Cool-downs are a part of most athletes' workouts. However, singers often do not use cool-downs (physical, mental, and vocal) at the end of a performance. A recent study looked specifically at the benefits of vocal cool-downs in singers and found that singers who used a vocal cool-down had decreased effort to produce voice the next day.[9]

Systemic hydration as a means to keep the vocal folds adequately lubricated for the amount of impact and friction that they will undergo has been previously discussed in this chapter. Compliance with adequate oral hydration recommendations is important and subsequently the minimization of agents that could potentially dry the membranes (e.g., caffeine, medications, dry air). The body produces approximately two quarts of mucus per day. If not adequately hydrated, the mucus tends to be thick and sticky. Poor hydration is similar to not putting enough oil in the car engine. Frankly, if the gears do not work as well, there is increased friction and heat, and the engine is not efficient.

Speak Well, Sing Well

Optimize the speaking voice utilizing ideal frequency range, breath, intensity, rate, and resonance. Singers generally are vocally enthusiastic individuals who talk a lot and often talk loudly. During typical conversation, the average fundamental speaking frequency (times per second the vocal folds are impacting) for a male varies from 100 to 150 Hz and 180 to 230 Hz for women. Because of the delicate structure of the vocal folds and the importance of the layered microstructure vibrating efficiently and effectively to produce voice, vocal behaviors or outside factors that compromise the integrity of the vibration patterns of the vocal folds may be considered phonotrauma.

Phonotraumatic behaviors can include yelling, screaming, loud talking, harsh sneezing, and harsh laughing. Elimination of phonotraumatic behaviors is essential for good vocal health. The louder one speaks, the further apart the vocal folds move from midline, the harder they impact, and the longer they stay closed. A tangible example would be to take your hands, move them only six inches apart, and clap as hard and as loudly as you can for ten seconds. Now, move your hands two feet apart and clap as hard, loudly, and quickly as possible for ten seconds. The farther apart your hands are, the more air you move and the louder the clap, and the skin on the hands becomes red and ultimately swollen (if you do it long enough and hard enough). This is what happens to the vocal folds with repeated impact at increased vocal intensities. The vocal folds are approximately 17 mm in length and vibrate at 220 times per second on A3, 440 on A4, 880 on A5, and over 1,000 times per second when singing a high C. That is a lot of impact for little muscles. Consider this fact when singing loudly or in a high tessitura for prolonged periods of time. It becomes easy to see why women are more prone than men to laryngeal impact injuries due to the frequency range of the voice alone.

In addition to the amount of cycles per second the vocal folds are impacting, singers need to be aware of their vocal intensity (volume). Check the volume of the speaking and singing voice and for conversational speech and consider using a distance of three to five feet as a gauge for how loud you need to be in general conversation (about an arms-length distance). Cell phones and speaking on a Bluetooth device in a car generally result in louder-than-conversational vocal intensity and singers are advised to minimize unnecessary use of these devices.

Singers should be encouraged to take "vocal naps" during their day. A vocal nap would be a short period of time (five minutes to an hour) of complete silence. Although the vocal folds are rarely completely still (because they move when you swallow and breathe), a vocal nap minimizes impact and vibration for a short window of time. A physical nap can also be refreshing for the singer mentally and physically.

Avoid Environmental Irritants: Alcohol, Smoking, Drugs

Arming singers with information on the actual effects of environmental irritants so that they can make informed choices on engaging in exposure to these potential toxins is essential. The glamour that continues to be associated with smoking, drinking, and drugs can be tempered with the deaths of popular stars such as Amy Winehouse and Cory Monteith who engaged in life-ending choices. There is extensive documentation about the long-term effects of toxic and carcinogenic substances, but here are a few key facts to consider when choosing whether to partake.

Alcohol, although it does not go over the vocal folds directly, does have a systemic drying effect. Due to the acidity in alcohol, it may increase the likelihood of reflux, resulting in hoarseness and other laryngeal pathologies. Consuming alcohol generally decreases one's inhibitions and therefore you are more likely to sing and do things you would not typically do under the influence of alcohol.

Beyond the carcinogens in nicotine and tobacco, the heat at which a cigarette burns is well above the boiling temperature of water (water boils at 212°F; cigarettes burn at over 1,400°F). No one would consider pouring a pot of boiling water on their hand, and yet the burning temperature for a cigarette results in significant heat over the oral mucosa and vocal folds. The heat alone can create a deterioration in the lining resulting in polypoid degeneration. Obviously, cigarette smoking has been well documented as a cause for laryngeal cancer.

Marijuana and other street drugs are not only addictive but can also cause permanent mucosal lining changes depending on the drug used and the method of delivery. If you or one of your singer colleagues is experiencing a drug or alcohol problem, research or provide information and support on getting appropriate counseling and help.

SMART PRACTICE STRATEGIES FOR SKILL DEVELOPMENT AND VOICE CONSERVATION

Daily practice and drills for skill acquisition are an important part of any singer's training. However, overpracticing or inefficient practicing may be detrimental to the voice. Consider practice sessions of athletes: they may practice four to eight hours per day broken into one- to two-hour training sessions with a period of rest and recovery in between sessions. Although we cannot parallel the sports model without adequate evidence in the vocal athlete, the premise of short, intense, focused practice sessions is logical for the singer. Similar to physical exercise, it is suggested that practice sessions do not have to be all "singing." Rather, structuring sessions so that one-third of the session is spent on warm-up; one-third on vocalise, text work, rhythms, character development, and so on; and one-third on repertoire will allow the singer to function in a more efficient vocal manner. Building the amount of time per practice session—increasing duration by five minutes per week, building to sixty to ninety minutes—may be effective (e.g., Week 1, twenty minutes three times per day; Week 2, twenty-five minutes three times per day, etc.).

Vary the "vocal workout" during your week. For example, if you do the same physical exercise in the same way day after day with the same intensity and pattern, you will likely experience repetitive strain-type injuries. However, cross-training or varying the type and level of exercise aids in injury prevention. So when planning your practice sessions for a given week (or rehearsal process for a given role), consider varying your vocal intensity, tessitura, and exercises to maximize your training sessions, building stamina, muscle memory, and skill acquisition. For example, one day you may spend more time on learning rhythms and translation and the next day you spend thirty minutes performing coloratura exercises to prepare for a specific role. Take one day a week off from vocal training and give your voice a break. This does not mean complete vocal rest (although some singers find this beneficial), but rather a day without singing and limited talking.

Practice Your Mental Focus

Mental wellness and stress management are equally as important as vocal training for vocal athletes. Addressing any mental health issues is paramount to developing the vocal artist. This may include anything from daily mental exercises/meditation/focus to overcoming performance anxiety to more serious mental health issues/illness. Every person can benefit from improved focus and mental acuity.

VOCAL WELLNESS TIPS FOR THE FOLK ARTIST

For the folk artist, the most common complaint reported is vocal fatigue. In a recent study, some of the most common vocal problems reported were related to inadequate stamina and loss of the high frequencies in their singing voice.[10] Also, approximately one-third of the respondents did not have health insurance, which would make them potentially less likely to seek medical attention for their voice problem. Specifically, many folk singers will sing for several hours at a time (either in rehearsal or performance) and then take a week or more off. However, they do not exercise their voice the rest of the week. A physical analogy can be made to this type of singing. If you only go to the gym and exercise for two hours on two days per week, then you are more likely to fatigue and get injured than if you spread out your two hours of training over several days. Therefore, as a folk singer, try to sing for twenty to forty-five minutes daily to keep your voice conditioned and "in shape."

Similar to contemporary pop singers, folk musicians are required to connect with the audience from a vocal and emotional standpoint. Therefore, both physical and vocal fitness should be foremost in the minds of anyone desiring to perform folk music today. Folk singers should be physically and vocally in shape to meet the necessary performance demands, as they are often required to play multiple instruments in addition to singing.

Performance of folk music requires that the singer has a flexible, agile, dynamic instrument with appropriate stamina. The singer must have a good command of their instrument as well as exceptional underlying intention in what they are singing, as it is about relaying a message and connecting with the audience. The voices that convey the folk song must reflect the mood and intent of the song, requiring dynamic control, vocal control/power, and an emotional connection to the text.

Similar to other commercial music vocalists, folk singers may often use microphones and personal amplification. If used correctly, amplification can maximize vocal health by allowing the singer to produce voice in an efficient manner while the sound engineer mixes, amplifies, and adds effects to the voice. Understanding both the utility and limits of a given microphone and sound system is essential for the singer both for live and studio performances. Also, the microphone type when playing a string instrument (guitar, banjo) and/or harmonica should be considered with all performance aspects in mind. Using an appropriate microphone can not only enhance the singer's performance, but can reduce vocal load. Emotional extremes (intimacy and exultation) can be enhanced by appropriate microphone choice, placement, and acoustical mixing, thus saving the singer's voice.

Not everything a singer does is "vocally healthy," sometimes because the emotional expression may be so intense it results in vocal collision forces that are extreme. Even if the singer does not have formal vocal training, the concept of "vocal cross-training" (which can mean singing in both high and low registers with varying intensities and resonance options) before and after practice sessions and services is likely a vital component of minimizing vocal injury.

FINAL THOUGHTS

Ultimately, the singer must learn to provide the most output with the least "cost" to the system. Taking care of the physical instrument through daily physical exercise, adequate nutrition and hydration, and maintaining focused attention on performance will provide a necessary basis for vocal health during performance. Small doses of high-intensity singing (or speaking) will limit impact stress on the vocal folds. Finally, attention to the mind, body, and voice will provide the singer with an awareness when something is wrong. This awareness and knowledge of when to rest or seek help will promote vocal well-being for the singer throughout his or her career.

NOTES

1. W. LeBorgne et al., "Prevalence of Vocal Pathology in Incoming Freshman Musical Theatre Majors: A 10-year Retrospective Study" (Fall Voice Conference, New York, 2012).

2. J. Brinckmann et al., "Safety and Efficacy of a Traditional Herbal Medicine (Throat Coat) in Symptomatic Temporary Relief of Pain in Patients with Acute Pharyngitis: A Multicenter, Prospective, Randomized, Double-Blinded, Placebo-Controlled Study." *Journal of Alternative and Complementary Medicine* 9, no. 2 (2003): 285–98.

3. N. Roy et al., "An Evaluation of the Effects of Three Laryngeal Lubricants on Phonation Threshold Pressure (PTP)." *Journal of Voice* 17, no. 3 (2003): 331–42.

4. K. Tanner et al., "Nebulized Isotonic Saline versus Water Following a Laryngeal Desiccation Challenge in Classically Trained Sopranos." *Journal of Speech, Language, and Hearing Research* 53, no. 6 (2010): 1555–66.

5. C. Brown and S. Graham, "Nasal Irrigations: Good or Bad?" *Current Opinion in Otolaryngology, & Head and Neck Surgery* 12, no. 1 (2004): 9–13.

6. T. Nsouli, "Long-Term Use of Nasal Saline Irrigation: Harmful or Helpful?" American College of Allergy, Asthma and Immunology (Annual Scientific Meeting, Abstract 32, 2009).

7. M. Shadkam et al., "A Comparison of the Effect of Honey, Dextromethorphan, and Diphenhydramine on Nightly Cough and Sleep Quality in Children and Their Parents." *Journal of Alternative and Complementary Medicine* 16, no. 7 (2010): 787–93.

8. L. Hill et al., "Esophageal Injury by Apple Cider Vinegar Tablets and Subsequent Evaluation of Products." *Journal of the American Dietetic Association* 105, no. 7 (2005): 1141–44.

9. R. O. Gottliebson, "The Efficacy of Cool-Down Exercises in the Practice Regimen of Elite Singers" (PhD dissertation, University of Cincinnati, 2011).

10. Molly Erikson, "The Traditional/Acoustic Music Project: A Study of Vocal Demands and Vocal Health." *Journal of Voice* 26, no. 5 (2012): 664e7–664e23.

8

USING AUDIO
ENHANCEMENT TECHNOLOGY

Matthew Edwards

In the early days of popular music, musicians performed without electronic amplification. Singers learned to project their voices in the tradition of vaudeville performers with a technique similar to operatic and operetta performers, who had been singing unamplified for centuries. When microphones began appearing on stage in the 1930s, vocal performance changed forever, since the loudness of a voice was no longer a factor in the success of a performer. In order to be successful, all a singer needed was an interesting vocal quality and an emotional connection to what he or she was singing. The microphone would take care of projection.[1]

Vocal qualities that may sound weak without a microphone can sound strong and projected when sung with one. At the same time, a singer with a voice that is acoustically beautiful and powerful can sound harsh and pushed if he or she lacks microphone technique. Understanding how to use audio equipment to get the sounds a singer desires without harming the voice is crucial. The information in this chapter will help the reader gain a basic knowledge of terminology and equipment commonly used when amplifying or recording a vocalist as well as providing tips for singing with a microphone.

THE FUNDAMENTALS OF SOUND

In order to understand how to manipulate an audio signal, you must first understand a few basics of sound, including frequency, amplitude, and resonance.

Frequency

Sound travels in waves of compression and rarefaction within a medium, which for our purposes is air (see figure 8.1). These waves travel through the air, into our inner ears via the ear canal. There they are converted, via the eardrums, into nerve impulses that are transmitted to the brain and interpreted as sound. The number of waves per second is measured in Hertz (Hz), which gives us the frequency of the sound that we have learned to perceive as pitch. For example, we hear 440 Hz (440 cycles of compression and rarefaction per second) as A4, the pitch A above middle C.

Amplitude

The magnitude of the waves of compression and rarefaction determines the amplitude of the sound, which we call its "volume." The larger the waves of compression and rarefaction, the louder we perceive the sound to be. Measured in decibels (dB), amplitude represents changes in air pressure from the baseline. Decibel measurements range from zero decibels (0 dB), the threshold of human hearing, to 130 dB, the upper edge of the threshold of pain.

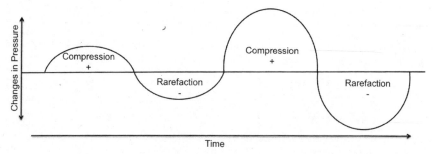

Figure 8.1. Compression and rarefaction. *Courtesy of Creative Commons*

Harmonics

The vibrating mechanism of an instrument produces the vibrations necessary to establish pitch (the fundamental frequency). The vibrating mechanism for a singer is the vocal folds. If an acoustic instrument, such as the voice, were to produce a note with the fundamental frequency alone, the sound would be strident and mechanical, like the emergency alert signal used on television. Pitches played on acoustic instruments consist of multiple frequencies, called overtones, which are emitted from the vibrator along with the fundamental frequency. For the purposes of this chapter, the overtones that we are interested in are called harmonics. Harmonics are whole number multiples of the fundamental frequency. For example, if the fundamental is 220 Hz (A3), the harmonic overtone series would be 220 Hz, 440 Hz (fundamental frequency times two), 660 Hz (fundamental frequency times three), 880 Hz (fundamental frequency times four), and so on. Every musical note contains both the fundamental frequency and a predictable series of harmonics, each of which can be measured and identified as a specific frequency. This series of frequencies then travels through a hollow cavity (the vocal tract) where they are attenuated or amplified by the resonating frequencies of the cavity, which is how resonance occurs.

Resonance

The complex waveform created by the vocal folds travels through the vocal tract, where it is enhanced by the tract's unique resonance characteristics. Depending on the resonator's shape, some harmonics are amplified and some are attenuated. Each singer has a unique vocal tract shape with unique resonance characteristics. This is why two singers of the same voice type can sing the same pitch and yet sound very different. We can analyze these changes with a tool called a spectral analyzer as seen in figure 8.2. The slope from left to right is called the spectral slope. The peaks and valleys along the slope indicate amplitude variations of the corresponding overtones. The difference in spectral slope between instruments (or voices) is what enables a listener to aurally distinguish the difference between two instruments playing or singing the same note.

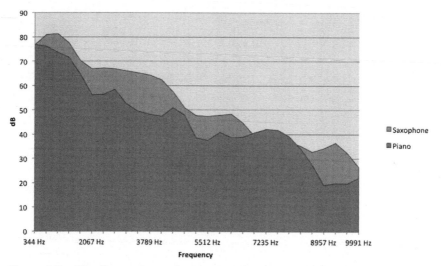

Figure 8.2. The figure above shows two instruments playing the same pitch. The peak at the far left is the fundamental frequency and the peaks to the right are harmonics that have been amplified and attenuated by the instrument's resonator resulting in a specific timbre. *Courtesy of Matthew Edwards*

Because the throat and mouth act as the resonating tube in acoustic singing, changing their size and shape is the only option for making adjustments to timbre for those who perform without microphones. In electronically amplified singing, the sound engineer can make adjustments to boost or attenuate specific frequency ranges, thus changing the singer's timbre. For this and many other reasons discussed in this chapter, it is vitally important for singers to know how audio technology can affect the quality of their voice.

SIGNAL CHAIN

The signal chain is the path an audio signal travels from the input to the output of a sound system. A voice enters the signal chain through a microphone, which transforms acoustic energy into electrical impulses. The electrical pulses generated by the microphone are transmitted through a series of components that modify the signal before the speakers transform it back into acoustic energy. Audio engineers and producers understand the intricacies of these systems and are able to make an infinite variety of alterations to the vocal signal. While some engineers strive to replicate the original sound source as accurately as possible, others use the capabilities of the system to alter the sound for artistic effect. Since more components and variations exist than can be discussed in just a few pages, this chapter will discuss only basic components and variations found in most systems.

Microphones

Microphones transform the acoustic sound waves of the voice into electrical impulses. The component of the microphone that is responsible for receiving the acoustic information is the diaphragm. The two most common diaphragm types that singers will encounter are dynamic and condenser. Each offers advantages and disadvantages depending on how the microphone is to be used.

Dynamic. Dynamic microphones consist of a dome-shaped Mylar diaphragm attached to a free-moving copper wire coil that is positioned between the two poles of a magnet. The Mylar diaphragm moves in response to air pressure changes caused by sound waves. When the diaphragm moves, the magnetic coil that is attached to it also moves. As the magnetic coil moves up and down between the magnetic poles, it produces an electrical current that corresponds to the sound waves produced by the singer's voice. That signal is then sent to the soundboard via the microphone cable.

The Shure SM58 dynamic microphone is the industry standard for live performance because it is affordable, nearly indestructible, and easy to use. Dynamic microphones such as the Shure SM58 have a lower sensitivity than condenser microphones, which makes them more successful at avoiding feedback. Because of their reduced tendency to feedback, dynamic microphones are the best choice for artists that use handheld microphones when performing.

Condenser. Condenser microphones are constructed with two parallel plates: a rigid posterior plate and a thin flexible anterior plate. The anterior plate is constructed of either a thin sheet of metal or a piece of Mylar that is coated with a conductive metal. The plates are separated by air, which acts as a layer of insulation. In order to use a condenser microphone, it must be connected to a soundboard that supplies "phantom power." A component of the soundboard, phantom power sends a 48-volt

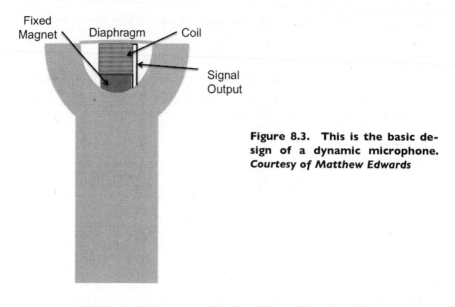

Fixed
Magnet   Diaphragm   Coil

Signal
Output

Figure 8.3. This is the basic design of a dynamic microphone. *Courtesy of Matthew Edwards*

power supply through the microphone cable to the microphone's plates. When the plates are charged by phantom power, they form a capacitor. As acoustic vibrations send the anterior plate into motion, the distance between the two plates varies, which causes the capacitor to release a small electric current. This current, which corresponds with the acoustic signal of the voice, travels through the microphone cable to the soundboard where it can be enhanced and amplified.

Electret condenser microphones are similar to condenser microphones, but they are designed to work without phantom power. The anterior plate of an electret microphone is made of a plastic film coated with a conductive metal that is electrically charged before being set into place opposite the posterior plate. The charge applied to the anterior plate will last for ten or more years and therefore eliminates the need for an exterior power source. Electret condenser microphones are often used in head-mounted and lapel microphones, laptop computers, and smartphones.

Recording engineers prefer condenser microphones for recording applications due to their high level of sensitivity. Using a condenser microphone, performers can sing at nearly inaudible acoustic levels and obtain a final recording that is intimate and earthy. While the same vocal effects can be recorded with a dynamic microphone, they will not have the same clarity as those produced with a condenser microphone.

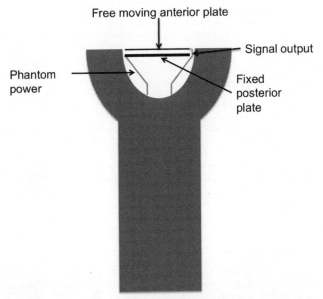

Free moving anterior plate

Signal output

Phantom power

Fixed posterior plate

Figure 8.4. This is the basic design of a condenser microphone. *Courtesy of Matthew Edwards*

Frequency Response. Frequency response is a term used to define how accurately a microphone captures the tone quality of the signal. A "flat response" microphone captures the original signal with little to no signal alteration. Microphones that are not designated as "flat" have some type of amplification or attenuation of specific frequencies, also known as cut or boost, within the audio spectrum. For instance, the Shure SM58 microphone drastically attenuates the signal below 300 Hz and amplifies the signal in the 3 kHz range by 6 dB, the 5 kHz range by nearly 8 dB, and the 10 kHz range by approximately 6 dB. The Oktava 319 microphone cuts the frequencies below 200 Hz while boosting everything above 300 Hz with nearly 5 dB between 7 kHz and 10 kHz (see figure 8.5). In practical terms, recording a bass singer with the Shure SM58 would drastically reduce the amplitude of the fundamental frequency while the Oktava 319 would produce a slightly more consistent boost in the range of the singer's formant. Either of these options could be acceptable depending on the situation, but the frequency response must be considered before making a recording or performing live.

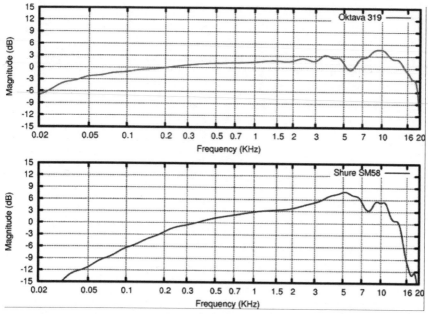

Figure 8.5. **Example frequency response graphs for the Oktava 319 and the Shure SM58.** *Courtesy of Wikimedia Commons*

Amplitude Response. The amplitude response of a microphone varies depending on the angle at which the singer is positioned in relation to the axis of the microphone. In order to visualize the amplitude response of a microphone at various angles, microphone manufacturers publish polar pattern diagrams (also sometimes called a directional pattern or a pickup pattern). Polar pattern diagrams usually consist of six concentric circles divided into twelve equal sections. The center point of the microphone's diaphragm is labeled 0° and is referred to as "on-axis" while the opposite side of the diaphragm is labeled 180° and is described as "off-axis."

Although polar pattern diagrams appear in two dimensions, they actually represent a three-dimensional response to acoustic energy. You can use a round balloon as a physical example to help you visualize a three-dimensional polar-pattern diagram. Position the tied end of the balloon away from your mouth and the inflated end directly in front of your lips. In this position, you are singing on-axis at 0° with the tied end of the balloon being 180°, or off-axis. If you were to split the balloon in

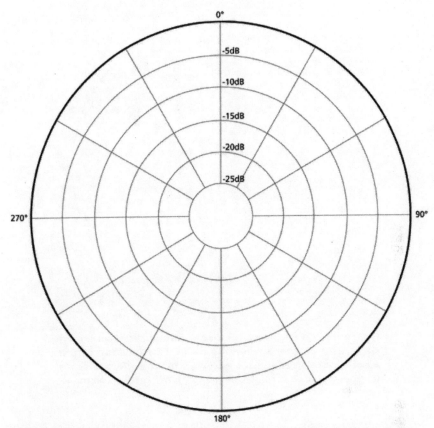

Figure 8.6. An example of a microphone polar pattern diagram. *Courtesy of Wikimedia Commons*

half vertically and horizontally (in relationship to your lips), the point at which those lines intersect would be the center point of the balloon. That imaginary center represents the diaphragm of the microphone. If you were to extend a 45° angle in any direction from the imaginary center and then drew a circle around the inside of the balloon following that angle, you would have a visualization of the three-dimensional application of the two-dimensional polar pattern drawing (see figure 8.6).

The outermost circle of the diagram indicates that the sound pressure level (SPL) of the signal is transferred without any amplitude reduction, indicated in decibels (dB). Each of the inner circles represents a -5 dB reduction in the amplitude of the signal up to -25 dB. For example, look at figure 8.7 below.

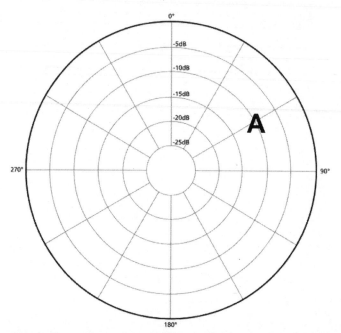

Figure 8.7. If the amplitude response curve intersected with point A, there would be a -10 dB reduction in the amplitude of frequencies received by the microphone's diaphragm at that angle. *Courtesy of Wikimedia Commons*

The examples below (figures 8.8, 8.9, and 8.10) show the most commonly encountered polar patterns.

When you are using a microphone with a polar pattern other than omnidirectional (a pattern that responds to sound equally from all directions), you may encounter frequency response fluctuations in addition to amplitude fluctuations. Cardioid microphones in particular are known for their tendency to boost lower frequencies at close proximity to the sound source while attenuating those same frequencies as the distance between the sound source and the microphone increases. This is known as the "proximity effect." Some manufacturers will notate these frequency response changes on their polar pattern diagrams by using a combination of various lines and dashes alongside the amplitude response curve.

Sensitivity.   While sensitivity can be difficult to explain in technical terms without going into an in-depth discussion of electricity and elec-

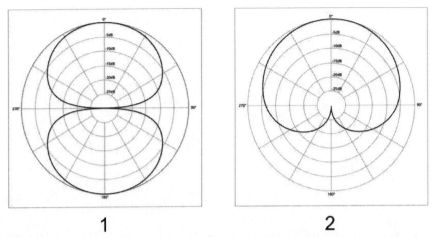

Figure 8.8. Diagram 1 represents a bidirectional pattern; diagram 2 represents a cardioid pattern. *Courtesy of Creative Commons*

trical terminology, a simplified explanation should suffice for most readers. Manufacturers test microphones with a standardized 1 kHz tone at 94 dB in order to determine how sensitive the microphone's diaphragm will be to acoustic energy. Microphones with greater sensitivity can be placed farther from the sound source without adding excessive noise to the signal. Microphones with lower sensitivity will need to be placed closer to the sound source in order to keep excess noise at a minimum.

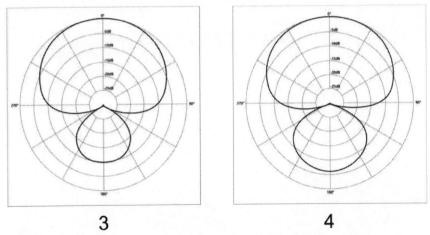

Figure 8.9. Diagram 3 represents a supercardioid pattern; diagram 4 represents a hypercardioid pattern. *Courtesy of Creative Commons*

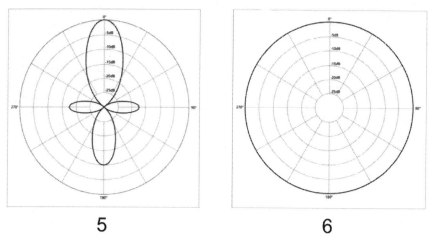

5   6

Figure 8.10. Diagram 5 represents a shotgun pattern; diagram 6 represents an omnidirectional pattern. *Courtesy of Creative Commons*

When shopping for a microphone, the performer should audition several next to each other, plugged into the same soundboard, with the same volume level for each. When singing on each microphone, at the same distance, the performer will notice that some models replicate the voice louder than others. This change in output level is due to differences in each microphone's sensitivity. If a performer has a loud voice, they may prefer a microphone with lower sensitivity (one that requires more acoustic energy to respond). If a performer has a lighter voice, they may prefer a microphone with higher sensitivity (one that responds well to softer signals).

Equalization (EQ)

Equalizers enable the audio engineer to alter the audio spectrum of the sound source, and make tone adjustments with a simple electronic interface. Equalizers come in three main types: shelf, parametric, and graphic.

Shelf Shelf equalizers cut or boost the uppermost and lowermost frequencies of an audio signal in a straight line (see figure 8.11). While this style of equalization is not very useful for fine-tuning a singer's tone quality, it can be very effective in removing room noise. For example,

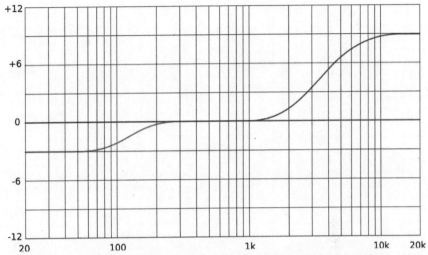

Figure 8.11.   The frequency amplitude curves above show the effect of applying a shelf EQ to an audio signal. *Courtesy of Wikimedia Commons*

if an air-conditioner creates a 60 Hz hum in the recording studio, the shelf can be set at 65 Hz, with a steep slope. This setting eliminates frequencies below 65 Hz and effectively removes the hum from the microphone signal.

Parametric   Parametric units simultaneously adjust multiple frequencies of the audio spectrum that fall within a defined parameter. The engineer selects a center frequency and adjusts the width of the bell curve surrounding that frequency by adjusting the "Q" (see figure 8.12). He or she then boosts or cuts the frequencies within the bell curve to alter the audio spectrum. Parametric controls take up minimal space on a soundboard and offer sufficient control for most situations. Therefore, most live performance soundboards have parametric EQs on each individual channel. With the advent of digital workstations, engineers can now use computer software to fine-tune the audio quality of each individual channel using a more complex graphic equalizer in both live and recording studio settings without taking up any additional physical space on the board. However, many engineers still prefer to use parametric controls during a live performance since they are usually sufficient and are easier to adjust mid-performance.

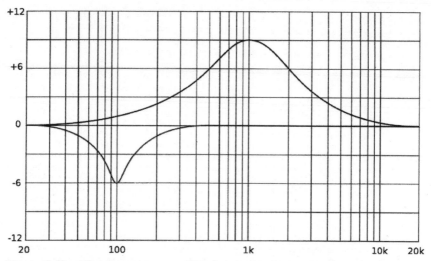

Figure 8.12. The frequency amplitude curves above display two parametric EQ settings. The top curve represents a boost of +8 dB set at 1 kHz with a relatively large bell curve—a low Q. The lower curve represents a high Q set at 100 Hz with a cut of -6 dB. *Courtesy of Wikimedia Commons*

Parametric adjustments on a soundboard are made with rotary knobs similar to those in figure 8.13 below. In some cases, you will find a button labeled "low cut" or "high pass" that will automatically apply a shelf filter to the bottom of the audio spectrum at a specified frequency. On higher-end boards, you may also find a knob that enables you to select the high-pass frequency.

Graphic Graphic equalizers enable engineers to identify a specific frequency for boost or cut with a fixed frequency bandwidth. For example, a ten-band equalizer enables the audio engineer to adjust ten specific frequencies (in Hz): 31, 63, 125, 250, 500, 1k, 2k, 4k, 8k, and 16k. Graphic equalizers are often one of the final elements of the signal chain preceding only the amplifier and speakers. In this position, they can be used to adjust the overall tonal quality of the entire mix (see figure 8.14).

Utilizing Equalization Opinions on the usage of equalization vary among engineers. Some prefer to only use equalization to remove or reduce frequencies that were not a part of the original sound signal. Others will use EQ if adjusting microphone placement fails to yield

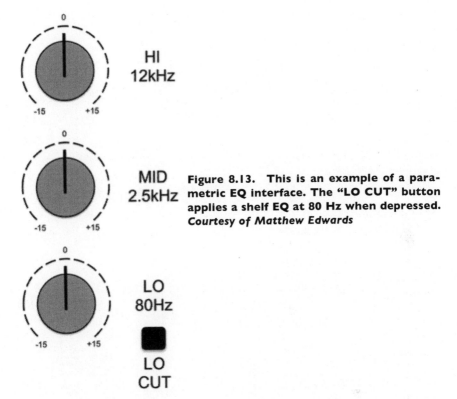

Figure 8.13. This is an example of a parametric EQ interface. The "LO CUT" button applies a shelf EQ at 80 Hz when depressed. *Courtesy of Matthew Edwards*

acceptable results. Some engineers prefer a more processed sound and may use equalization liberally to intentionally change the vocal quality of the singer. For instance, if the singer's voice sounds dull, the engineer could add "ring" or "presence" to the voice by boosting the equalizer in the 2 kHz–10 kHz range.

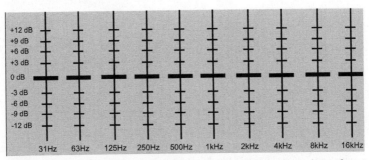

Figure 8.14. This is an example of a graphic equalizer interface. *Courtesy of Matthew Edwards*

Compression

Many singers are capable of producing vocal extremes in both frequency and amplitude levels that can prove problematic for the sound team. To help solve this problem, engineers often use compression. Compressors limit the output of a sound source by a specified ratio. The user sets the maximum acceptable amplitude level for the output, called the "threshold," and then sets a ratio to reduce the output once it surpasses the threshold. The typical ratio for a singer is usually between 3:1 and 5:1. A 4:1 ratio indicates that for every 4 dB beyond the threshold level, the output will only increase by 1 dB. For example, if the singer went 24 dB beyond the threshold with a 4:1 ratio, the output would only be 6 dB beyond the threshold level (see figure 8.15 below).

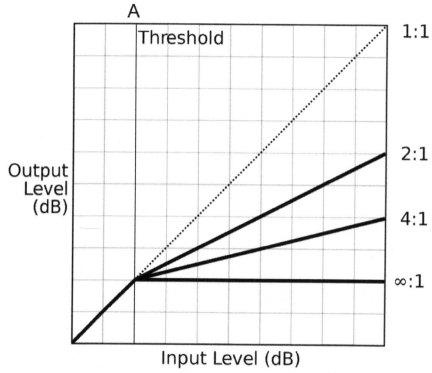

Figure 8.15. This graph represents the effects of various compression ratios applied to a signal. The 1:1 angle represents no compression. The other ratios represent the effect of compression on an input signal with the threshold set at line A. *Courtesy of Wikimedia Commons*

Adjusting the sound via microphone technique can provide some of the same results as compression and is preferable for the experienced artist. However, compression tends to be more consistent and also gives the singer freedom to focus on performing and telling a story. The additional artistic freedom provided by compression is especially beneficial to singers who use head-mounted microphones, performers who switch between vocal extremes such as falsetto and chest voice, and those who are new to performing with a microphone. Compression can also be helpful for classical singers whose dynamic abilities, while impressive live, are often difficult to record in a manner that allows for consistent listening levels through a stereo system.

If a standard compressor causes unacceptable alterations to the tone quality, engineers can turn to a multiband compressor. Rather than affecting the entire spectrum of sound, multiband compressors allow the engineer to isolate a specific frequency range within the audio signal and then set an individual compression setting for that frequency range. For example, if a singer creates a dramatic boost in the 4-kHz range every time she sings above an A4, a multiband compressor can be used to limit the amplitude of the signal in only that part of the voice. By setting a 3:1 ratio in the 4-kHz range at a threshold that corresponds to the amplitude peaks that appear when the performer sings above A4, the engineer can eliminate vocal "ring" from the sound on only the offending notes while leaving the rest of the signal untouched. These units are available for both live and studio use and can be a great alternative to compressing the entire signal.

Reverb

Reverb is one of the easier effects for singers to identify; it is the effect you experience when singing in a cathedral. An audience experiences natural reverberation when they hear the direct signal from the singer and then, milliseconds later, they hear multiple reflections as the acoustical waves of the voice bounce off the sidewalls, floor, and ceiling of the performance hall.

Many performance venues and recording studios are designed to inhibit natural reverb. Without at least a little reverb added to the sound, even the best singer can sound harsh and even amateurish. Early reverb

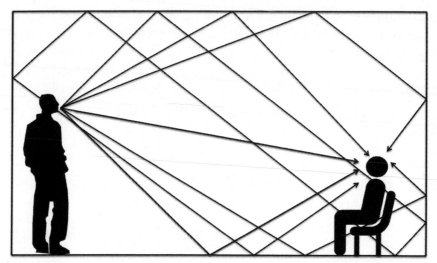

Figure 8.16.   This diagram illustrates the multiple lines of reflection that create reverb. *Courtesy of Matthew Edwards*

units transmitted the audio signal through a metal spring, which added supplementary vibrations to the signal. While some engineers still use spring reverb to obtain a specific effect, most now use digital units. Common settings on digital reverb units include wet/dry, bright/dark, and options for delay time. The wet/dry control adjusts the amount of direct signal (dry) and the amount of reverberated signal (wet). The bright/dark control helps simulate the effects of various surfaces within a natural space. For instance, harder surfaces such as stone reflect high frequencies and create a brighter tone quality while softer surfaces such as wood reflect lower frequencies and create a darker tone quality. The delay time, which is usually adjustable from milliseconds to seconds, adjusts the amount of time between when the dry signal and wet signals reach the ear. Engineers can transform almost any room into a chamber music hall or concert stadium simply by adjusting these settings.

Delay

Whereas reverb blends multiple wet signals with the dry signal to replicate a natural space, delay purposefully separates a single wet signal from the dry signal to create repetitions of the voice. With delay, you will hear the original note first and then a digitally produced repeat of the note several milliseconds to seconds later. The delayed note may be heard one time or multiple times and the timing of those repeats can be adjusted to match the tempo of the song.

Auto-Tune

Auto-Tune was first used in studios as a useful way to clean up minor imperfections in otherwise perfect performances. Auto-Tune is now an industry standard that many artists use, even if they are not willing to admit it. Auto-Tune has gained a bad reputation in the last few years and whether or not you agree with its use, it is a reality in today's market. If you do not understand how to use it properly, you could end up sounding like T-Pain.[2]

Both Antares and Melodyne have developed auto-tune technology in both "auto" and "graphical" formats. "Auto" Auto-Tune allows the engineer to set specific parameters for pitch correction that are then computer controlled. "Graphical" Auto-Tune tracks the pitch in the selected area of a recording and plots the fundamental frequency on a linear graph. The engineer can then select specific notes for pitch correction. They can

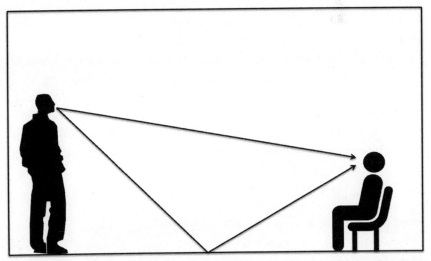

Figure 8.17.   This diagram illustrates how a direct line of sound followed by a reflected line of sound creates delay. *Courtesy of Matthew Edwards*

also drag selected pitches to a different frequency, add or reduce vibrato, and change formant frequencies above the fundamental. To simplify, the "auto" function makes general corrections while the "graphic" function makes specific corrections. The "auto" setting is usually used to achieve a specific effect (for instance "I Believe" by Cher), while the "graphic" setting is used to correct small imperfections in a recorded performance.

Digital Voice Processors

Digital voice processors are still relatively new to the market and have yet to gain widespread usage among singers. While there are several brands of vocal effects processors available, the industry leader as of this printing is a company called TC-Helicon. TC-Helicon manufactures several different units that span from consumer to professional grade. TC-Helicon's premiere performer-controlled unit is called the Voice-Live 3. The VoiceLive 3 incorporates over twelve vocal effects, eleven guitar effects, and a multi-track looper with 250 factory presets and 250 memory slots for user presets. The VoiceLive 3 puts the effects at the singer's feet in a programmable stomp box that also includes phantom power, MIDI in/out, a USB connection, guitar input, and monitor out. Onboard vocal effects include equalization, compression, reverb, and "auto" Auto-Tune. The unit also offers μMod (an adjustable voice modulator), a doubler (for thickening the lead vocal), echo, delay, reverb, and several other specialized effects.[3]

One of the most impressive features of digital voice processors is the ability to add computer-generated harmonies to the lead vocal. After the user sets the musical key, the processor identifies the fundamental frequency of each sung note. The computer then adds digitized voices at designated intervals above and below the lead singer. The unit also offers the option to program each individual song, with multiple settings for every verse, chorus, and bridge.

THE BASICS OF LIVE SOUND SYSTEMS

Live sound systems come in a variety of sizes from small practice units to state-of-the-art stadium rigs. Most singers only need a basic knowledge of the components commonly found in systems that have one to eight inputs. Units beyond that size usually require an independent sound engineer and are beyond the scope of this chapter.

Following the microphone, the first element in the live signal chain is usually the mixer. Basic portable mixers provide controls for equalization; volume level; auxiliary (usually used for effects such as reverb and compression); and, on some units, controls for built-in digital effects processors. Powered mixers combine an amplifier with a basic mixer, providing a compact solution for those who do not need a complex system. Since unpowered mixers do not provide amplification, you will need to add a separate amplifier to power this system.

The powered mixer or amplifier connects to speaker cabinets, which contain a "woofer" and a "tweeter." The woofer is a large round speaker that handles the bass frequencies, while the tweeter is a horn-shaped speaker that handles the treble frequencies. The crossover, a component built into the speaker cabinet, separates high and low frequencies and sends them to the appropriate speaker (woofer or tweeter). Speaker cabinets can be either active or passive. Passive cabinets require a powered mixer or an amplifier in order to operate. Active cabinets have an amplifier built in and do not require an external amplifier.

If you do not already own a microphone and amplification system, you can purchase a simple setup at relatively low cost through online vendors such as Sweetwater.com and MusiciansFriend.com. A dynamic microphone and a powered monitor are enough to get started. If you would like to add a digital voice processor, Digitech and TC-Helicon both sell entry-level models that will significantly improve the tonal quality of a sound system.

Monitors are arguably the most important element in a live sound system. The monitor is a speaker that faces a performer and allows them to hear themselves and/or the other instruments on stage. Onstage volume levels can vary considerably, with drummers often producing sound levels as high as 120 dB. Those volume levels make it nearly impossible for singers to receive natural acoustic feedback while performing. Monitors can improve aural feedback and help reduce the temptation to over-sing. Powered monitors offer the same advantages as powered speaker cabinets and can be a great option for amplification when practicing. They are also good to have around as a backup plan in case you arrive at a venue and discover they do not supply monitors. In-ear monitors offer another option for performers and are especially useful for those who frequently move around the stage.

MICROPHONE TECHNIQUE

The microphone is an inseparable part of the singer's instrument. Just as there are techniques that improve singing, there are also techniques that will improve microphone use. Understanding what a microphone does is only the first step to using it successfully. Once you understand how a microphone works, you need hands-on experience.

The best way to learn microphone technique is to experiment. Try the following exercises to gain a better understanding of how to use a microphone when singing.

- Hold a dynamic microphone with a cardioid pattern directly in front of your mouth, no farther than one centimeter away. Sustain a comfortable pitch and slowly move the microphone away from your lips. Listen to how the vocal quality changes. When the microphone is close to the lips, you should notice that the sound is louder and has more bass response. As you move the microphone away from your mouth, there will be a noticeable loss in volume and the tone will become brighter.
- Next sustain a pitch while rotating the handle down. The sound quality will change in a similar fashion as when you moved the microphone away from your lips.
- Now try singing breathy with the microphone close to your lips. How little effort can you get away with while producing a marketable sound?
- Try singing bright vowels and dark vowels and notice how the microphone affects the tone quality.
- Also experiment with adapting your diction to the microphone. Because the microphone amplifies everything, you may need to under-pronounce certain consonants when singing. You will especially want to reduce the power of the consonants [t], [s], [p], and [b].

FINAL THOUGHTS

Since this is primarily an overview, you can greatly improve your comprehension of the material by seeking other resources to deepen your knowledge. There are many great resources available that may help clarify some of these difficult concepts. Most important, you must experiment. The more you play around with sound equipment on your own, the better you will understand it and the more comfortable you will feel when performing or recording with audio technology.

NOTES

1. Paula Lockheart, "A History of Early Microphone Singing, 1925–1939: American Mainstream Popular Singing at the Advent of Electronic Amplification." *Popular Music and Society* 26, no. 3 (2003): 367–85.

2. For example, listen to T-Pain's track "Buy You a Drank (Shawty Snappin')."

3. "VoiceLive3," *TC-Helicon*. Accessed May 2, 2016. http://www.tc-helicon.com/products/voicelive-3/.

BIBLIOGRAPHY

Abraham, Roger D., ed. *A Singer and Her Songs: Almeda Riddle's Book of Ballads*. Baton Rouge: Louisiana State University Press, 1970.

Allen, William Francis, Charles Pickard Ware, and Lucy McKim Garrison. *Slave Songs of the United States*. New York: A. Simpson, 1867. Reprint, New York: Dover, 1995.

Anthony, Ted. *Chasing the Rising Sun: The Journey of an American Song*. New York: Simon & Schuster, 2007.

Arnett, Hazel. *I Hear America Singing! Great Folk Songs from the Revolution to Rock*. New York: Praeger Publishers, 1975.

Barnwell, Ysaye M., and George Brandon. *Singing in the African American Tradition*, rev. ed. Woodstock, NY: Homespun Tapes, 1998.

Bohlman, Philip V. *The Study of Folk Music in the Modern World*. Bloomington: Indiana University Press, 1988.

Brand, Oscar. *The Ballad Mongers: Rise of the Modern Folk Song*. New York: Funk & Wagnalls, 1962.

The Broadman Hymnal. Nashville, TN: Broadman Press, 1940.

Brocken, Michael. *The British Folk Revival, 1944–2002*. Farnham, UK: Ashgate, 2013. First published 2003.

Cantwell, Robert. *When We Were Good: The Folk Revival*. Cambridge, MA: Harvard University Press, 1996.

Carlin, Richard. *Worlds of Sound: The Story of Smithsonian Folkways*. New York: HarperCollins, 2008.

Carlin, Richard, and Bob Carlin. *Southern Exposure: The Story of Southern Music in Pictures and Words.* New York: Billboard Books, 2000.

Cohen, Ronald D., ed. *Alan Lomax: Selected Writings 1934–1997.* New York: Routledge, 2003.

Cohen, Ronald D., and Rachel Clare Donaldson. *Roots of the Revival: American and British Folk Music in the 1950s.* Urbana: University of Illinois Press, 2014.

Dunaway, David King, and Molly Beer: *Singing Out: An Oral History of America's Folk Music Revivals.* New York: Oxford University Press, 2010.

Erbsen, Wayne. *Hymns of the Old Camp Ground: Old Time Gospel Songs with Words, Music and History.* Asheville, NC: Native Ground Music, 2008.

Erbsen, Wayne. *Rural Roots of Bluegrass: Songs, Stories and History.* Asheville, NC: Native Ground Music, 2003.

Filene, Benjamin. *Romancing the Folk: Public Memory & American Roots Music.* Chapel Hill: University of North Carolina Press, 2000.

Glassie, Henry, Clifford R. Murphy, and Douglas Dowling Peach. *Ola Belle Reed and Southern Mountain Music on the Mason-Dixon Line.* Atlanta, GA: Dust-to-Digital, 2015.

Gospel Hymns: Numbers 1 to 6 Revised. Grabill, IN: Gospel Hymn Publishing, 1966.

Heavenly Highway Hymns. Luther G. Presley, compiler. Franklin, TN: Brentwood-Benson Music Publishing, 1956.

Jackson, George Pullen. *White Spirituals in the Southern Uplands: The Story of the Fasola Folk, Their Songs, Singings, and "Buckwheat Notes."* Chapel Hill: University of North Carolina Press, 1933. Reprint, New York: Dover, 1965.

Jamison, Phil. *Hoedowns, Reels, and Frolics: Roots and Branches of Southern Appalachian Dance.* Urbana: University of Illinois Press, 2015.

Kent, Ray D., and Charles Read. *Acoustic Analysis of Speech,* 2nd ed. Albany, NY: Delmar, 2002.

Kimbrough, S. T. Jr., ed. *Beams of Heaven: Hymns of Charles Albert Tindley.* New York: General Board of Global Ministries, The United Methodist Church, 2006.

Kingsbury, Paul, and Alanna Nash, eds. *Will the Circle Be Unbroken: Country Music in America.* New York: DK Publishing, 2006.

Klein, Joe. *Woody Guthrie: A Life.* New York: Knopf, 1980.

Leary, James P. *Folksongs of Another America: Field Recordings from the Upper Midwest, 1937–1946.* Madison: University of Wisconsin Press; Atlanta, GA: Dust-to-Digital, 2015.

Lomax, John. *Cowboy Songs and Other Frontier Ballads,* new ed. New York: Sturgis & Walton, 1917.

Lomax, John, and Alan Lomax. *American Ballads and Folk Songs*. New York: Macmillan, 1934. Reprint, New York: Dover, 1994.

Lomax, John, and Alan Lomax. *Our Singing Country: Folk Songs and Ballads*. New York: Macmillan, 1941. Reprint, New York: Dover, 2000.

Lornell, Kip. *Exploring American Folk Music: Ethnic, Grassroots, and Regional Traditions in the United States*. Jackson: University Press of Mississippi, 2012.

Lornell, Kip. *The NPR Curious Listener's Guide to American Folk Music*. New York: Penguin, 2004.

Louvin, Charlie, with Benjamin Whitmer. *Satan Is Real: The Ballad of the Louvin Brothers*. New York: HarperCollins, 2012.

Malone, Bill C. *Country Music U.S.A.: A Fifty-Year History*. Austin: University of Texas Press, 1968. Reprint, 1975.

Malone, Bill C. *Music from the True Vine: Mike Seeger's Life and Musical Journey*. Chapel Hill: University of North Carolina Press, 2011.

Marshall, Erynn. *Music in the Air Somewhere: The Shifting Borders of West Virginia's Fiddle and Song Traditions*. Morgantown: West Virginia University Press, 2007.

Milnes, Gerald. *Play of a Fiddle: Traditional Music, Dance and Folklore in West Virginia*. Lexington: University Press of Kentucky, 1999.

Morrish, John, ed. *The Folk Handbook: Working with Songs from the English Tradition*. New York: Backbeat Books, 2007.

Petrus, Stephen, and Ronald D. Cohen. *Folk City: New York and the American Folk Music Revival*. New York: Oxford University Press, 2015.

Ritchie, Fiona, and Doug Orr. *Wayfaring Strangers: The Musical Voyage from Scotland and Ulster to Appalachia*. Chapel Hill: University of North Carolina Press, 2014.

Ritchie, Jean. *Singing Family of the Cumberlands*. New York: Oak Publications, 1955. Reprint, 1963.

Romalis, Shelly. *Pistol Packin' Mama: Aunt Molly Jackson and the Politics of Folksong*. Urbana: University of Illinois Press, 1999.

Sandberg, Larry, and Dick Weissman. *The Folk Music Sourcebook*. New, updated ed. New York: Da Capo, 1989.

Sandburg, Carl. *The American Songbag*. New York: Harcourt, Brace & World, 1927.

Seeger, Pete. *American Favorite Ballads: Tunes and Songs as Sung by Pete Seeger*. New York: Oak Publications, 1961.

Seeger, Pete. *Pete Seeger in His Own Words*. Selected and edited by Rob Rosenthal and Sam Rosenthal. Boulder, CO: Paradigm Publishers, 2012.

Seeger, Pete. *Where Have All the Flowers Gone: A Singalong Memoir*. 2nd ed. Bethlehem, PA: Sing Out!, 2009.

Seeger, Ruth Crawford. *American Folk Songs for Children*. New York: Oak Publications, 1948. Reprint, 2002.

Seeger, Ruth Crawford. *American Folk Songs for Christmas*. North Haven, CT: Linnet Books, 1953. Reprint, 1999.

Seeger, Ruth Crawford. *The Music of American Folk Song*. Edited by Larry Polansky. Rochester, NY: University of Rochester Press, 2001.

Simos, Mark. *Songwriting Strategies: A 360° Approach*. Boston: Berklee Press, 2014.

Sims, Walter Hines, ed. *Baptist Hymnal*. Nashville, TN: Convention Press, 1956.

Slobin, Mark. *Folk Music: A Very Short Introduction*. New York: Oxford University Press, 2011.

Van Ronk, Dave, with Elijah Wald. *The Mayor of MacDougal Street: A Memoir*. Cambridge, MA: Da Capo Press, 2005.

Warner, Anne. *Traditional American Folk Songs from the Frank and Anne Warner Collection*. Syracuse, NY: Syracuse University Press, 1984.

Wolfe, Charles K., and Ted Olson, eds. *The Bristol Sessions: Writings about the Big Bang of Country Music*. Jefferson, NC: McFarland, 2005.

Woliver, Robbie. *Hoot! A 25-Year History of the Greenwich Village Music Scene*. New York: St. Martin's Press, 1986.

Work, John W., ed. *American Negro Songs and Spirituals: A Comprehensive Collection of 230 Folk Songs, Religious and Secular*. New York: Bonanza Books, 1940.

INDEX

ABOUT THE AUTHOR

Valerie Mindel is a longtime folk musician, teacher, and workshop leader, known for bringing out the best in singers, whatever their level. Her specialty is the close buzzy harmony that characterizes bluegrass, country, and other forms of American roots music. In addition to a busy workshop schedule, she teaches at numerous music camps, including Allegheny Echoes, Ashokan Music and Dance Camps, the Festival of American Fiddle Tunes, the Augusta Heritage Center's Vocal Week, Grand Targhee Music Camp, and Village Harmony, and in Britain at Sore Fingers Summer Schools and the Scotland-based Harmony Week. She teaches regularly in New York City at Brooklyn's growing old-time music school, Jalopy Theatre & School of Music, and she also teaches and performs in various combinations, including with California-based Any Old Time, with daughter and old-time country musician Emily Miller and her husband, Jesse Milnes, and with Joe Newberry. She lives in Marlboro, Vermont. For more, visit www.valandemmy.com.